T0345593

In Performance

EDITED BY
CAROL MARTIN

In Performance is a book series devoted to national and global
theater of the twenty-first century. Scholarly essays providing
the theatrical, cultural, and political contexts for the plays and
performance texts introduce each volume. The texts are written
both by established and emerging writers, translated by
accomplished translators and aimed at people who want to put
new works on stage, read diverse dramatic and performance
literature and study diverse theater practices, contexts, and histories in light of globalization.

In Performance has been supported by
translation and editing grants from the following organizations:

The Book Institute, Krakow
TEDA Project, Istanbul
The Memorial Fund for Jewish Culture, New York
Polish Cultural Institute, New York
Zbigniew Raszewski Theatrical Institute, Warsaw

INSTRUCTIONS FOR BREATHING

AND OTHER PLAYS

CARIDAD SVICH

LONDON NEW YORK CALCUTTA

Seagull Books, 2014

Instructions for Breathing © by Caridad Svich, 2009
Wreckage © by Caridad Svich, 2009
Fugitive Pieces (*A Play with Songs*) © Caridad Svich, 2000, revised 2002
Thrush (*A Play with Slaughter Songs*) © Caridad Svich, 2006
Rift © Caridad Svich, 2010, revised 2011
Steal Back Light from the Virtual © Caridad Svich, 2001, revised 2010
Luna Park © Caridad Svich, 2005, revised 2010

For performance rights enquiries for this authors' work, contact New Dramatists Alumni, 424 West 44th Street, New York, NY 10036; e-mail: newdramatists@new-dramatists.org, csvich21@caridadsvich.com.

Fugitive Pieces and *Luna Park* have been previously published as licensed acting editions by Playscripts, Inc., and are reprinted with Playscripts' permission.

ISBN 978 0 8574 2 111 1

British Library Cataloging-in-Publication Data
A catalog record for this book is available from the British Library

Book designed by Bishan Samaddar and Niharika Jatia, Seagull Books, Calcutta, India
Printed and bound by Hyam Enterprises, Calcutta, India

CONTENTS

ACKNOWLEDGMENTS | **vi**

Introduction | **vii**
CRUEL MERCIES AND TENDER ECSTASIES
Tamara Underiner

INSTRUCTIONS FOR BREATHING | **1**

WRECKAGE | **53**

FUGITIVE PIECES | **108**
A PLAY WITH SONGS

THRUSH | **161**
A PLAY WITH SLAUGHTER SONGS

RIFT | **228**

STEAL BACK LIGHT FROM THE VIRTUAL | **304**

LUNA PARK | **362**

ACKNOWLEDGMENTS

The seven plays in this volume represent more than ten years of my life, labor and love in the American theater. Each play has been nurtured over time by a roving band of artists I am fortunate to call collaborators from New York City to Austin, Texas, to Los Angeles to San Francisco, Chicago, and many points in-between. Among the many artists who must be thanked for their faith and commitment toward realizing the shared visions of these plays are Catherine Coray, Dan Cozzens, Eisa Davis, Annie Dorsen, Lee Eddy, Randy Gener, Frank Harts, Carla Harting, Kate Hopkins, Anne Kaufman, Juliana Francis Kelly, Jocelyn Kuritsky, Judson Jones, O-Lan Jones, Jenny Larson, Polly Lee, Todd London, Florencia Lozano, Alfredo Narciso, Jason Neulander, Stefan Novinski, Emily Morse, J. Dakota Powell, Jean Randich, Matthew Rauch, Gerry Rodriguez, Heidi Schreck, Seret Scott, Keith Randolph Smith, Stephen Squibb, Adam Sultan, Michael Tisdale, Daniella Topol, Roberto Gutierrez Varea, Chris Wells, Mark Wing-Davey, Marissa Wolf, Aaron Yoo, and Jose Zayas. Among the many organizations that must also be thanked for the development of these plays are A.S.K. Theater Projects, Center Theatre Group and the Latino Theatre Initiative, Crowded Fire, French-American International High School of San Francisco, Hartt School for the Arts, HotINK, Kitchen Dog Theater, William Inge Center for the Arts, LoNyLa Lab, Nautilus Music Theater, NoPassport Theatre Alliance & Press, Passage Theatre Company, Radcliffe Institute for Advanced Study at Harvard University, Salvage Vanguard Theater, New Dramatists, and the New York University Graduate Acting Program. Special thanks to Carol Martin, Chiori Miyagawa, and Tamara Underiner.

As always, this is for my parents.

INTRODUCTION

CRUEL MERCIES AND TENDER ECSTASIES

As a playwright, songwriter, editor, and translator living between many cultures, including inherited ones, the idea of departure has always been not only an actual or metaphorical basis for writing the work, but also an idea made manifest through the enactment of writing, its performance, and my living of it. Born in the US of Cuban-Argentine-Spanish-Croatian parents, I have felt in a strange kind of exile even while growing up as an "American."

Caridad Svich[1]

Explorations of exile led Caridad Svich to an MFA in playwriting from the University of California, San Diego, in 1988, and a residency with the legendary María Irene Fornés at the INTAR Hispanic Playwrights-in-Residence Laboratory in New York, from 1988 to 1992. Between then and now, Svich has written more than thirty plays, many of which include songs of her own composition, and has translated more than twenty others, including works by Lope de Vega, Calderón de la Barca, Julio Cortazár, Ugljesa Sajtinac, Federico Garcia Lorca, and Isabel Allende. In a career now entering its third decade, Svich has gained recognition within the Latina/o theatrical community, and from both national and international theatrical circles. Her works are often set in Latin/o American landscapes limned in shades of upheaval, whether from war, border-crossing, or falling in love—or all of the above—and accompanied by the sights and sounds of global popular culture.

---

1 Caridad Svich, homepage for personal website. Available at: www.caridad-svich.com (last accessed on December 1, 2013).

According to scholar Lillian Manzor, Svich's plays function as "an expressionistic allegory of the uncertainty of (post)modern times: displaced human beings reconfigure the maps of home in a nonlinear fashion so that we can inhabit our imaginary communities of Mexico–Hollywood–Buenos Aires–Granada–Havana–New York."[2]

In the 1980s, when Svich was first learning how to write plays, few women playwrights enjoyed success in the US. Wendy Wasserstein, Beth Henley, and Marsha Norman were commercially successful even as their plays were critiqued as the kind of plays "a woman was expected to write."[3] In other words, plays about women, set in places women often find themselves, focusing on their relationships with their sisters, mothers, and men—without an examination of the more complex global economic structures of sexual politics. Svich broke this expectation by writing about sex as something for sale in desperate economies of necessary exchange that sometimes includes love as part of the transaction. She attributes her break with conventions of female playwrighting to Fornés's influence: "When I sit down at the writing table and start a new play, whether in longhand or on my laptop, it is Fornés's charge to tell the truth that stays with me. Inside that call to duty is another one: write the stories you need to write, and don't let anyone tell you that a woman can't say this or that on and for the stage."[4]

---

2 Lillian Manzor, "Caridad Svich," *The Oxford Encyclopedia of Latinos and Latinas in the United States Cultures*, VOL. 1. New York: Oxford University Press, 2005, pp. 184–6.

3 Lavonne Mueller, interviewed by Stratos E. Constandinidis, "Playwriting and Oral History: An Interview with Playwright Lavonne Mueller," *Journal of Dramatic Theory and Criticism* 9(1) (Fall 1994): 145–55, here p. 149. I believe this critique has as much to do with the systems of production then (and even now) that brought these playwrights to visibility as it does the work itself.

4 Caridad Svich, "A Dream of Making," *Theater Journal* 62(4) (December 2010): 511–14, here p. 513.

Identified with and by a Latina/o theatrical community, Svich's works often are set in vaguely recognizable Latina/o American landscapes, but not always or only there. Sometimes it is possible to plot her characters' coordinates along the axes of time (history) and space (the political geography of global capital), but a good part of every Svich play is devoted to exposing the narrative conventions that fix characters in place and time. Each of Svich's plays offers its own instructions for breathing in the flinching face of loss, as well as in the tender ecstasies of hope, as her characters find ways to connect and belong in the midst of disorientation and dislocation.

INSTRUCTIONS FOR READING

The seven plays in this volume can be read in a variety of ways. Each play stands on its own as an examination of human relationships in extreme situations that serve as the cause or context for the characters' various dilemmas. Personally, I like to lose myself in the poetry of Svich's plays in order to stage them in my mind so that I can hear the distinct voice that I have come to recognize as hers: a poetic voice that both advances and accompanies the story, like a rhythm section in a band. Again, Fornés is a key influence: "Fornés pushed each of her writers [. . .] to resist ease and comfort, to challenge language to its limits, and to test the resonant spaces of words themselves and their ability to shift energy and motion in a play."[5] This suggests that another way to read these plays is to read them aloud, either alone or with friends. What often happens is that what appears on the page as heightened or exaggerated, when read out loud sounds curiously like people talking, when they are speaking the truth. Seen here is Sondra in *Rift*, the madam of a brothel in a war-torn country, breaking up a fight between two of her girls:

5 Caridad Svich (ed.), "The Legacy of Maria Irene Fornés: A Collection of Impressions and Exercises," *PAJ 93: A Journal of Performance and Art* 31(3) (September 2009): 1–32, here p. 2.

SONDRA. Take that smile off your face, girl, or you'll see my animal. Or don't you think I have one? Mama Sondra got plenty animal inside her. And this no conjure talk. This ain't somethin' you can DISMISS with a swivel of the hips and a wave of the hand. I got ancient animal inside me, kind that can rise up and cry havoc mighty enough to wake up the dead. You with your petty anger, your shit jealousies, what gods do you wake?

FATIMA. Whatever.

Or Minerva in *Thrush*, introducing herself to Bette:

MINERVA. I've hid under for a while. Yeah. Buried myself in dirt so as to not get caught.

Soldier come by once, he dug me up. He was a mad one, wrecked one, all fury.

He had part of his arm blown off. Scabs and scars all over. Felt sorry for him. I did. Thought he could use a prayer or some sign of heaven. But he wouldn't listen.

He just wanted to dig up, have his way, and move on. I let him, right? He was a mad one. Wrecked boy. I give him a dirt smile.

He didn't know what . . .

He shot himself. Right in front of me.

I buried him. I put him in the ground where I'd been, covered him up in dirt and leaves.

If anybody ask? I never seen him. You see?

I bury everything. I bury, and do good. That's what I'm like.

No hosanna. No hosanna here.

BETTE. . . . You're a mess of a girl.

MINERVA. I'm not.

Svich views US dramaturgy as searching for a "more 'real' realism,"[6] in its search for dramatic structure and rhythm. This search must be continually renewed as historical subjects change. For Svich, the most pressing contemporary subject is displaced—whether by choice or force—human beings. Despite its homogenizing influence, the flow of global capital has produced a movement of people who must learn to make their way across divides of culture, class, and language. At the same time, these same people carry with them specific histories that pulse through their experience wherever they are; these histories may or may not serve their new futures, but are constantly manifest in ways that shape their experience and the experience of those around them. How does a playwright capture the psyche of such a subject, whose consciousness is informed as much by dislocation as location, by virtual as well as material reality, by personal and political trauma?

Svich's approach may vary from play to play, but there's a family resemblance in her approach that suggests a new form: "hauntological realism." "Hauntology" is a term coined by Derrida that has since been taken up in literary, cultural, and performance studies, as well as in contemporary music—all domains in which Svich moves easily—that takes up where ontology leaves off in its charge to explain the nature of what is.[7] Whereas the latter is preoccupied with being, hauntology privileges what lurks at the borders of being—the ghost, the echo, the revenant, the reverberation—those presences that are here but not here, related to an original source that is dimly discernible and of which they partake, but do not share an identity. Introducing the social into the metaphysical, hauntology seeks to describe what exists outside the order of consensual knowledge, but exerts a force, a pull, perceptibility in the material world.

---

6 Jason Grote, Caridad Svich, and Anne Washburn, in conversation with Ken Urban, "Contemporary American Playwriting: The Issue of Legacy," *PAJ 84: A Journal of Performance and Art* 28(3) (September 2006): 11.

7 See Michael Sprinker (ed.), *Ghostly Demarcations: A Symposium on Jacques Derrida's "Spectres de Marx"* (London: Verso, 1999).

Hauntological presences appear in some way in all of the plays collected here. Sometimes they are central to the world of the play, as in *Instructions for Breathing* (2009), where a child has gone missing: her fate not known, her presence is palpable in her absence, in her parents' anguish, in the way their friends cannot hide their relief in the fact that the horror is vicarious—she is not their child. In the end, the disembodied voice that opens the play is joined to that of a girl who appears years later. Her story, which could be that of the missing child's, offers the promise of the play's title. In *Luna Park* (2005, revised 2010), a young man goes missing during a terrorist attack on a seaside amusement park that is a metonym for the US, pre- and post-9/11, on a too-perfect day with a chill of premonition: the future haunting the present. Like the parents in *Instructions for Breathing*, the circle of young friends who survive must find their own, individual ways of dealing with their sadness and anger, which for some is personal, for others, political.

Sometimes, Greek myth supplies the haunting narratives that animate a contemporary tale. Characters in *Instructions for Breathing*, for example, discuss Euripides's *Ion*, another tale of a child left behind. In *Wreckage* (2009), *Medea* suffuses the contemporary tale. If, as literary scholars Peter Buse and Andrew Stott have written, "the question of the *revenant* [one who returns from the dead] neatly encapsulates deconstructive concerns about the impossibility of conceptually solidifying the past,"[8] consider the opening scene of *Wreckage*. Here, two bodies that have been swept ashore awake to repeat a variation on the deadly cycle liberally drawn from the ancient play. They pursue their individual paths through what may or may not be the afterlife, with sexual partners who may or may not be what they appear to be. One is taken in by an older woman who calls him "daughter," and uses him to taunt her husband; the

---

8 Peter Buse and Andrew Stott (eds), Introduction to *Ghosts: Deconstruction, Psychoanalysis, History* (New York: St. Martin's Press, 1999): 1–23, here p. 11. Emphasis in the original.

other becomes a sex worker who services that husband. The play allegorizes the agonies and ecstasies attendant on the coming of age, and exposes the vacuity of "marriage, a fine house, money, social standing, power, privacy, at the expense of lust, sensation, and knowledge." *Wreckage* is a meditation on the ongoing relationship between archetype and fate: to what degree can we escape the myths that make us? As the boys' (after) lives unfold, a radio newscast tracks the story of a teenage princess who has killed her baby when she learns his father has been cheating on her.

Justin Maxwell has suggested that Svich's adaptations are not about "retelling old stories, but finding an ancient spark and letting it ignite her very contemporary aesthetics. The sources of Svich's adaptations live in the deep recesses of Jungian cultural memory, like shared dreams." [9] The ability of ancient myth to effect contemporary realities is also part and parcel of *Steal Back Light from the Virtual* (2001, revised 2010), where characters wander through a labyrinth of the world's urban capitals where seven young men have been sacrificed "for the good of the city," an archetypal city that could be any city. A man with the face of a bull was spotted, and possibly captured on film by a young woman, trying to beat death by recording it again and again, all around the world. The characters, all of whose lives will intersect each other's over the course of the play, include a journalist named Mesmer, who stages crimes so he can secure the scoop on them; his kept wife, obsessed with whether he is cheating on her; a lost young man nearly killed in an accident, rescued by a young woman; another young woman who eats only ice cream while watching nothing but slasher movies, who loves a young cross-dressing man who, like others in the play, sells his body, and who, in turn, loves Mesmer, the play's final, beautiful, sacrifice. *Steal Back Light from the Virtual* makes manifest the dizzying disorientations

---

9 Justin Maxwell, "Cartography Lessons with Caridad Svich," *American Theater* (July–August 2009). Available at: www.tcg.org/publications/at/julyaugust09/cartography.cfm (last accessed on December 1, 2013).

that go along with being a citizen of the world today with all its promise of isolating connectivity. What tethers us to each other? What is the thread we unravel to find our way to each other and out of this or that dead end?

Between the plays that bookend this collection, hauntings take on many other shapes, forms and figures. *Fugitive Pieces* (2000, revised 2002), *Thrush: A Play with Slaughter Songs* (2006), and *Rift* (2010, revised 2011) form a "land and country" trilogy in which characters wander over and through heaths newly blasted by war, atrocity, and resource exploitation, archetypal landscapes littered with the shards of global and US dreams, through which the characters pick their way toward mercy, survival, and redemptive love. Two troubled wanderers who hop a freight train bound anywhere, are haunted by both past traumas and ravenous, pop-culture inflected dreams. A country like the US is ghosted as it is briefly glimpsed through the windows of the train—a scarecrow here, a little girl's dress on a clothesline there, the corpse of an undocumented man thrown into a ravine. From afar, the sounds of a carnival serve as a grotesque backdrop to lives lived in a fragmented flight from, and yearning toward, justice and its cruel mercies. Will this road trip lead to wholeness? The play ends with them going off not into a sunset, but into the huge screen of a drive-in movie.

Sometimes such here-but-not-here figures are used as part of the play's land- and soundscape, as in the near-apocalyptic *Thrush*, where, in a country ravaged by war, "A young woman walks the fields. A young man trails her. The ghost voices of the fallen rise up in ballads, hymns, blues and swing as if torn from roots of mad sorrow." [10] *Thrush* explores what it means to be human during times of wrenching displacement. The young woman, Minerva, and Bette, like Brecht's Mother Courage, sell water (and themselves) to

---

[10] Quoted in Salvage Vanguard Theatre press release, 18 August, 2006: Available at: www.salvagevanguard.org/press/press-20060915.shtml (last accessed on December 1, 2013).

the soldiers passing through. When, in an attempt to cross the border into (possibly) safer territory, one of them kills Bette, Minerva must resolve to carry on, often ruthlessly. In a detention center she encounters a Ghost Child (a "willful apparition") who sounds like (and is played by the actor playing) Bette, in Svich's upending of reality. Bette also appears as a kind of spirit guide and rogue ferry guard who will help Minerva and her new traveling companion—a soldier on the lam who is haunted by those he has slaughtered—to escape.

In *Rift* haunting is central to the principal character's journey. The ghost/vision of Ilona's lover Maurice, with whom she has inadvertently committed an act of revolutionary atrocity, haunts her because she, like Antigone, has not been able to bury his body. In the world of *Rift*, live bodies matter only for their value in the sex trade, and a public-service broadcast cheerily announces executions: *"Executions at five o'clock; All plastic sheeting donations to the central square."* *Rift* examines the extremes of human exploitation as a metaphor for what happens in a world in which profit is the only moral imperative and greed its sanctioned engine. Some characters find their way back to being human, some cannot, and still others remain trapped (willingly or not) in the cycle of exploitation and survival.[11]

Svich's hauntological realism shows how the past (whether personal, historical, mythical, or literary) lives on in the present in ways that tear the seams that both unite and divide then and now, absence and presence, death and life. Writing on the centrality of the spectral

---

11 *Rift* was commissioned in 2009 by the graduate acting program at NYU's Tisch School for the Arts and developed through the Joint Stock method (named after the process employed by the British Joint Stock Theatre Group), in which actors research a topic over the course of several weeks; their improvisations provide material which the playwright later shapes into a script for ensemble performance. In this case the initial idea was "feral children." See Ilyse Liffreing's interview with Svich for the *San Francisco Examiner*. Available at: www.examiner.com/performing-arts-in-san-francisco/interview-with-playwright-caridad-svich (last accessed on December 1, 2013).

for the notion of hauntology, Colin Davis has noted that, "For Derrida, the ghost's secret is not a puzzle to be solved; it is the structural openness or address directed towards the living by the voices of the past or the not yet formulated possibilities of the future. The secret is not unspeakable because it is taboo, but because it cannot not (yet) be articulated in the languages available to us."[12]

Svich's contribution to US dramaturgy is an expansion of the type of language available to us in order to portray the unspeakable, but still perceptible. Like Svich's characters, readers have some choice in what they do with these sounds and presences that come to us from our distant and not-so-distant past. We can pave over the ruins of Luna Park and make our world all amnesiac-pretty again, move on, and get over; or we can find a way to maintain the ruins and remember the stories they hold, living and breathing together among them, in beauty and in grace.

---

12 Colin Davis, "État Présent: Hauntology, Spectres and Phantoms," *French Studies* 59(3) (2005): 373–9, here pp. 378–9.

CHARACTERS	
SARA	30s, wife and mother, working professional, upwardly mobile.
JON	30s, husband and father, working professional, upwardly mobile.
LESLIE	30s, friend of Jon, Sara, but closer friend to Les, married into and divorced with money.
LES (LESTER)	30s, friend of Jon's, works in same office (preferably black).
DON	30s, friend of Jon and Les, works in same office (preferably Latino).
THE GIRL	13, rootless.
VOICE OF THE CHILD	Voiceover.
TIME	Now. Several months later, and then several years later. And in and out of time.
SETTING	A neat space with clean lines: vaguely chic, minimalist, and safe. A rough shoreline bordered by rocks is kept at a distance, but is never really that far away.
PLACES	A room overlooking the ocean, a room of memory, perhaps somewhat reminiscent of a child's room in its dimensions but not in decor; the well-appointed but modest house of Sara and Jon; a public place, perhaps outside a grocery store; the office; the park, the beach in Gibraltar. All suggested with elegance and economy.

NOTE ON THE PLAY

This play was finalist for the 2010 PEN USA Award in Drama.

The scenes designated as being "In Time" are theatrically fluid—performed in stillness or with suggested movement. They may also occupy a virtual, mediated space. *Every effort should be made to cast the play inclusively, and thus reflective of the world.* Melody to original song lyrics in script may be obtained by contacting the playwright or reset by another composer. Words in paranthesis in the script are not meant to be spoken.

This script received its world premiere at Passage Theatre Company in New Jersey (artistic director: June Ballinger) in spring 2009 under Daniella Topol's direction with cast: Heidi Schreck, Bryan Close, Polly Lee, Frank Harts, Gerardo Rodriguez, Kate Hopkins. Sound design by Broken Chord Collective.

1. IN TIME

The memory room is lit. It is empty, save for a table and chair and a window.
A voice is heard.

VOICE OF THE CHILD. You walk into a small room overlooking an ocean.
    The room is in Gibraltar
    or maybe the Pyrenees or maybe Ushuaia.
    There is a rustic table in the room.
    It's near a window that overlooks an ocean.
    The table feels warm. It's been, as they say, lived in.
    Although this place, this room, this ocean, is far away,
    it feels as if it could be anywhere.
    Music is heard.
    It is as if it is playing along a border . . .
    It feels ancient, even though it was made only a year ago.
    This is an opening track, a ghostly prelude.
    Listen.

2. MISSING THE CHILD

The parents, Sara and Jon, try to make sense of things.

SARA. She was here

JON. She was right here

SARA. I don't know where Sonya

JON. Where she could

SARA. I didn't

JON. For a moment

SARA. We left
    We had to go to the

JON. We didn't think

SARA. I mean, Sonya was sleeping.

JON. She was sound . . .

SARA. . . . We tucked her in.

JON. (And now those words . . . to tuck in . . . they seem)

SARA. It wasn't like we were

JON. We're not

SARA. We've never been

JON. We're not like other

SARA. Leaving kids around
　　on their own
　　on playgrounds

JON. After school

SARA. On the street

JON. Getting into

SARA. Doing all sorts of

JON. I mean, we're not like that

SARA. We're good parents

JON. We invest time, quality time

SARA. Energy

JON. Loads of

SARA. We do the best we . . . I'm a good mother

JON. Always have been

SARA. So, you see, this

JON. Isn't happening
　　Okay? You understand?

SARA. Not to us.

JON. 'Cause we don't
　　It's not like we deserve

SARA. Does anyone deserve?

　　(*Silence.*)
　　I don't even remember what Sonya was wearing.

JON. The blue jumper.

SARA. Was it?

JON. With the bunnies.
  The blue jumper with the bunnies.
  Pink socks.
  The gold necklace Serena gave her.

SARA. The small scar on her left knee
  from when she fell in the playground at nursery.
  The way she holds her hand out when she wants something.
  Silence.

JON. We'll find her.

3. RUMORS OR A PICTURE OF SONYA

Leslie and Les and Don outside the upscale grocery store. They see a Xerox photo of Sonya (unseen by audience) on a missing-child flyer.

LESLIE. So beautiful.

DON. Yes.

LESLIE. Hard to imagine that she's just . . .

LES. Vanished. Her picture everywhere.

LESLIE. How could someone, a little girl, just go . . .?

LES. She was sleeping, apparently.

LESLIE. Huh?

LES. Before they left for the party. Sonya was sleeping.

LESLIE. You mean they?

LES. They have an alarm system.

LESLIE. Meaning what?

LES. They were only at the party—what?

DON. Minutes.

LES. Right down the street, for Chrissakes.

LESLIE. Les, would you leave Nissa alone? Would you?

DON. At least she's blond . . .

LESLIE. What?

DON. There's more of a chance that they'll find her because she's blond.

All the kids you see that go missing and whatnot . . . If they're blond, nine times out of a hundred, they get found. Blond kids get more attention. It's statistical.

LES. It's racist.

DON. It's part of it.

LES. It's ALL of it.

DON. Look, all I'm saying is, if it was Nissa that was missing (God forbid, but if it was).

LES. Not about my daughter, Don. The line is drawn. You get me?

DON. Hear me out, Les.

LES. I'm hearing.

DON. If it was Nissa, nine times out of a hundred, you could bet (and I say this with sadness, heavy on my heart) you could bet there'd be less of an effort to find her.

LES. I'd find her.

DON. By the populace, Les. The news, whatnot. I'm not saying it's right, okay? The truth is, it burns me up, but I recognize, you know, the country we live in. Even after all these years.

LESLIE. It's so sad. Just a little girl . . .

LES. What Jon and Sara must be going through . . .

DON. . . . Maybe we should call them, huh? Say something.

LESLIE. . . . We should leave them alone. Give them space.

LES. . . . If it was Nissa who was . . .

LESLIE. Nissa's fine. She's safe.

4. AND A LITTLE PRAYER

Sara is seen. She waits on a mobile phone call. She speaks to herself memories of the routine of her life with Sonya while she's on hold.

SARA. Wednesday: library day.
Thursday: market.
Friday: playtime.
Saturday: sleep in, finally.
Actually, no. No sleep in.
Cartoons: Skeletrina, Gloomy bear fuzzy face, Ciao ciao, Adios . . .
Sunday: waffles from the corner place, with strawberries.
Monday: come on, bunnytoes . . .

(*She's off hold*)

Yes? Yes I'm still here.
I've been waiting. Yes.
Sonya. Uh-huh.
No. No. S-o-n-y-a.
Yes.
. . .
Sorry?
A scrunchie?
Yes.

Sara closes mobile phone. A moment.

5. A GOOD MIRROR

Jon and Les and Don at the office. The silent hum of the workplace.

JON. I don't even know what this is.

LES. Hmm?

JON. This paper.
I can't make it out.
Paper in my hand and I can't . . .

LES. Let me see, Jon.

JON. No. I'll figure it out.

LES. Maybe you should take a break.

JON. Huh?

LES. Break.

JON. I'm fine.

LES. Okay.

They work for a while, then:

JON. What's that mean?

LES. Huh?

JON. Just now when you said . . .

LES. Nothing. What? Just a break.

JON. Break from what?

LES. Nothing. Christ. Jon. It's just a . . . whatchamacallit . . . phrase. "Take a break." You know. "Have yourself a break today."

JON. Have yourself? Yourself? What is that? Huh? Yourself?

LES. I don't know. Phrase, old jingle. On the TV, radio, whatever. A phrase. That's all. Right, Don?

DON. Yeah. I remember that one. (*Sings*) Have yourself a break today.

JON. You never said it before.

LES. Well, what the fuck, Jon, I'm saying it now. "Take a goddamn break."

JON. You think I can't do my job.

LES. Jon, I'm your friend, okay? I care.

JON. . . . No one's innately good.

LES. What is that? One of your college aphorisms? Some hand-me-down cynical bullshit? Cairo, Istanbul, Mumbai on a comparative socio-spatial geographic chart of dynamic urban growth gone to seed?

JON. What the hell are you talking about? Cairo, Istanbul . . . ?

LES. Well, we do business with them, don't we? So, as example, as ergo, you know, i.fucking.e . . . we know people from dealing with them, from doing business . . . right? So, it seems to me from this knowledge of people, people from all over the planet committed to the global market, to the global city, to goddamn growth and progress even under duress, under circumstances

that would indicate otherwise, that we'd understand—if anyone would, if anyone can—goodness, goodness in people.

DON. Their intrinsic value.

LES. Exactly. But you said, you said, No one person is good.

JON. I said "innately," Les.

LES. Innately, my ass. What the fuck does that mean?

JON. We love and hate; that's all.
We just love and hate each other.
Innate goodness doesn't exist.

LES. . . . You're a cannon, my friend.

JON. Don't.

LES. The way you think . . . the way you talk about LIFE . . . People
are good. I'm good. I know that. I look in the mirror and say
to myself "I'm good." Every day.

JON. Really?

LES. I have faith in myself, Jon.
Look, we all do, right?
Deep down we're rock solid, man. Unwavering.
And this what we do here in this job is what we do.
We sell nothing. We make nothing.
Hell, we make nothing out of nothing and convince other
people to buy it.
We're a brand. We live it up.
This is the office. Okay. Calls from wherever any time of
the day.
Entire countries on hold. The power, my friend. Goddamn
power.
And it's not evil. It's just business. Like me or you or anybody
else.
Taking a crap, making a dime, trying to get by.
This is good. We're good. Innately.
And believe me, I understand
if your faith has been . . . shook by this thing that you're going
through.
(I'd be the same)

But we're good. Down to the bone. People are good.
You're going through a rough time . . . I'm with you. I'm here.
I'm not on some cruise ship downing a margarita.
I'm here. And I'm comfortable with that.
I'm comfortable.

JON. You're right.

LES. Of course I'm right. Right, Don?

DON. It's a "categorical imperative," Les.

LES. See? Even Don.

JON. Fucking Kant. Are you quoting, Don?

DON. Look, he was on to something. Kant thought about goodness.

JON. I can handle things. I'm not a fuck-up.

LES. Jon . . .

JON. You and everybody else, looking at me . . . the minute I walk
in . . .

LES. Hey Jon.

JON. It was an accident. I'm a good father.

LES. I know.

JON. I work here.
I don't go around acting like I'm working, making a show of
things.
Like Don.

DON. Hey. I work.

JON. That's not me. That's not my game.
Not like everybody else:
taking the credit for things they haven't even done.
Hustling the next and next raise, while I'm here,
without a complaint, dutiful to a fault (always the dutiful son),
just doing my job,
fucking advocating for colleagues,
for you, Les (when no one else . . . no one else . . . you remember that?)

LES. I know, Jon.

JON. Like I'm made of gold or something,
like I've got a halo on my head . . .
But at the end of the day, at the end of the day, what?
The saints go home. The saints go to their graves.
And nobody, nobody, gives a shit.
And then you say "friends whatever. We're friends."

LES. We are friends, Jon.

JON. We play golf on the weekends, Les. We have a coupla beers.
It's not like you'd put your life on the line, Les.

LES. You're not even listening . . .

JON. "Take a break." You said THAT, didn't you?

LES. Let's just settle down, okay? You know how Michal can get . . .

JON. Yeah. Michal. Oh yeah. I'd like to see him, man . . .
with his fucking wherewithal, with his 72-fucking-par dick . . .

Michal crosses, unseen.

Hey, Michal!

LES. Jon . . .

JON. Hey!

Michael exits, unseen.

LES. We got golf on Sunday.

JON. So what? Let him win? Is that what you're saying?

LES. Just . . . ease up, you know.

JON. Be good?
. . . So full of shit with the goodness, the goodness, bleeding
out of you.

LES. What are you . . .?

JON. You look in the mirror every day? You say I'm good?
Who in their right mind does that? Huh?
No one. No one on this earth. Fucking evangelical.

LES. Jon, I'm Episcopalian.

JON. A child doesn't just disappear, Les.
A child doesn't run away from a good home.
And our home, our home, is good.

This isn't a "they fuck you up, your Mom and Dad" kind of thing.

DON. Like the poem. Philip Larkin.

JON. What the fuck is that?

DON. I'm just . . . referencing . . .

JON. Well, this isn't that . . . This isn't a reference! My LIFE is not a goddamn hyperlink in cyberspace.

LES. It's just a poem, Jon.

JON. We're not complicit. We're not culpable of anything.
I'm not a father who leaves his daughter alone in a park.

LES. You're saying I'm . . .?

JON. I remember, Les. I remember things.

LES. Look, Jon, you're torn up, I'm with you, man, but don't—

JON. You're gonna tell me you've never let Nissa alone for a second?

LES. Don't. Okay? Not about my daughter, Jon.

JON. That day at the park. I was there, Les. I was right there.
You turned around and where was she?
Precious Nissa doted on by her perfectly good, perfectly doting father
Stranded . . . three years old and the child is stranded, vanished somewhere in the neighborhood park.

LES. . . . Give me that.

JON. What?

LES. Fucking hard copy you've been fiddling with for the last half hour.

JON. I know where it goes, Les.

LES. You don't know shit.

Les wrests paper from Jon and puts it away in a file. Pause.

JON. So, this is what this is, eh?

LES. This is work, Jon. Work. We lose something, it wrecks the order, okay?

JON. Gotta have that.

LES. Yes. We do, Jon. It's not just your ass. We're all in this, right?
What you do, what I do, what Don does reflects on everything
here.

JON. I can do my job, Les. I'm doing my . . .

DON. You're doing fine, Jon.

LES. You think people are going to wait, Jon?
If they have to wait, they'll go somewhere else, man.

JON. I can do my job, Les.

LES. I'm just trying to help you. At the end of the day . . .

JON. I can do my job.

LES. Yeah.

6. LETTING IN THE QUIET

*Answering machine is heard: "You have five new messages," followed by
long beep, static, then a hang up.*

SARA. Goddammit.

> (*She throws bag of take-out food onto the floor.*
> *Long beep, static, hang-up.*)

Jon?

> (*She takes off jacket and handbag, throwing them on the floor*
> *Long beep, static, hang-up.*)

Every fucking day.

> (*Long beep, static, hang-up.*)

She goes within. Time shift.

7. WHAT WE DO AT HOME

*Jon walks in from another room inside the house. He seems slightly adrift.
Pause. Sara enters with bag of take-out food.*

SARA. They said a sock . . .

JON. What?

SARA. Now they found a sock.

JON. Is it . . .?

SARA. A child's sock.

JON. Is it pink? She had her pink socks on before-

SARA. They said a sock. They didn't say what color. They said dirty, muddy, something.

JON. Muddy how? It's not muddy around here.

SARA. It's what they said.

JON. If it's pink, if it's pink . . . it could be . . .

SARA. I got us something. Let's eat.

They begin to eat. Pause.

JON. A sock. How can a person lose a sock?

SARA. Dryer syndrome.

JON. Huh?

SARA. . . . Remember?

JON. . . . Where'd she come up with that?

SARA. I don't know.

JON. Crazy.

SARA. Smart.

JON. To come up with that . . . yeah.

SARA. And that other time . . . what was it?. . .

JON. At the beach.

SARA. Yeah.

How does a person get lost?

JON & SARA. Lochness disease.

They laugh. Pause.

JON. Things she'd come up with.

SARA. Pink elephants.

JON. Huh?

SARA. Story at bedtime.

JON. I don't remember that one.

SARA. She made it up.

JON. Never told me.

(*Pause*.)

Food's good.

SARA. It's crap.

Everything's plastic.

Look at these:

Little knives and forks and spoons that don't work, that don't cut.

But we use them anyway, 'cause there's nothing else, right?

You order from a place, you eat.

You open a can, you eat.

JON. Sara . . .

SARA. I don't want to cook.

I don't want to make things.

A sock. That's all I know.

('Cause the scrunchie wasn't hers.)

So, just a lone sock left somewhere.

Crap food, crap life, crap love, crap piss, crap looking . . .

Everyone looking at me . . . like I was . . . like I was . . .

JON. Shh. Come on now.

He holds her. They caress, kiss, let themselves discover each other again.

SARA. I always liked your hands.

When we met that day on the pier

and you scooped me up crazy-wonderful,

. . . it was your hands . . .

Sonya has your hands.

(*And then she pulls away, passion turning into confusion and rage*.)

I keep rewinding that night in my head:

your hand on my thigh, keys, door, kiss. Us. Just us.

JON. We went to Michal's party, that's all.

SARA. Five, ten minutes . . . For your fucking job.

JON. Not anymore, actually.

SARA. Huh?

JON. They gave me leave. At the office. I had an . . .
. . . outcry . . . "outburst"

SARA. What did you—?

JON. I spoke out of turn.
I wrecked the order. Can't have that.

SARA. Oh. Jon . . .

JON. Michal comes in
after I'd had my say and Les had his
and Don whatever . . .
Michal comes in with his clean smile and says "Hey. Jon"
And I knew. Right then.
The look on his face . . .
Leave of absence.

SARA. God.

JON. We'll be fine.

SARA. . . . with my job alone we can't . . .

JON. We have enough . . . we got credit, right? . . .

SARA. How long is . . . this leave . . .?

JON. Michal didn't say. He just cut me a check. I mean, Michal, you
know. He's good business.

SARA. What did you . . .?

JON. I just had some words, that's all.

SARA. With Les, right? Why do you have to . . .? Every time.

JON. I never—

SARA. What is Les to you? Why give him the satisfaction of knowing
. . . what's inside, what you're really . . . your heart?

JON. It wasn't like that.

SARA. I know you. You always . . .

JON. You want me to just take it, take his crap? He was talking about,
making light even of what we're . . . you want me to ignore
that? We spend half our lives ignoring . . .

SARA. What's that mean?

Are you talking about Sonya now? Are you talking about me and Sonya?

I never ignored her.

JON. Everybody ignores everybody.

SARA. I spent time. Plenty of time.

JON. My parents, my parents . . . my mother—

(*She slaps him. A moment.*)

She was with me. I remember. Hours and hours . . . wasteful hours . . . no schedule . . . no fucking clocks . . . just play . . .

SARA. Your parents had more money.

JON. Meaning what? They could afford to be with me?

We don't have enough money now, is that it?

SARA. . . .

Sara goes within. A moment.

JON. I'll find her, Sara. I'll go out every day and look for her.

(*Jon gets car keys out of his pocket and speaks to Sonya, in mind, out loud.*)

And we'll be big and strong. And we'll travel the world.

Give me your hand, bunnytoes. Tell me where to go.

(*He walks out, keys in hand.*

Time passes. Night.

Sara enters from within with Sonya's plush toy [perhaps a teddy bear or an elephant], and a children's book, perhaps Tish Rabe's [adapted from Dr. Seuss])

Oh, Baby, the Places You'll Go.

She sits on the floor, opens the book and reads a few pages out loud. She falls asleep while reading.

There's some light from outside coming in through the window but otherwise the house is dark. Jon walks in.

JON. Sara? . . . Sara?

(*Jon approaches her. Sara thrashes about violently in her sleep. Jon tries to subdue her. Sara wakes, startled.*)

I'm right here.

An embrace. They go within. The book is left behind.

8. A GIFT

Time passes.
Leslie and Les are seen in silhouette passing by Jon and Sara's house.
Don is seen in silhouette passing by Jon and Sara's house.
Time shift.
Leslie, with gift in hand, sits in a chair in Jon and Sara's house.

LESLIE. I wanted to call. I've been meaning to. It's just that I . . .

SARA (*from offstage*). That's all right.

LESLIE. No, it's not, it's not remotely . . . I mean, we're friends, we know each other. It's not like we're . . . like you're some . . . we know the same people, for crying out loud.

SARA (*from offstage*). Some. Yes.

LESLIE. I just don't want you to think . . .

SARA. I don't . . .

LESLIE. 'Cause I'm not . . . that kind of person, you know who . . . turns the cheek when the shit . . . You know what I'm saying? I'm not like . . . I've never been . . . So, I don't want you to think I'm . . .

SARA (*enters with tea*). I don't . . .

LESLIE. I should've called. Right away. I should've brought something.

SARA. You have.

LESLIE. Well, this. Yes. Well . . . it's nothing . . . please, don't open it now . . . I'll feel embarrassed . . . 'cause, really, it's just . . . I didn't know what to . . . no one I've known has ever . . . gone through . . . weeks now, hasn't it been?

SARA. Months, actually.

LESLIE. I don't how you . . . I don't have kids, but my dog . . . I know it's not the same, not remotely. Sorry, I don't mean to be insensitive . . . but just to say . . . I can imagine . . . if it were me . . .

SARA. You're not.

LESLIE. No. No. I know. I know we're not . . . I know that we don't really . . . Look, perhaps you don't even think of me as a friend. And I understand. I haven't been the most . . . It's just not my thing, you see. I don't do friendship very well. But I want you to know that I . . . I'm here, right? I've come all this way. I'm . . . whatever you need, you know?

SARA. Thank you.

LESLIE. Has there been any news?

SARA. A sock, that's all.

And it wasn't even her sock. So . . .

Sonya's invisible. That's what I tell myself. She's become invisible.

. . . I don't feel like a mother anymore.

Perhaps I never felt . . .

LESLIE. It's all right.

SARA. I don't know anything anymore.

LESLIE. We all have our . . . what we keep inside . . .

SARA. I know I didn't want kids. I didn't. Is that wrong?

LESLIE. I don't have kids.

SARA. I told Jon when we got together.

But he . . . he wanted . . . he kept . . . you see? And then I wanted . . .

But I keep telling myself now, the question keeps . . . was I a good mother?

If I'd been a better mother, would Sonya . . .

LESLIE. You can't think those things.

SARA. But I do. I do think them.

Stories. Memories. Things that go by in the mind.

Moments when she called out from another room and I said, Wait. Not now. Wait. Later. Sonya. Later. Later. Later . . .

and then it's . . . too late . . .
and you think WHAT was I doing? WHAT was so IMPOR-
TANT that . . .?
But of course in the moment, in that moment,
when she called from the other room,
I didn't think . . . because you don't. No one does.
Sonya's there. In her room. She's playing.
She's sleeping. She's fine.
I go to work to feel useful. I stare at Jon when I come home.
I make her bed over and over.
I bite random parts of my body for no reason.
I listen to her voice on the answering machine.
I replay the message over and over
until I can't listen to it anymore,
until all I want to do is erase . . .
But then some song comes on the radio
"Any Other World"[1]
And the song is absolutely made to . . .
And I do. I cry. Right on cue.

LESLIE. I get weepy at songs too.

SARA. And yet no matter how much I cry,
everyone still thinks Sara messed up. It's her fault.

LESLIE. I don't think—

SARA. Don't lie to me. There's nothing worse than . . .
At a time like this . . . at any time . . .
You think I don't hear them? The rumors? Gossip?
This fucking town . . .
She was drunk, they say. She was a bad mother.
She, she, she . . .

LESLIE. I brought you a . . .

SARA. Yes, thank you. A gift. Thanks. I'll open it later, as instructed.
God forbid I think it's awful and tell you to your face.

---

1 The reference is to a pop song by Mika from his 2007 album *Life in Cartoon Motion.*

Pause.

LESLIE. Look, I think you think things about people, about me,
and of course I'm not saying you shouldn't,
you've every right to think anything you'd like
(I mean I can see from this house, the state of it, that
your perspective on things is not entirely . . .)

SARA. . . . Her things. I like having them around.

LESLIE. Of course.

SARA. Coloring books, toys . . . report cards . . .
first grade . . . she got straight A's.

LESLIE. That's great.

SARA. Is it? Are A's that important? I ask myself these things. I spent
hours asking . . . While you and all the rest (say) . . . She, she,
she . . .

LESLIE. I don't.
I'm reaching out, okay?
You may not want it, you may not approve,
I may not the person you thought should be here,
but whatever you may think, I'm here.
'Cause I know what it's like to be,
Shall we say, ignored;
I know what people think of me,
Ever since the so-called inappropriate marriage.
Inappropriate because what? I didn't deserve him?
He wasn't in my strata? I loved him, you know.
Even after the house and the clothes and the dog,
Even after the split, and more clothes, and the same dog
I loved him. So, I know. You see? I know about being left.
And I thought, well, well, there she is, there's Sara in her
tragedy,
And who the hell is coming forth, you know?
Who is actually offering anything to her
Except far-away concern, worry and sad smiles;
Like your child was one of those kids on late-night TV ads,
You know, those kids from far-away countries

with terribly sad, beautiful faces,
And I know Sonya's not . . . She's not far away.
She couldn't have just . . . It's too painful to think . . .
So, I came here to . . . okay? Offer something.

(*Phone rings. Sara lets it ring.*)

Aren't you gonna?

SARA. No.

LESLIE. You want me to?

SARA. Let the machine.

Slight pause. Child's voice is heard on the answering machine:
"We're not home. Leave a message," followed by machine beep fol-
lowed by staticky silence.

LESLIE. I don't think she's far away at all.

SARA. Vision, eh?

LESLIE. Just a feeling.

SARA. I don't know what to feel anymore.

LESLIE. We make plans, we live our lives,
we don't think that anything (awful)'s going to happen.
I don't know why that is, but we just don't.
We think things are given to us perhaps? But really, nothing is.
All we have in the end is what we (can) hope for.
Silly, I suppose.
But it's all we have, right?
Take care, Sara. Take care.

Leslie exits.

9. IN TIME (2)

Sara is seen in the memory room.

VOICE OF THE CHILD. You sit in the room overlooking the ocean.
You hear a voice.
The voice leans into your ear.

It speaks a language you don't understand.
Perhaps it is a made-up language.
You follow it anyway.
You move your arms. You raise them in prayer.
This is church, you tell yourself.
This room, this lived-in table, this looking out,
Waiting, waiting . . .
This is church
Now.

A gesture of praying.

10. IN PARALLEL TIME

Jon picks up discarded items, clutter, etc. in the living area.

JON. You walk through the room looking for a sign.
(She says) Forgot, Daddy. I left my book in the playground.
I left my jumper in the laundry.
I leave so many things.
Go play. Go play with Mommy,
I'll take care of everything,

(*He goes within for a brief moment to discard elsewhere all items in hand.*
And then reappears to pick up the plush toy left behind, and speaks to it)

and later I'll tell you a story about the world.

Jon goes within with the plush toy.

11. AFTER THE GAME, A WORTHWHILE APOLOGY

Les, Don and Jon in the park.

LES. Like the hand of God. I swear. Did you see that fastball?

DON. Inhuman.

LES. Like a fucking god, man.

JON. That kid should play in the bigs.

LES. As long as he doesn't mess up (he will).

DON (*sings chorus from Elton John song*). "Rocket man burning out his fuse up here alone."

LES. What the hell are you singing, man?

DON. Huh?

LES. What is that? You hear that, Jon?

JON. Yeah.

DON. What? I can sing.

LES. I'm not saying (you can't), Don. Just saying, What, you know.

JON. That was some fastball.

LES. Yeah. Yeah, it was. Miss you, man.

JON. Is that right?

LES. Yeah, man, it's like . . .

DON. What do we do without you at the office?

JON. You really think that, Don?

DON. Oh. Yeah. Paper clips.

JON. Bullshit.

DON. No, man, I mean it. Your desk was so organized. Even the paper clips were in the right place.

JON. You'd steal my paper clips, Don?

DON. I'd never . . .

JON. Bull fucking shit.

LES. It's true, man, we miss you.

JON. Poker clutch in the back room. The money you took off me.

LES. Hey, I can't help it if you can't play.

JON. I play. I just don't cheat.

LES. Now, Jon . . .

JON. Yeah yeah.

LES. I'm sorry, you know. I didn't know Michal would . . .

JON. He did what he had to do, Les, what he felt was right.

LES. Yeah, but it's shitty. Don't you think?

JON. I don't judge people, Les.

LES. Come on, you know it is.

DON. The whole world's shitty.

LES. Is that right, Don?

DON. Catastrophic orbit.

JON. How's that?

DON. World. Creation is catastrophe, after all. Constant rupture, chaos and remaking.

LES. Don, you get out here and your mind . . .

DON. What? Park's nice. You can breathe the air.

LES. We should've gone to the bar.

JON. And what? Run into Michal?

LES. Yeah. You're right. See enough of him . . .
It pisses me off. What he did. I should talk to him.

JON. You'd do that?

LES. Get him on a good day, you know . . .

DON. That'd be when?

LES. He has good days, Don.

JON. You don't have to . . .

LES. I want to. Just because you flared up a bit . . .
Hell, Alex in accounting, he does nothing but flare up.

DON. Gets bank, too.

LES. Skimming off the top, he is.

DON. Is he?

LES. I should talk to Michal. Maybe this weekend at the club.

JON. Well, that'd be . . .

LES. Least I can do. With what you're going through . . .

JON. What's that?

LES. Huh?

JON. What am I going through, Les? Huh? Tell me. What is it that I'm going through?

LES. You know.

JON. No, I don't. Why don't you tell me?

LES. Jon . . .

JON. Can't even say it. Can't even get the nerve to . . .

DON. Okay, guys, okay.

JON. What is it with you, Don? Huh?

DON. We're out here. We're having a time. Let's have it. That's all.

JON. You're a case.

LES. Don's always been a case.

DON. Rag on me all you like. Go on. But you need me. You need Don around.

LES. Look, Jon . . . I'm here for you, right? I'm here.

JON. You talk to Michal, then? You tell him to give me back my job?

LES. Listen, you're getting something, aren't you?

JON. What's that?

LES. With the leave . . . I mean, you're covered for a while, right?

JON. You think I like this? Hanging around? With nothing?
Driving my car for hours 'cause it's something to do,
'cause maybe just maybe there'll be some sign of Sonya,
some rare fucking glimpse she's alive;
you know how many miles I drive every day?
I go to whole other towns way out fucking nowhere.
And I get back and everything's the same.
And you sit here with "Hey man . . ." Fuck you.

LES. Hey.

JON. Fuck you, Les. Fuck you up the fucking ass.

LES. Okay. Look. Look. You're drunk.

JON. Yeah. I'm drunk. I'm roaring. I'm riled. I was drunk that night and I'm still—

DON. You weren't drunk that night.

JON. Huh?

DON. At the party.

JON. What's this, Don? You have some words of wisdom now from over there in paper-clip-thieving land?

DON. All I'm saying is . . . I saw you. You were fine. A little buzzed maybe but . . .

JON. Oh, so it's my fault that . . .

DON. I'm not saying . . .

JON. Then what? What?

DON. Look, in time, Jon, everything will find its place, you know.

JON. In time?

DON. I just mean you'll have a better hold on things, on how time flows through us, out of us, so forth, and where we all stand in the grand scheme.

JON. What the fuck are you on?

DON. Just beer . . .

JON. In time, eh?

DON. That's right. You'll see things for what they are.

JON. And I'll be the wiser, is that it? Is that your pearl (of wisdom) from the oracle of Mount Shit?

DON. Hey. Hey. Don't push me.

LES. Okay, guys.

JON. Can't take it?

DON. I can take.

JON. Yeah? Let's see, then.

DON. What?

JON. Let's see what you can fucking take.

LES. Okay, guys. Okay.

JON. Cut out, Les. This is me and Don here. Me and Don, right?

DON. Yeah.

JON. Well, then. Come on. Don.

DON. I defer . . .

JON. Defer, my ass. I'm not going to stand here, be the bully; this isn't grade school we're out in the yard and Mrs. Grabinski is keeping score.

DON. If you could see yourself . . .

Jon clocks Don. Don falls.

LES. Jesus, Jon. What the—?

JON. I see myself fine, Don. Y'hear me?

LES. Jesus, Jon . . . .

JON. Get up. Come on. Get up, Don.

LES. Don. Don. Don.

DON. Okay. Les. Okay. I'm . . .

LES. Goddammit, Jon.
What's with you, man? What's got into you? Huh?
You know, I vouch for you all the time.

JON. You mean at work? With Michal? Is that what you mean, Les?

LES. I vouch for you, okay? But this . . .

JON. . . . Hey. Don, (are) you all right?

DON. Yeah.

JON. Look, I'm . . . .

DON. I don't want your (apology) . . .

JON. Fucking beer, man.

DON. Uh-huh.

Pause. Jon offers Don another beer. Don accepts. Silence. They drink.

It's like that story.

JON. Huh?

DON. Like the ancients. Greeks and them all.

LES. What is, Don?

DON. This. This here. Story of a kid left in a cave.

LES. Huh?

DON. Abandoned by his own mother.

JON. Sara did not abandon Sonya.

DON. Story, that's all. Fiction. Myth.

JON. . . . So, what's the story, Don?

DON. You wanna talk now, eh?

JON. Look, I said . . .

DON. Yeah yeah . . . . I hear you, Jon. . . . Story is, a mom leaves her kid in a cave, the same cave where she gave birth to him. Leaves him for dead, right?

JON. Christ.

DON. Yeah, it's pretty awful, but then, it turns out, as these stories go, that a god's been watching over everything.

JON. What god?

DON. Some god. You know, the Greeks had all sorts of gods . . . And this god, he takes pity on the kid and takes him under his wing, see? Leaves the kid at the doorstep of this other god-like person. An act of grace. And the kid, you know, he's rescued. He has a home. A home he doesn't know, but a home nonetheless and this kid, he grows up just fine, no worries, no trauma, none of that.

JON. Except?

DON. You know this story?

JON. No but there's always . . .

DON. An "except," yeah. Well, except, time goes by, right? And this kid starts to wonder where the hell he came from. And around the same time his mother comes around.

JON. She knows . . .?

DON. No. No. It's a . . . whatchamacallit . . . a coincidence. She happens to be visiting.

LES. Not knowing they're . . .?

DON. Exactly. But in the end, in the end, they figure things out and faith is restored. See? That which was lost . . .

LES. . . . You are so full of shit.

DON. Honest to God.

LES. Fucking Greeks and Romans.

DON. Hey. It's not my story. I didn't invent it.

JON. So, what, you're telling me we're gonna find Sonya in ten, twelve years' time?

DON. I'm just saying it takes a certain kind of faith. If you think about the story—what's lost, what's recovered, even after a period of blindness, as it were (blindness; you hear me, Jon?). It's beautiful in a way. The kid left in a cave is reunited with his family. After years. After not knowing. They're returned to each other. They escape tragedy . . . Hey. Hey. Jon. Hey. What's this? Huh? Don't cry on me now.

JON (*weeping*). Fucking story . . .

DON. It's a story. That's all. Just a story.

JON. I want to believe . . . want to believe something. Shit. I'm all . . .

DON. It's all right.

JON. I'm so . . .

LES. It's all right.

JON. I'm so drunk.

LES. . . . Church, man.

JON. Don't give me religion, Les.

LES. It works for some people. Sara's going, right?

JON. Yeah.

LES. Like every day or something.

JON. You following her?

LES. No. Just, you know.

JON. Sara's a good person, okay?

LES. Yeah, but she's not a saint. I mean, back in the day . . .

JON. Back in the day, nothing, asshole. You USE her name, you talk about her with that tone again and I swear to God, I swear . . . you'll be meat, my friend. Pulp when I'm through with you.

LES. I just—

JON. NOTHING. NOT A WORD.

LES. . . . You've got some fucking in with me, man.

JON. No.

LES. Seems it.

JON. Just . . . telling you straight, that's all.

LES. Straight up, eh?

JON. . . . Fuck off.

LES. Hey. Come on. Truce, all right?

JON. And you tell Michal, you tell your beloved boss, asswipe.

LES. Hey, don't insult me, man.

JON. Tell him he'll never see me in that office again, not even if he goddamn begs.

LES. Jon . . .

JON. NEVER . . . y'hear me? I'm out. You and everybody else in this town . . . I'm going home.

DON. Want me to drive you?

JON. No, Don. No.

LES. Do what you have to do, man.

JON. Les, you are so full of shit.

Jon leaves. Pause.

LES. All I wanted to do was say I'm sorry, you know.

DON. Jon'll hear ya. In time. He'll hear us all.

They leave.

12. WHAT WE DO WHEN WE WAIT OR ANATOMY OF A MARRIAGE

Sara stacks all chairs, furniture pieces in a corner. There is a kind of super-energy in evidence here, the kind found often in sleeplessness. She cleans the floor with fervor. Jon enters.

SARA. Late.

JON. I didn't think you'd still be up. You should sleep.

SARA. I don't sleep anymore.

JON. There's work in the morning.

SARA. I quit.

JON. Huh?

SARA. I left them.

I couldn't work there anymore, Jon. I couldn't keep looking at
numbers, watching other houses go up for sale, for foreclosure,
for the banks to maybe bail them out. And I'm sitting there,
doing the books, just another desk, another phone, another
screen to be idle by while the weeks and weeks roll on like
liturgy . . .

JON. How are we supposed to . . .?

SARA. We'll sell things.

JON. The house?

SARA. Furniture. We don't need all these things, Jon.

End table. Why do we need an end table?

JON. Things. They're our things. Years we've been . . . You could've
waited, you know . . . to have your life's (revelation) . . . I can't
drive around and . . .

SARA. We'll drive around together.

JON. No. No.

SARA. We'll both look for her.

JON. . . . no . . .

SARA. Why not?

JON. It's not something you . . .

SARA. I can drive.

JON. That's not what I mean.

SARA. What, then?

JON. When I'm out there, when I'm . . . I just drive, you know . . .
it's different . . . you see?. . . Space . . .

SARA. . . .

JON. Look, I'm not gonna—we'll talk—I just I can't . . . think right now.

SARA. So, you walk away.

JON. What do you want from me? You want me to go to church with you? You want me to pray? I don't do that, Sara. I can't sit somewhere looking at some stained-glass ceiling while my kid's in some cave.

SARA. Sonya's not . . .

JON. Story. Old story.

SARA. I like going to church, Jon.

JON. I look up and all I see is grey. Sheer grey.

SARA. It's quiet. Safe.

JON. I drive around and seek out every little sign

SARA. I hear her

JON. Every path

SARA. She speaks to me. She tells me things

JON. People think he's crazy, he's lost all sense.
But what they don't understand is . . .

SARA. I need to believe

JON. Fuck that kind of thinking
And anything that makes everything seem okay

SARA. 'Cause if I don't, if I don't . . . I won't be able to move

JON. I won't stay between what was and what is.

SARA. Just safe. I'm trying to get safe.

He goes within. Silence. She remains.

13. A SONG OF GOING/DREAMING (A CRADLE SONG IN ¾ TIME)

In continuous time, Sara sings to stave off chaos.

SARA. If I go
    When I go
    All the world will know.

    If I go
    When I go
    Oh so very slow.

    There you'll be
    On a boat
    On an endless shoal.
    (*softly*) Shiver me,
    Little hope.
    Let all go.

    And we'll dream
    And we'll float
    On a boat of song.

14. OF A TIME/A SLEEPING WORLD

Time passes: a montage of months.
Jon sits in the memory room.
Sara observes from a slight distance.
He rests his head on the table, in an attempt perhaps to conjure a memory,
An attempt at connection of some kind.
He opens a slim drawer of the table and finds a tiny paper parasol like
the kind used to adorn cocktail drinks. He opens it. A gesture of hope.
He walks out of the memory room and into the living area of the house.
Shift.
Sara is seen in the memory room.
She prays silently, but the prayer fails her.

IMAGE 1.1 **Sara (Heidi Schreck) prays.**

Instructions for Breathing, directed by Daniella Topol at Passage Theatre Company, New Jersey (2009).

Photograph by Cie Stroud (Courtesy Passage Theatre Company press office).

Jon sees her from a slight distance,
She tries again.
There is an overwhelming sound of static.
Jon approaches her.
She walks away.

Shift.
Sara walks through the house.
Night.
The fading history of stars guides her.
Jon catches Sara with his eyes.
A moment between them.
She turns away slowly.
He wanders, restless, unsure of what to do with himself,
Of how to reach out to his beloved.
Shift.
The soft language of shells.
The sound of the beach.
Rustling and sounds of faint laughter.
Sounds that resonate, that call out.
Perhaps this is a shared conjuring, perhaps this is Sara's conjuring.
Broken words parse through the wind.

15. WAITING

Waiting consumes Sara and Jon.

SARA. Years.

JON. It's been

SARA. Two years

JON. Two days,

SARA. Four hours.

JON. And now

SARA. We wait
    as her day

JON. Another birthday

SARA. Passes.

JON. With no cake

SARA. No candles

JON. And no songs

SARA. Of gloomy bears

JON. And magic bunnies

SARA. Just

JON. Waiting.

SARA. . . . I'm starting to think . . . what if she . . .?

JON. We can't think that.

SARA. It's been such a long time, Jon. No word. No sign. Not even the sock was . . .

IMAGE 1.2 **Sara (Heidi Schreck) and Jon (Bryan Close) struggle with their loss.**
Instructions for Breathing, directed by Daniella Topol at Passage Theatre Company, New Jersey (2009)
Photograph by Cie Stroud (Courtesy Passage Theatre Company press office).

JON. Could've been . . .

SARA. I don't even dream anymore. Remember when we used to . . .?

JON. It's been a long time.

SARA. There was that game we used to play.

JON. What game?

SARA. Remember? Close your eyes, open the atlas and . . .

JON. See where you land.

SARA. And we'd always end up in these

JON. Crazy-ass places.

SARA. Ushuaia.

JON. The Pyrenees.

SARA. Gibraltar.

JON. We were like kids.

SARA. We'd say "one day, one day we'll go to all those places."

JON. Just go.

SARA. . . . Close the house, sell it, lose it, just go?

JON. Can't stay here

SARA. Looking at all her things

JON. Day after day

SARA. No word, no nothing,

JON. Just waiting and waiting

SARA. I see her sometimes. I close my eyes and I see her in some other place, in one of those places we used to dream about

JON. End-of-somewhere place

SARA. In a room near an ocean,

JON. Rough, remote

SARA. Rustic, beautiful,
And I think

JON. If that's where she is

SARA. That's where we should be.

JON. Just go.

A gentle embrace.
For no more than an instant,
the mere glimpse of the Child (Sonya) is seen, in the distance.

16. OUT OF TIME

Several years later. Don is seen

DON. I saw her. That day. I saw Sonya through the window.
I was walking over to Michal's. Heading over to the party.
It was a clear night. Really beautiful.
The lights were on in Sara and Jon's house.
I liked looking at their house.
Not 'cause it was special in any way.
Other houses—Leslie's for instance—they're built to impress.
But I don't go in for that. I like simple things.
Sara and Jon's—yeah—it was simple.
Warm kinda glow, you know?
I remember I looked up.
There was a soft light on upstairs.
And for a moment I swear it looked like Sonya was dancing in
her room.
Really happy.
Just dancing, you know, moving about—twirling a parasol?
Funny what stays in the brain. After all these years, I still think
about that:
The random happiness of an only child.

17. GIBRALTAR

Sara and Jon are seen on the beach.

SARA. It's good here.

JON. Been good. Yes.

SARA. So calm.

JON. The ocean.

SARA. Gibraltar.

JON. You're so warm.

SARA. The heat . . .

JON. I just want to be inside you all day.

> *Kiss.*

SARA. Your lips are sweet.

JON. Breakfast.

SARA. Still?

JON. I haven't brushed my teeth.

SARA. Dirty boy.

JON. You like it.

SARA. I'm afraid I do.

> *Kiss.*

JON. Go for a swim?

SARA. Later.

JON. Sun's out.

SARA. I just want to be here.

JON. Breathe, eh?

SARA. Yeah.

JON. Not think of anything.

SARA. I want to stay here.

JON. We are here.

SARA. Permanently.

JON. You mean stay stay?

SARA. Yes.

JON. And get by how?

SARA. How we've gotten by so far.

JON. Eking it out, moving on the cheap, like nomads.

SARA. Except we wouldn't move anymore. Just stay.

JON. And what? Sell knick-knacks? Souvenirs from Gibraltar . . .?

SARA. Why not?

JON. Not for me.

SARA. Haven't you ever wanted to—?

JON. I lived that life already.

SARA. Not really.

JON. I don't want to be responsible for anything anymore.

SARA. I just think . . .

JON. Just look at the water.

SARA. I'd really like to be in one place, Jon. Feels like we're floating.

JON. I thought you liked floating. Today, Gibraltar. Tomorrow, Finisterre. We got the whole atlas, darlin' . . .

SARA. But it's been years, Jon.

JON. We could go on this hike later, down some ancient path this guy was telling me about . . . it's nothing but rocks . . . and the drop is apparently unbelievable . . .

SARA. Jon.

JON. It'll be fun.

SARA. . . . I'd like to have a baby. I'd like to be mom again.

JON. What?

SARA. It's not like we have, I have, all the time in the world, y'know. And I'd like to . . . try again.

JON. . . . I don't want a . . . I don't want a replacement, Sara.

SARA. It wouldn't be . . .

JON. It would. To me, it would . . .
Having one . . . losing . . . not ever knowing . . . not even after years . . .

SARA. We can't just keep floating.

JON. Look, let's just go for a swim, okay?

SARA. I see her, Jon. I still see her. When I close my eyes . . . But I also see what could be, you know . . . in time . . .

JON. Set up house?

SARA. We could try. Yes.

JON. And if things don't . . .

SARA. We can't think about that. I want to have a child, Jon. I need to have a child. I can't keep on like this. I'm sorry, but I . . .

JON. I love you.

SARA. Jon.

JON. Just us, right?

SARA. It's been us for a long time.

Look, maybe you're not . . . But I have to . . .

Good, bad, indifferent, flawed, messed-up, beautiful, stupid, strange,

whatever you want to call it, but I can't keep pointing at the atlas

in hope that the next and next place will be . . . enough

to keep me from yelling and screaming,

and making love over and over again without the thought of, any thought of . . .

I'm sorry, Jon. I'm sorry.

She leaves. He is left.

18. THE RETREATING WORLD OR WATCHING THE CHILDREN

Time passes. Les, Leslie, and Don in the park with a view to the play-ground.

The children in this scene (Nissa, Mia) should preferably be unseen.

LES. Nissa! Nissa! What are you—? Stop that! Nissa. Stop it!

LESLIE. Don't worry. She'll be fine. She's just acting out.

LES. I don't like her acting out. She's been doing it a lot lately. It's not good.

LESLIE. She's getting older.

LES. No excuse for acting out.

LESLIE. Les, when you were her age, didn't you—?

LES. Yes, but that's different.

LESLIE. What's that mean?

LES. Boys, you know . . .

LESLIE. Boys are different?

LES. Yes. What? I'm not biased. This isn't some gender-bias thing. You know me, Leslie.

LESLIE. Uh-huh.

LES. But facts are facts.

DON. Actually, girls take more risks.

LES. What?

DON. Girls. They need to shove outdoors as much as boys.

LES. Where'd you get that?

DON (*Blackberry in hand*). Research.

LES. Don. Don.

DON. Hey, it's proven.

LESLIE. Well, all I know is, she should act out as much as she wants. You hear that, Nissa?

LES. Don't encourage her. Nissa's my child. I'll deal with her. You deal with Mia.

LESLIE. Mia can do what she likes. I don't mind if she acts out.

LES. And to think once you weren't going to have kids.

LESLIE. I know. But now I've Mia. Where's the guidebook, huh? That's what I want to know. Where's the book to tell you how to be a parent?

DON. There are lots of books.

LESLIE. You know what I mean. THE book.

LES. There isn't one. You have to make things up as you go along.

LESLIE. And if it's just you . . .

LES. Exactly.

LESLIE. I just hope I don't raise Mia the way I was raised. I'm really trying to avoid all the mistakes my parents made.

LES. You can't.

LESLIE. I can try. (*Sees Sara in near distance*)
Is that . . . ?

DON. . . . Sara. Yes.

LESLIE. I thought they went away.

DON. They did. (But I guess . . .)

LES. She looks . . .

LESLIE. Older. I know. Well, what can you expect, she went through the wringer . . .

DON. And they never did . . .

LESLIE. No, they never did find her. It was awful. When I think of Mia . . .

LES. Or Nissa.

LESLIE (*to Mia*). HIT HIM, HIT HIM, HIT HIM. That's right, Mia. Good girl.
Sara? Sara!
(*Sara comes into view.*)
I thought it was you. God. Long time.

SARA. Yes. Yes, it is.

LESLIE. So, how are you?

SARA. Fine. Just fine.

LESLIE. You look

LES. Great. You look great.

SARA. Thanks, Les.

LES. It's so good to see you.

SARA. Good to see you too.

LESLIE. . . . I just can't believe it. Such a long time.

SARA. Yes. Well . . .

LESLIE. So, what, you're moving back here?

SARA. No. I . . . I just needed to . . . sometimes you need to get away from getting away, you know.

DON. Retrace the steps.

SARA. Not exactly, but . . .

LES. I think it's great you're back. Even if it's just for a visit.

SARA. It's amazing. Everything looks the same.

LES. Slow wheels of progress around here. More layoffs, but other than that, same ol' same ol'.

LESLIE. And Jon? Did he . . .?

SARA. Oh, no, he . . . he's uh . . . he couldn't make it.

LES. I'm sorry.

SARA. Is that . . .?

LES. Nissa. Can you believe it?

SARA. She looks . . .

She's overcome for a moment (a memory of Sonya).

LES. What?

SARA. She's beautiful.

Pause.

LESLIE. Oh. God. I just remembered . . . I have to go to that thing. I totally forgot. Mia! Mia! Come on. Let's go.

SARA. Is that your—?

LESLIE. Yes. That's my Mia. Come on, Mia darling.
Good to see you, Sara. Really good.

Leslie leaves. Pause.

LES. You know, I . . . I've always wanted to say . . .

SARA. You don't have to . . .

LES. I know, but I . . . I think Jon thinks I got him fired somehow . . . and I had nothing to do with that . . . in the end, Michal made the decision . . . and there was nothing I could do . . .

SARA. That was years ago.

LES. Yes. Well . . . I'm sorry, you know. Sorry. Nissa! Let's go, hon. You don't want to be late. The pig's gonna leave for England.

SARA. Pig?

LES. It's a game we play. . . . Don, you coming along?

DON. What?

LES. I'm dropping you off, remember? At the club?

DON. Oh. Yeah. Yeah. Listen, I know we've never talked much, but . . . it's nice you've come back. For what it's worth and what-not—this town could use to see you.

LES. Don.

DON. I'm there, Les. Right there.

Les and Don leave. Sara remains.
The only sound: the creak of an empty swing
that's just been vacated by a child.
The swing stops swinging.
Sound of car driving off.
Sara sobs. It is extended, messy and uncontrollable:
a great, necessary release.
It should take as long as it needs to, even if it takes two minutes.
The Girl, about 13 years old, is revealed. She looks at Sara.

GIRL. Tissue?

SARA. Huh?

GIRL. I always carry tissue. Just in case.

SARA. Yes. Thanks. I'm a mess.

GIRL. Yeah.

SARA. I'm gonna use up all your tissue.

GIRL. That's all right. I can get more.

SARA. I don't know what . . . I just couldn't stop . . .

GIRL. Crying's weird like that sometimes. I cried once for hours. And then I stopped. Don't think I've cried since.

SARA. Really?

GIRL. Yeah. It was a long time ago. I don't even remember what it was about.

SARA. I think it's just being here.

GIRL. What? The playground?

SARA. Yeah.

GIRL. You don't like them or something?

SARA. I hate them.

GIRL. That's weird.

SARA. I used to come here with my daughter.
When I had time. We used to play. On the swings.

GIRL. And what? You don't play anymore?

SARA. No.

GIRL. Why not?

SARA. Just don't.

GIRL. . . . Something happened to her.

SARA. It was a long time ago.

GIRL. I'm sorry.

SARA. I wish I wasn't such a messy cryer. I must look a sight.
You don't happen to have a mirror or—?

GIRL. I got a lip-gloss case. It's got kinda—a mirror.

SARA. That'll work.

GIRL. . . . You have to flip it.

SARA. Huh?

GIRL. To open it. You have to flip the top part of the . . . Here. Let
me show you . . . See?

SARA. Now that you tell me . . .

GIRL. I know. They make them kinda screwed up. This girl I know
says they make them like that so we can spend hours wasting
our time.

SARA. Smart girl.

GIRL. I hate her.

SARA. Don't say things like that.

GIRL. Why not?

SARA. 'Cause you don't mean them.

GIRL. I do mean them. What do you know about me, huh? Who are you to tell me anything? You don't know me. I hate when people tell me things. Tell me what to do and stuff. I just want to send them all to hell.

SARA. That's why you're here?

GIRL. What?

SARA. Shouldn't you be in school or something?

GIRL. Fuck that.

SARA. You shouldn't . . .

GIRL. What? Don't tell me. Watch my mouth. That's what you're gonna say? Hey, girl, watch your mouth, or I'll wash it out for ya.

SARA. I wasn't going to say anything.

GIRL. I talk shit. I don't mean it. Lip gloss looks good on you. Keep it.

SARA. It's yours.

GIRL. Keep it. I want you to have it.

SARA. Thanks . . . Why do you always carry tissue around?

GIRL. Huh?

SARA. You said . . . before . . .

GIRL. I don't know. Something I do, I guess. Like if my nose bleeds or if I have snot or something . . .

SARA. I used to tell my daughter to always . . .
It's actually something my mom always used to tell me . . .
Things handed down, you know . . . I always used to tell her to . . .

GIRL. Before she died?

SARA. I didn't say she . . .

GIRL. Oh. Sorry. I just thought . . . Sorry. Fucking hole. Should keep it shut.

SARA. Look, I know I don't know you and . . . so I've no right to tell you anything, really, but . . . you shouldn't say things like that.

GIRL. What? Words? I just use them. They don't mean anything.

SARA. They do.

GIRL. People say things all the time. They don't mean them. They lie straight to your face and they tell you they're telling you the truth. Like this lady that took care of me once, she was always going on and on about how much she loved me, but she'd still beat the crap out of me any time she felt like. And this other lady, long time ago, she . . . So one day I just ran off. Got up in the middle of the night and just started walking as far as I could. Miles and miles. I figured if she didn't have time for me, I wouldn't have time for her.

I must've walked to a whole other country. That's what it felt like. My clothes were all raggedy-ass and sticking to me, and I must've lost my shoes somewhere along the way. And I was so thirsty. Like, desert kind of thirst. Weird, huh? To feel the desert when you're not even there. And there was this little ol' lady with a funny accent, kinda scary looking but sorta nice, and she come up to me and she gave me things. Water and things. And she took me into her house for a while. And she made my hair all different and she was funny . . . I liked her I think. 'Cause she spoke true. At least I thought she did. She said things, she meant them. She had time. She made time. And pretty soon I forgot everything about everything. I even forgot why I started walking in the first place. But she died, this little ol' lady. Like, real sudden. Walked into the house one day and she was dead. So I got put somewhere else with some relative of hers. Yeah. She was the liar, the real liar. But I left her, so it's cool. I left her and came here. And it's all right. I get along with people. I say things. People say things back. Nobody means anything. But that's all right. That's how we live, right?

SARA. I'm sorry.

GIRL. What for?

SARA. I'm so sorry.

GIRL. You're weird. You live around here?

SARA. Used to.

GIRL. It's a nice town.

SARA. It's all right.

GIRL. People, right?

SARA. Huh?

GIRL. They're kinda screwed up here.

SARA. Yeah.

GIRL. They act all normal and everything but they're so fucked up.

SARA. They're more than fucked up.

GIRL. Yeah?

SARA. Yeah.

> *They laugh: a shared outburst of feeling.*
>
> We really shouldn't . . .

GIRL. Why not? They don't care about us.

I bet all the time you lived here, no one around here really cared . . .

So, why should we give a fuck?

SARA. I wish you wouldn't . . .

GIRL. Words? . . . If it bothers you that much . . .

SARA. It's not that it bothers me . . . well, it does, but not in the way you think . . .

It's just . . . words are important, okay? Sometimes they're all we have.

GIRL. You're such a mom.

SARA. Am I?

GIRL. Come on, you don't even know me, and you're all being a mom.

. . . I used to dream I used to live in this house,

this real nice house somewhere,

Maybe, like, near the beach or something, far away, you know,

Maybe a whole other country,

And in this house, the people would be real straight up, you know,

No lies, no crap, no . . . in some hurry all the time,
And we could just hang out, you know,
Hang out and get to know each other.

SARA. Come 'ere.

GIRL. Huh?

SARA. Just come 'ere.

Sara embraces The Girl. A long embrace.

19. IN TIME (3)

Jon is seen in the memory room.

VOICE OF THE CHILD. You sit in the room overlooking the ocean.
You're in Gibraltar.
Though you wish sometimes
You were somewhere else.
You wait. You listen.
The room creaks. It makes sounds.
A part of you wants to stop all the noise,

. . .

You look out
As she goes
And you try to catch her with your eyes.

20. NOW

*We see the view now
from the window of the rustic room that overlooks the ocean.
We see Sara and Jon, and at a slight distance, the Girl.
The beach is empty, serene. The Girl holds a wooden Chinese parasol.
Sara and Jon walk toward her.
As they do so, a voice is heard. It is the Voice of the Child, Sonya's voice.
The Girl speaks the lines live with the voiceover.*

VOICE OF THE CHILD / THE GIRL. When I was born I was made of harsh wings

And you had to grab at me to stop me from cutting things,

Isn't that right?

Isn't that what you told me, Mommy?

I remember. You told me things.

You released your thoughts into me.

All's inside. See? Skin holds all sorts of things.

Don't worry. This will be easy.

Just listen. Just follow me.

See? It's like breathing.

Breathe, breathe, breathe, breathe . . .

And soon we'll be . . .

And as the Girl twirls and twirls the parasol: blackout.

The End.

WRECKAGE

CHARACTERS	
FIRST SON	Teen, homeless, slightly brooding, sensitive, passionate, wary.
SECOND SON	Teen, homeless, open, fluid, androgynous.
WOMAN	30s–40s, fierce, attractive, sensual, elegant.
NURSE	Played by male. 40s, slightly off-kilter, darkly humorous, honest, somewhat prescient.
HUSBAND	30s–40s, strong, powerful, contained, and caustic.
BROADCAST (VOICEOVER)	The clear, emotionally detached voice on the airwaves, male.
PLACES	The private beach, the gleaming house, the road, the boardwalk, and the convenience store of the jeweled city along the isthmus.

NOTE ON THE PLAY

Melodies to original song fragments in the text may be obtained by contacting the playwright, or the lyrics may be reset by another composer.

SCRIPT HISTORY

This script was written on a residency at the William Inge Center for the Arts in Kansas. Subsequently the play received a rehearsed reading at New Dramatists in New York under the direction of Annie Dorsen. A revised draft of the script received a mini-workshop at New Dramatists as part of the PlayTime Studio for New Plays under the direction of Stefan Novinski. The cast comprised Florencia Lozano (Woman), Alfredo Narciso (First Son), Aaron Yoo (Second Son), Chris Wells (Nurse), and Keith Randolph Smith (Husband). It also received a workshop at The Hartt School / University of Hartford as part of their New Play Festival and development with Highwire Theatre's reading series in NYC.

The play premiered at Crowded Fire Theatre in San Francisco under Erin Gilley's direction in May 2009. It received its Midwest premiere at Caffeine Theatre in Chicago in spring 2011.

This work is inspired, in part, by Jeff Buckley's cover version of Hank Williams' song "Lost Highway."

1

Waves. White hot sun. A cold beach. A distant broadcast is heard midst the waves.

VOICEOVER. The bodies of two boys were found yesterday morning. They were retrieved from the sea at about 9 a.m. Both boys had been struck with a blunt object, but otherwise, outside of a little blood, their bodies showed no other significant signs of violence. It is not known how long they were in the water, or who is responsible for their deaths.

(Waves. Two boys are seen on the beach, blood-marked in beauty. They are draped across each other, eyes closed, entwined. They wear simple street clothes and are barefoot. They awaken slowly, and stare at the water.)

A surveillance camera at a convenience store near the site recorded the last known appearance of the boys, who are believed to be brothers. Circumstances surrounding the deaths are unknown, although both boys are said to have been wearing vaguely feminine attire when they were found. In other news, the weather report promises highs in the low 80s, perfect for a day at the beach.

Silence.

SECOND SON. Was it like this?

FIRST SON. What?

SECOND SON. Swimming?

FIRST SON. Don't know.

SECOND SON. Don't you remember?

FIRST SON. I don't remember anything.

SECOND SON. Not even me?

FIRST SON. Of course I remember you. You're here.

SECOND SON. I remember a kiss. A woman's lips on my hands. Very sweet.

FIRST SON. When was this?

SECOND SON. I don't know. Not long ago.

FIRST SON. You're dreaming.

SECOND SON. No. This is what I remember.

FIRST SON. Well, I don't recall anyone kissing you.

SECOND SON. That's because you don't recall anything.

FIRST SON. A woman?

SECOND SON. Yes.

FIRST SON. What was she like?

SECOND SON. Tall. Strong. Pretty. She had tears in her eyes.

FIRST SON. How come?

SECOND SON. She was angry.

FIRST SON. Not mournful?

SECOND SON. No. Not grieving. She was furious, and sweet at the same time. Don't you remember?

FIRST SON. No.

SECOND SON. She held me.

FIRST SON. A cuddle?

SECOND SON. More than that. An embrace.

FIRST SON. Full on?

SECOND SON. Very warm. Very tender. I think she loved me.

FIRST SON. You're making it up.

SECOND SON. I'm not.

FIRST SON. Some woman held you?

SECOND SON. I was in her arms for a long time.

FIRST SON. And then?

SECOND SON. She kissed me.

FIRST SON. A kiss is important. A kiss is everything sometimes.

Pause.

SECOND SON. Do you want to?

FIRST SON. What?

SECOND SON. Kiss.

FIRST SON. Somebody might see.

SECOND SON. There's no one here.

FIRST SON. Might be. You don't know.

SECOND SON. What of it?

FIRST SON. You don't know how to kiss. You've no practice.

SECOND SON. I remember.

FIRST SON. A woman's lips on your hand? That's not a real kiss.

SECOND SON. What'd you mean?

FIRST SON. Hands don't count. Lips are what do.

SECOND SON. Who said? . . . You don't want me to kiss you.

FIRST SON. I didn't say that.

SECOND SON. You're shy.

FIRST SON. I'm not. Never have been. I'm not remotely shy.

SECOND SON. You don't act it.

FIRST SON. Kiss me. Go on. But not on my hands. I want a real kiss, yeah. Tongue and everything.

Second Son kisses First Son lightly. Pause.

SECOND SON. Well?

FIRST SON. I don't know.

SECOND SON. Did it feel like anything?

FIRST SON. It was all right.

SECOND SON. That's all?

FIRST SON. It was fine. What'd you want? You want to be reciprocated for your affection?

SECOND SON. What are you talking about?

FIRST SON. Words, right? I remember. They're in my brain. Tons of them waiting to be let out. "Affection" is a fine word.

IMAGE 2.1 **Second Son (Detroit Dunwood) embraces First Son (Eric Kerr).**
Wreckage, directed by Erin Gilley at Crowded Fire Theatre, San Francisco (2009)
Photograph by Marissa Wolf and Crowded Fire Theatre press office.

Pause. First Son kisses Second Son. Pause.

Aren't you going to say anything?

SECOND SON. You bit me. I've got blood . . .

FIRST SON. I didn't mean . . .

SECOND SON. It was nice. I liked it.

FIRST SON. Want another?

SECOND SON. No. I'm fine.

Pause.

FIRST SON. I can't tell what you are.

SECOND SON. Sorry?

FIRST SON. You're familiar to me.

SECOND SON. So are you.

FIRST SON. But I can't . . .

SECOND SON. Split somehow . . .

FIRST SON. Yes. My memory's split. That's a good word. "Split." It's
perfect, really.
Sounds exactly like what it means.
Look at you.

SECOND SON. What?

FIRST SON. You look like everything.

SECOND SON. What d'you mean?

FIRST SON. Beauteous.
(*From memory*) "Beauteous babe, you have a city,
where far from me and my sad lot you will live."

SECOND SON. What are you going on about?

FIRST SON. Words. Figments. Fragments.

SECOND SON. You're funny.

FIRST SON (*from memory*). "Behold my lover's laughing eyes."

SECOND SON. I'm not your lover.

FIRST SON. Aren't you?

SECOND SON. I don't think so.

FIRST SON. What, then?

Second Son heads to the water.

SECOND SON. Come on, silly. Let's go for a swim.

FIRST SON. No.

SECOND SON. Just for a bit.

FIRST SON. I'm not going in.

SECOND SON. Are you afraid?

FIRST SON. No.

SECOND SON. Then why not?

FIRST SON. I don't like the sea.

SECOND SON. But we're here. Look at it. Isn't it just . . .?

FIRST SON. Yes. It is.

SECOND SON. But you still won't . . .?

FIRST SON. No.

SECOND SON. I'd like to go in.

FIRST SON. Go on, then.

SECOND SON. Will you watch me?

FIRST SON. Why should I?

SECOND SON. You're older than me.

FIRST SON. So?

SECOND SON. So, you're supposed to take care of me. Older boys take care of younger boys.

FIRST SON. Are you a younger boy?

SECOND SON. Of course. Don't I look it?

FIRST SON. I suppose.

SECOND SON. Well, you're older. That's clear.

FIRST SON. I'm not old.

SECOND SON. No, but you're older. Definitely. So, you've got a duty.

FIRST SON. To take care?

SECOND SON. That's the law.

FIRST SON. Since when?

SECOND SON. Always.

FIRST SON. That's a burden.

SECOND SON. Look, are you going to watch me or not?

FIRST SON. All right.

SECOND SON. Swear.

FIRST SON. You're so serious for such a young boy.

SECOND SON. Promise.

Second Son extends his hand to First Son.

FIRST SON (*taking his hand*). . . . I do.

SECOND SON. . . . I'm going in. Straight into the sea. Watch me.

(Short pause. They let go of each other. Second Son walks away.)

Are you watching?

FIRST SON. Yes.

The Second Son walks further away.

SECOND SON. Are you watching?

FIRST SON. Yes.

Second Son goes into the water. Pause. First Son looks away.

2

Some time passes. First Son rests on the sand. Woman dressed in ultra-chic evening wear approaches. She carves space and time as she walks. She regards First Son.

WOMAN. Well, look at you.

FIRST SON. I fell asleep.

WOMAN. I know. I watched you. You have soft eyelids.

FIRST SON. Do I?

WOMAN. Like a child. A beauteous babe.

FIRST SON. Hmm?

WOMAN. Isn't that your name?

FIRST SON. No.

WOMAN. I could've sworn . . .

FIRST SON. Not beauteous. Not babe. I'm just me. The first.

WOMAN. I can't call you that.

FIRST SON. Call me what you like, then.

WOMAN. Lost?

FIRST SON. I'm not. I know exactly where I am.

WOMAN. Where are you?

FIRST SON. Beach. White shimmering sand. Bit cold, but sun hot. And you're dressed for the evening. Am I right?

WOMAN. Quite right.

FIRST SON. First of firsts. That's me. First to get everything. First to get hit, first to get kissed. Sure of my stride.

WOMAN. And the younger?

FIRST SON. What?

WOMAN. Have you forgotten him already? There was a younger boy here too.

FIRST SON. When was this?

WOMAN. Don't lie to me. I saw him.

FIRST SON. . . . He went for a swim.

WOMAN. And then?

FIRST SON. . . . He went away. To the city, I think. He was hungry.

WOMAN. Young boys are always hungry.

FIRST SON. That they are.

WOMAN. . . . Are you a boy?

FIRST SON. Of course.

WOMAN. You don't look it. Not at first glance.

FIRST SON. Do you mind?

WOMAN. I don't mind anything.

FIRST SON. I wish I could be like that. Unmindful of things. I try. But I get tired somehow. The waves come up fierce-like. After a while, I can't look at them. All these words come into my head. And I have to close my eyes.

WOMAN. What kind of words?

FIRST SON. Hapless ruinous words. Fragrant and sweet upon the breath, but full of sorrow.

WOMAN. You shouldn't be here.

FIRST SON. I'll go.

He starts to walk away. She pulls him back.

WOMAN. Where are you going to go? You're nothing without me.

FIRST SON. I don't understand.

WOMAN. Somebody's got to watch me.

FIRST SON. Why?

WOMAN. I might do something awful. And then where would we be?

FIRST SON. Heaven.

    Pause.

WOMAN. You care about me. A woman senses these things.

FIRST SON. What else do you sense?

WOMAN. You're playing games with me. You're lying.

FIRST SON. I wouldn't . . .

WOMAN. Lying is your habit, your addiction. You revel in it.

FIRST SON. You're wrong about me.

WOMAN. I wish I were. Damned child, son of a doomed mother.

FIRST SON. . . . What do you know about me?

WOMAN. Only what I sense.

FIRST SON. You're the liar.

WOMAN. Quick boy. Quick with the lip. Up to no good, are you?

FIRST SON. Look, I just want to—

WOMAN. What?

FIRST SON. . . . Aren't you going to kiss me?

WOMAN. I'm taken already. I can't have you.

FIRST SON. Husband?

WOMAN. No one else comes in-between.

FIRST SON. Something sweet. Tender skin. You could hold me.

WOMAN. Is that all you want?

FIRST SON. More than anything.

WOMAN. . . . What a funny boy you are standing on my beach.

FIRST SON. Don't you feel anything for me?

WOMAN. You're trespassing.

FIRST SON. This beach is yours?

WOMAN. Everybody knows that. It's private. What'd you think? Pristine sand just takes care of itself? You've got a lot to learn. Where'd you come from?

FIRST SON. The sea.

WOMAN. Water angel? Is that what you are?

FIRST SON. I don't know.

WOMAN. Lost boy.

FIRST SON. I'm not.

WOMAN. You've got blood on you.

FIRST SON. Don't . . .

WOMAN. I'm only . . .

FIRST SON. It's a stain; nothing more.

WOMAN. You should wash it off. You should be cleaned.
You can't walk around like that. What will people say?

FIRST SON. They'll say what they say.

WOMAN. We're civilized here. Understand? As soon as blood comes
upon us, we get rid of it. We erase everything . . . These brief
days we forget, and only after do we lament. Come on now,
let's get you clean . . . What is it? What are you looking at?

FIRST SON. . . . Did you really see him?

WOMAN. Who?

FIRST SON. The younger . . .

WOMAN. . . . Funny boy. What a funny boy you are. Are you a boy?

FIRST SON. Yes.

WOMAN. You don't have to be.

She takes his hand. They go within.

3

*From outside, Second Son spies on First Son, who is within (the house)
with Woman. Faint music is heard from within.*
*Woman is showing First Son around, engaged in the niceties of social
entertaining: drinks, appetizers, a dance.*
Second Son watches with fascination.

SECOND SON. I see him now.

He is inside the bosom of the house.
He is dancing close with his mannequin.
He glides. He laughs.
I reach out,
But he can't see me.
He is blind now.
He moves in another's orbit,
Touched by another's lightning.
I follow him in my own way.
I learn from what I see, from what he teaches me.
I have only been taught to follow
Since the day I was born.
I remember. You see?
The younger boy imitates the older boy,
The second son imitates the first.
Seek none other, for he makes your path.
It has been writ down time immemorial.
In the green eye
Of the poisoned world
Hell came
And stayed for a visit.
Behold me here:
The unmade son
Awake to his demise,
And not afraid to meet it.
Drown me. Come on.
I'm willing.
For I will rise
And be sovereign one day.

Second Son looks toward the house, and then runs away.

4

Waves. The coming night. The broadcast is heard now, a little closer.

VOICEOVER. No word still on whether the two young boys found two days ago were murdered or were victims of a ritual sacrifice, but all roads to the beach have been closed as investigation continues on the incidents surrounding this bizarre crime. There are no suspects thus far. And police are viewing the convenience-store tapes for any clues that may help them piece together the facts of this sad case. Meanwhile, cross-examination has begun in the trial of the teen princess accused of strangling her lover's baby. An official statement is expected from the young woman's mother later today.

5

Inside the house all is white and gleaming. Woman bathes First Son: a ritual cleansing.

WOMAN. First the face:
  Beautiful
  Expectant
  Innocent.
  Clear, pure water. Yes.
  And a hint of lemon
  On the temples
  And the hairline.
  Such a smooth forehead.
  You've the perfect age, you know.
  There's a time in a boy's life
  When he is a radiant being;
  Men grow to be handsome,
  But this . . . radiancy . . . this . . . beauty . . .
  It doesn't come back. You don't believe me?

FIRST SON. I think you're falling in love with me.

IMAGE 2.2 **Woman (Laura Jane Cole) cleanses First Son (Eric Kerr).**
Wreckage, directed by Erin Gilley at Crowded Fire Theatre, San Francisco (2009)
Photograph by Marissa Wolf and Crowded Fire Theatre press office.

WOMAN. I'm taken, remember?

FIRST SON. So, where is he?

WOMAN. Over there. You can't see him, but he's there. He always watches me.

FIRST SON. What?

WOMAN. Don't worry. We've an arrangement.

FIRST SON. What kind?

WOMAN. Are you going to let me do this properly?
Relax now. . . . And the torso . . . you're strong, aren't you? I can feel it. Right here.
Are you ticklish?

FIRST SON. No.

WOMAN. You're blushing. Just like a girl. How sweet you are. Such slim hips . . .

FIRST SON. Stop it.

WOMAN. What's wrong?

FIRST SON. I should leave.

WOMAN. I'm not done yet.

FIRST SON. I don't need to be bathed. I'm fine as is.

WOMAN. Come now. Don't be angry. Young boys shouldn't be marred by anger.

FIRST SON. I'm not as young as you think.

WOMAN. Indulge me, first of firsts.

FIRST SON. Why?

WOMAN. I care for you. And you need me.

FIRST SON. I don't need anybody.

WOMAN. How are you going to get by in this world? Tell me.

FIRST SON. I'm strong. I can do things.

WOMAN. Like . . .?

FIRST SON. I've got skills.

WOMAN. What kind?

FIRST SON. I've a good eye for things.

WOMAN. Numbers, you mean, the economy?

FIRST SON. Yeah. Maybe. I can figure things out.

WOMAN. You don't know anything. It's nothing to be ashamed of. Ignorance is a kind of fuel, really. You can't imagine how far you can go in this world with your kind of ignorance.

FIRST SON. . . . . Teach me things.

WOMAN. I will.

FIRST SON. Teach me now.

WOMAN. We've plenty of time.

FIRST SON. Do we?

WOMAN. So scared, you are. Why is that? Are you frightened of me?

FIRST SON. No. I like you.

WOMAN. . . . Let me anoint you.

FIRST SON. What are you doing?

WOMAN. First the limbs . . . hands . . . the tips of your fingers . . .

She kisses his hands.

FIRST SON. Why'd you do that?

WOMAN. To feel your skin with my lips.

FIRST SON. I don't like it. I don't want anybody kissing my hands.
You understand me?
I won't have it.

WOMAN. What would you have, then?

FIRST SON. Kiss on the lips, yeah. Neck, shoulders . . .

WOMAN. Forehead?

FIRST SON. If you like. Sure.

(*She kisses his forehead gently. Husband is seen in the background; he has a discreet view.*)

. . . You're good to me. So very good. Why is that?

WOMAN. Because I want to be. Isn't that enough?

FIRST SON. Nobody's good for long. Nobody's innocent.

At the least provocation, everything can turn.

WOMAN. Is that what you remember?

FIRST SON. I remember words, yeah. Sorrow's breath.

I remember being loved once
and that love transforming itself into a monster.

WOMAN. Is that what you think I am?

FIRST SON. You could be anything. We've all got a changing shape.

WOMAN. Here. Put this on.

She offers him a necklace.

FIRST SON. It's yours.

WOMAN. It was a gift. Let it be my gift to you: an ornament for your naked beauty.

FIRST SON. I don't understand you.

WOMAN. You don't have to. Just take it.

FIRST SON. What kind of stone is—?

WOMAN. Amber.

FIRST SON. But it's violet.

WOMAN. It's a rare kind.

FIRST SON. Precious, then?

WOMAN. Very.

FIRST SON. It feels nice.

She drapes an ankle-length garment on him.

What are you dressing me as?

WOMAN. The noblest of men.

FIRST SON. Do men wear such things?

WOMAN. Such things and more. If you'll have me.

FIRST SON. I thought you were taken.

WOMAN. Untake me.

FIRST SON. You want to destroy me.

WOMAN. I want what's best for you. Don't you see?
There's this woman who killed her son.
They say she killed him just like that.
Without a thought. Without the slightest remorse.
She had everything arranged.
The sooner the child was out of her life, the better.
They say she kissed him and stifled his breath,
And watched his eyes fade from light. They say she will not be forgiven.
Would you forgive me?

FIRST SON. I don't know what you mean.

WOMAN. If I were a monster, would you forgive me? Would you protect me?

FIRST SON. Is this what you do: steal boys from your beach?

Steal them away and make of them meat?

WOMAN. Oh, sweet boy, act the dutiful daughter, and not the vengeful son.

Do not let fear be your guide as you wake now to this new world.

There's no need to be afraid, my dear boy,

for you are learning to speak the language of the dead.

She kisses him on the mouth, overtaking him. Husband disappears from view.

6

Second Son is at road's edge. He is met by Nurse, a man in well-worn beach clothes: capri pants, a colorful shirt, and sandals.

NURSE. I think she pushed those boys in. Yeah. Right into the water.

Left them to drown like that, all gussied up like girls.

I'm sure it was her, this woman I saw. I'm sure she did it.

She's got the look of a murderer. A real elegant type.

She was driving a car. Fancy. Latest model.

I can't afford that. I haven't the money, know what I mean?

I'm not in her class.

But she . . . oh yeah. She had jewels on. Emeralds and amber . . .

I saw her. Not at the convenience store, but after . . .

I don't know why nobody will interview me. I'm a witness, right?

I could tell things and make a fortune.

But nobody will ask me. They just say those boys are dead and that's that.

And it means nothing to nobody 'cause boys die all the time:

In woods, ravines, trenches, mines . . .

Some boys are dead even when they're alive;

They come home from wars and lock ups

And they're dead inside. Know what I mean?

. . . You're a boy, aren't you? You're a pretty little thing waiting to be screwed.

You've got fresh face, and small hands. Long limbs.

. . . I could go up right inside you. Would you like that? Damned boy. Don't you speak?

SECOND SON. I don't need words.

NURSE. How much, then?

SECOND SON. What'll you give me?

NURSE. Is this what you know?

SECOND SON. Pure love doesn't exist. I know that.

There was a young boy who told an older boy to take care of him, but the older boy turned the other way, and only took care of himself.

What was the younger boy to do

but turn himself away, away to another world, too?

What use have I for sweet words, or for love?

NURSE. You talk like you're in disguise.

SECOND SON. Do you mind?

NURSE. You can use another's tongue but you best learn it right. Best not slip.

SECOND SON. I'll take your advice.

NURSE. I wouldn't take it to heart. I'm a failure at life.

Anxious hands, anxious deeds, a bit of screwing and some crystal does me.

Do you want to go for a ride?

SECOND SON. Where to?

NURSE. Spin round the city, see the sky, I got a portable wonderland, right?

SECOND SON. You'll protect me?

NURSE. I don't get boys like you into trouble. It's not in my nature.

SECOND SON. Swear?

NURSE. I promise.

SECOND SON. . . . . All right.

NURSE. . . . You're an easy type. We're going to get on just fine. What is it? You're cold?

SECOND SON. A little.

NURSE. Need some good hands to do you a survey?
"Survey the merchandise. Make sure that it's clean."
That's what my mom always said.
My mom was an angel. Was yours an angel, pigeon?

SECOND SON. I don't remember.

NURSE. Orphan boy. Is that what you are? An orphaned thing
Spit out from mother ocean?

SECOND SON. Sent back to shore, I think.

NURSE. A prince, a right sovereign.
How far must you have come, my pigeon . . .
How very far to find yourself here in this tatty world.
Got yourself a name?

SECOND SON. No.

NURSE. . . . . "I have no name
I am but two days old.—
What shall I call thee?
I happy am.
Joy is my name,—

Sweet joy befall thee!
Pretty joy!
Sweet joy but two days old.
Sweet joy I call thee."[1]

SECOND SON. Joy. Yes. Joy is my name.

NURSE. Wet kiss, then?

SECOND SON. I've not much practice.

NURSE. You're slipping, pigeon.
Keep your disguise, dear Joy, sweet Joy of mine.

---

[1] William Blake, "Infant Joy," *Songs of Innocence and Experience* (1789)

Listen to your nurse. She knows you from the womb,
From your day of making.

SECOND SON. How much did you see, sweet Nurse?

NURSE. You mean of the elegant lady and the like? Of the real live
story?

SECOND SON. Yes.

NURSE. I saw everything, my little one, that I did.
Come now, be released, dear Joy. Be released through me.

And Nurse leads Second Son away.

7

*Night. First Son walks proudly through the silvery house while Woman
and Husband make love.*

FIRST SON. I walk through the house of familiar objects
Wearing the clothes of a beauteous daughter.
I smell of honey, and myrtle
And cling to the amber that adorns me.
This is my home now, I tell myself.
This is how I shall live in this new world
That has taken me in
And has saved me from wandering the curved earth
In search of a false memory.
I hear the woman and her husband make love in the barren
room.
And I remember the smell of sex,
And how a younger boy kissed me because he knew no one
else
And how I returned his kiss with pride and diffidence.
Words, you see. They come back to me.
I am piecing together who I can be
From this I hear, and this I see:

The passionate scream, and the silver tray resting on the stone
centerpiece,
The guttural moan, and the golden rings woven into the
obscene tapestry.
I remember everything and nothing,
As I continue walking
Through the resplendent house
Of empty rooms surrounded by the sea.
Look at me, I cry.
Look at me, I sing.
I am your guardian; I am your mercenary.
Stir my limbs and fill me with vengeance
Even as I act the daughter dear,
The delicate thing,
Made for your sport
And your errant amusement.
Hold me up on a sublime pedestal.
Venus' envy am I.
And then I remember the younger boy
Who sought his comfort in my anxiety.
He was familiar to me, too.
A twinned self, a blood thing
Lost in the waves, drowned by my inconstancy.
Poor boy, I whisper
To no one.
How I miss your unpracticed tongue,
Your tender lips,
And open heart.
Poor lost boy,
What has become of you here in this new world
Which prizes nothing except the warmth of flesh
Against the cold massacre of night?

8

Sex-spent, and wanting more, Second Son is fed by Nurse, and then readied for trade.

NURSE. You're a ravenous one.

SECOND SON. I crave . . .

NURSE. Too much. Sucked at my tit, and left me empty, you have.

SECOND SON. Been long time since . . .

NURSE. No need to say it. Here. Here's a bit of sugar. That'll keep
  you for a while.
  Don't ever say you don't know nothing.
  Not to anybody else, y'hear?
  'Cause it won't get you anywhere, Joy,
  And you want to go places, don't you? You want to see things?

SECOND SON. Whole world. Yes. That's what I want.
  Never seen anything except what's before me.
  Tall woman once—like you—you remind me of her, you do—
  She held me for days and then no more.
  It was like I'd been sent to a dark place.
  A place of full of tears that knows no end, because weeping
  doesn't stop,
  And history isn't over, even if we think it is. Isn't that right,
  Nurse?

NURSE. You're getting ideas in your head. I don't know what to make
  of it.

SECOND SON. Make of it what you will. Trade me for what I'm worth,
  Which is plenty, and you know it.

NURSE. Worth a bundle, if you keep your sweetness intact.
  Ripe boy, you are. That's true enough.

SECOND SON. I'm ripe for the taking, even after I've been took.

NURSE. Sweet Joy, you're made a man.

SECOND SON. Through and through.

NURSE. And yet worth more as a girl,
  As a changeable thing

For precious Joy is what we seek come nightfall,
Come daybreak.
Precious dear and awfully willing.
Men get shot, boys get killed,
And it's the girl ones, who keep going.
Remember that.
For after I'm gone, you will need to know these things
So as not to swim in the dark ocean full of tears
Like a lost babe
Caught in the current
Ready to be swept out to Hades.
Promise me you'll remember.

SECOND SON. I do.

NURSE. There, there. Such vacant eyes need rest. Sugar's sleep is what you need.

SECOND SON. Tit in mouth is what I want. Suckle me, sweet Nurse. Send me back to the womb.

NURSE. Fist, Joy. Hard fist now. No more suckling.
Done enough for tonight.
I know you want and want, but I'm empty, y'hear?
I get sick fast, see? That's my calamity.
Best you go on now; put on clothes that suit your trade.
Pick something there. I've got fresh market goods.

SECOND SON. Jeans and halters?

NURSE. No. Not for you, Joy. You need some sheer lace to show off your torso,
The cut of your figure must be appreciated by all.
There. That's a smile. You like compliments, eh?

SECOND SON. I like being told nice things.

NURSE. Don't get too accustomed to it, dear. Compliments spoil us.
Rough words sometimes do better than kind.
Those tap pants are nice. Silk, eh?

SECOND SON. You mind?

And Second Son starts to put on the lingerie, the old clothes for his new life . . .

NURSE. No. You need vintage style to remind us all of the past,
Of the good rolling times
Of quick money,
And all manner of ripe pickings
Just waiting round the corner
Singing sweet jazz,
Coming foul in the mouth,
And letting all the workers down low
Rise up to the high life,
To riches and glory, right?
Do you know what I'm talking about, pigeon?
Do you what I mean by jazz?
I'm teaching you things, Joy.
I'm teaching you how to get by in this life.

SECOND SON (*dressed now*). I'm grateful, sweet Nurse.

NURSE. As well you should be, pigeon.
I've no riches except what comes from a lifetime of work and caring,
And of being a good nurse to all those in need, you see?

SECOND SON. One day I'll be . . .

NURSE. No. Not you. Not a nurse. You're a prince, dear.
You've got shining future ahead of you.
I can see this. I have visions.
Just like I'd seen that lady in the car and those boys . . .
I see things. You're to go far, pigeon.

SECOND SON. I've visions, too. I've seen things.

NURSE. Past hauntings?

SECOND SON. Future ones, I think.

NURSE. What do you see, child?

SECOND SON. A divine image:
A boy stands veiled in blood,
unsure of himself, unsure of everything.
He trembles. He waits. A shiver song caught in his throat.

A tall woman appears. She looks at him with soft eyes. She holds him.

And sings him to sleep.

Nurse pulls Second Son toward him, and sings "Orphan Boy"

NURSE. Poor orphan boy.
Come right out of water
Seeking where to dream.
Come right out of water
Looking for where he'd been.

Orphan, orphan boy
Rest your pretty head.
No reason to this world.
No reason once you're dead.

Lights dim on Nurse and Second Son. In the house, Woman and First Son are illuminated. First Son looks at himself in a mirror. He wears a new garment.

FIRST SON. How you love me . . .

WOMAN. Yes.

FIRST SON. Because I'm the most beautiful?

WOMAN. Perhaps.

FIRST SON. You know it's true.

WOMAN. You are exquisite.

FIRST SON. I am ravishing.

WOMAN. Careful now.

FIRST SON. What'd you mean?

WOMAN. You must not yield to your beauty.

FIRST SON. Why not?

WOMAN. Remember: it will be short-lived.

FIRST SON. What of it? It's what we make of things that counts.

WOMAN. In the here and now?

FIRST SON. Yes.

WOMAN. Cursed boy.

FIRST SON. Ravishing boy.

WOMAN. . . . Don't lose yourself, dear.

FIRST SON. What'd you mean?

WOMAN. Let me keep you here. This is sanctuary.

FIRST SON. Admire me, then. Worship me. For I am what you make of me.

WOMAN. Greedy boy . . . What am I going to do with you?

FIRST SON. Take care of me. Sing to me.

Woman sings another section of "Orphan Boy" song, while the First Son revels.

WOMAN. The weight of water,
Oh tender child,
Leaves ancient sorrow
Far behind.
The still of sundown
On borrowed time
Will ease your trouble
. . . Clear your mind.

Fade up on Nurse and Second Son. Nurse sings.

NURSE. Orphan, orphan boy
Dream a thing or two,
For there will be another
Who dreams a dream of you.

Nurse cradles Second Son. First Son stands in adoration before Woman who caresses him. Lights fade.

9

Waves. The broadcast is heard, a little closer still.

VOICEOVER. Police continue to investigate the alleged murder of the two boys found on the beach the other day. No mention has been made yet of the boys' names or where they were from.

Media attention focuses instead on the trial of the teen princess, who will take the stand in her defense tomorrow morning. Sources say that the young woman has been distraught the last few days, and worried about her appearance. Check your local stations for up-to-the-minute news on this and other breaking stories. Weather in the 90s, winds to the north, and rain expected later in the week.

10

It is near daybreak. Inside the house, First Son is seen through the glass.

FIRST SON. I sleep, and pretend I am you and he as one and the same.
I slip off my daughter's clothes—my clean things—
And imitate your sounds.
My mouth opens. Fire breathes . . .
Never leave, I wish. Never leave, I cry.
Stare at my eyelids. Watch me.
I am your remnant of memory.
Reach out your hand, open my senses. Lead me.
You do everything out of love.

The glass turns and Husband and Woman are seen, entwined.

HUSBAND. He moves.

WOMAN. He waits for us.

HUSBAND. He listens.

WOMAN. He won't stop until he's had his fill.

HUSBAND. He's addicted.

WOMAN. Yes.

HUSBAND. To our sex.

WOMAN. To our needs.

HUSBAND. What shall we do?

WOMAN. Love him. What else can we do?

HUSBAND. . . . Before there was no one.

WOMAN. And now there is another, here, with us.

HUSBAND. Between us.

WOMAN. Joining us.

HUSBAND. Closer.

WOMAN. And even closer.

HUSBAND. . . . He needs us.

WOMAN. He has no one.

HUSBAND. Poor boy.

WOMAN. He sings.

HUSBAND. Very softly. What is it?

WOMAN. A song without words. A song of yearning for two bodies, not one . . . .

HUSBAND. Let's show him.

WOMAN. Let's teach him everything. Such a good daughter . . . Such a good son . . .
. . . Is he gone?

HUSBAND. He's still.

WOMAN. He's transfixed. Tender child . . .

HUSBAND. He watches you like one. Full of love. Pure love.
I can't look at him anymore. His eyes burn into me.
You've brought this boy here to vex my heart.

WOMAN. I've done nothing of the kind. Know this: I love you now more than before.
His presence stirs me . . .
The thread which crosses through him to you is destined for me,
For he is like you: made for me.
And I am the path from thread to line, from line to thread and back.
I am complete.

HUSBAND. What words are these?

WOMAN. A lover's words.

HUSBAND. A mother's words.

WOMAN. If unconditional love is what you seek . . .? Then yes, perhaps yes, a mother's words.

HUSBAND. And for me, for your lover, what words are there left?

WOMAN. The same words, only red, violet, and orange in hue.

HUSBAND. . . . I dream in red, the color of blood, yes but I also dream of regret and of waking to not find you.

WOMAN. But I'm here, right here . . . What is it? Tell me.

HUSBAND. The boy's staring.

WOMAN. You imagine him.

HUSBAND. No. He's here. Right here, behind the glass.

WOMAN. He's on the sand; he's strolling the beach, stretching his legs . . . He's finding himself slowly. Let him be.

HUSBAND. He's in my eyes. His sweetness is consuming. Hungry boy . . .

WOMAN. Call to him, then.

HUSBAND. What for?

WOMAN. Let's ravage him. Split him.

HUSBAND. Gut him.

WOMAN. Lover dear, husband dear . . .

HUSBAND. Claw . . .

WOMAN. Bite. Scratch.

HUSBAND. Woo me anew.

WOMAN. With spite.

HUSBAND. I fell in love with you through and through. From first I saw. That was clear.
You were my cup of sweet poison, my rich jewel ready to be worn.

WOMAN. And haven't I given you everything, husband dear?

HUSBAND. Too much . . . your bitter taste cuts through me . . .

WOMAN. Lustful boy.

HUSBAND. Man, not boy. A boy is he who stands there like a little girl waiting for us to part.

WOMAN. Loose yourself . . . Abandon yourself to me.

Consume me in your fire, make of me ash, for out of it we shall both rise.

HUSBAND. In triumph, dear, exceeding . . .

Husband and Woman make love.

11.

Morning. The house is serene. Woman and First Son are eating. Silence.

FIRST SON. The harlot of the blood knot.

WOMAN. Those are cheery words. Did you sleep all right?

FIRST SON. I didn't sleep at all. I couldn't sleep, could I? You were with him.

WOMAN. He is my husband. I told you when we met that I was taken. I've never lied to you. Do you want me to start now?

FIRST SON. No.

WOMAN. Then don't sulk. Please. It's not becoming. Keep your face up.

FIRST SON. Yes, dear.

WOMAN. You're brooding. It's to be expected, I suppose.

FIRST SON. Why? 'Cause I'm a boy?

WOMAN. You're still learning the ways of the world.

FIRST SON. Crap world this. Rotten, aching . . . blisters on the sand.

WOMAN. Drink your tea.

FIRST SON. Are you going to play "the mother" now?

WOMAN. I don't play roles. I'm not an actor.

FIRST SON. And yet you change. From one moment to the next . . .

WOMAN. So do we all. Terror, cruelty, and jealousy all have a human face.

FIRST SON. What am I? Eh? What am I to you?

WOMAN. You're beautiful. That's enough. You're my angel, my sacred apparition, my first of firsts.

FIRST SON. . . . Silly harlot.

WOMAN. Watch your tongue.

FIRST SON. Why should I?

WOMAN. Because this is my house.

FIRST SON. His house, where he beds you.

WOMAN. And goes inside me, yes. Don't forget.
You're well-kept, and fed, and you're safe here. What more do
you want, dear boy?

FIRST SON. More than more. I want everything.

WOMAN (*tenderly*). Have a pear.

FIRST SON. I'm not hungry.

WOMAN. You need to fill yourself.

FIRST SON. With what? Poison? I have that already. Have plenty. It's
all inside me.
I can feel it. My blood's swimming in poison.

WOMAN. Do you think I am giving my affection to a third party when
it should rightfully be given to you?

FIRST SON. What's that? Babble-talk?

WOMAN. It's a question, that's all. I claimed you, but you do not claim
me. My affection is free. My attention and love are granted as
I please.

FIRST SON. And what do I get?

WOMAN. The best tea, this house, the beach . . .
The perfect attainment of your beauty, such as it is, for it will
be short-lived.
. . . How I do grieve for you . . .

FIRST SON. Already?

WOMAN. I grieve eternally. My suffering knows no bounds. Can't
you see?

FIRST SON. I see someone who seizes ruin,
Whose heart gives way to secrecy.
Idle hope you should have that I will ever nurse

You in your old age and deck your corpse with loving hands.
I'll do no such thing. I'm not made for it.
I'll not repay you in kind for any mercy granted me.
You will lose me in time; I'll see to it.
And I'll never again look at you with fond eyes.
Bitterness and sorrow will be your company at your life's end.
That's what I see in my tabloid memory.

WOMAN. Pity me, my dear boy; see me through and through, as I see
you.
We are both wronged in ecstasy. We both crave, and seal our
fate
With too much love, so much ardor, zealous we are in our
jalousie.
For in love, this love,
In its faint ray we regard
Anger
Blame
Doubt
Ignorance
Virtue
Safety
And privacy
While we entertain
Abuse
Duty
Panic
Despair
Freedom
And pollution.
Our presence, my presence and yours too, is a pollution
And yet we make of it something holy, yes. A pollution of
saints
Bound by love.
You see, sweet boy? Strange boy . . .
My son and daughter at once,

So much have you to learn,
And so much you have learned already
At my hands
By my bed
Through my dignity.
Steel your heart now; you will be the better for it.

FIRST SON. . . . It's early.

WOMAN. So it is.

FIRST SON. Day's just begun.

WOMAN. And what's in store for us?

FIRST SON. Whatever you wish.

12

Husband behind the glass.

HUSBAND. Woo him with my words.
Take him into your heart.
Clever glittering creature,
Wrap him tight
And dispose of me.
You are a changing being.
This is what I see:
You let the boy in.
You toy with him as if he were your son,
"Our son,
The first of firsts,"
And you watch him move like an errant daughter.
You wrap him inside your tongue
Which has a serpent's will.
And he follows
Unknowing
Blissful
As if in a dream.

Sweet boy he is . . . your boy . . . not mine . . .
For he is meant for me, and not for me.
Fear disintegrates my throat,
And you eat happily,
As I contemplate a barren feast.
What is he to you
But a little nothing?
How can a woman love so completely and without shame?
I see you true, my passionate beast.
You who were my soul's fire
Have turned into a bauble,
A mock lover,
Bent on deceiving me.
Mutilated hours
mark my days.
Cold evenings
Wreck my heart.
Our sex is but a feverish lightning.
Damp sheets, crushed pillows
And the imprint of your body.
We live on a broken ship,
Mastless
And bereft of sails.

13

*On the boardwalk where the boys cruise as girl-boys at morning's rise,
Second Son wears his new-life clothes. Nurse is his guide. They hustle for
johns.*

(This is played in the spirit of a bawdy vaudeville turn.)

SECOND SON. I'd like to contribute to the future discourse

NURSE. on mourning

SECOND SON. I can tell you a thing or two
about negotiating with the dead

NURSE. and living at times in the Underworld.

SECOND SON. I've been fetched, you see, by demons and daemons.
My history is not revealed easily.

NURSE. Some say history is over but I don't believe them.
I think all you have to do is look at the fine print

SECOND SON. all around

NURSE. and it's clear

SECOND SON. that history is alive,

NURSE. and doing its repetitive dance

SECOND SON. of death, mayhem, joy,

NURSE. and good old-fashioned ecstasy.
Take our siren, this siren here,

(*Second Son poses.*)

our dame of note:
she has her hooks in, her locks in place and she's ready to roll.
What care anyone for a little blood spilt?
We must all have our sacrifice,
our sweet honey jazz. Look here,

SECOND SON. Look here,
See what we're made of—you and I:

NURSE. the same stuff

NURSE & SECOND SON. Altogether

SECOND SON. That's right

NURSE. And if you think different

SECOND SON. woe to you

NURSE. Sweet honey woe
What destiny awaits you if you think you're above the melee.

SECOND SON (*calling out to a potential john*) Hey Babycakes come over
here, and put your flesh on the line. It's time to serve your
country, to be dutiful and proud and not look back at what
history can teach you, at what surely awaits us all if we pay
attention to what's gone before, past, over and out.
Hey Sugar press your lips for the grand economy of style.

NURSE. for petrol, tobacco, rum, cold sex, and sweet cane the world over

SECOND SON (*to Nurse*). (given up by Cain the brother in ancient time; but that was old blood, right? We'll have none of it now)
(*back to the clientele*) I wave my hand, Babycakes secure in the knowledge that no one will know that tomorrow

NURSE. in Pakistan, or in the new China, which has superseded Barcelona *und* Berlin, as the It spot of it spots where one needs to be seen,

SECOND SON. a boy will be found strangled by his own economic dreams.

NURSE. This is the way of the sorry-ass world

SECOND SON. This is what we crave:

NURSE. blood and death

SECOND SON. blood and sex blood

NURSE. and more blood . . . on an immaculate tray.

And Second Son strikes a burlesque pose on a makeshift pedestal.

14

On the boardwalk Husband sees Second Son in his new guise, and takes him aside
Out of slight view
For an exchange
Of anonymous sex
And no talk.
Just passionate fury
And extreme release

Woman sees Husband and Second Son make love in her mind's eye

WOMAN. Doubt enters. It fills me up. It burrows deep. My heart is torn by doubt.

I can't touch him now without thinking he's with someone else.

I am ravaged by thoughts and whispers.

I punish myself. But punishment serves no purpose when doubt remains.

Doubt is a poison. It infects the blood. And once it is in your veins,

There is little you can do but give in to it slowly, and let everything fade.

I say goodbye to him each morning.

I kiss his empty pillow and become accustomed to his absence.

I am learning how to live without love.

This lesson I am teaching myself, so I can go on.

Each day I doubt him more.

One day I will lose him completely. I am consumed.

My vision is corrupted. I breathe doubt. I taste it. I hold it on my tongue.

I ask nothing and imagine everything.

While in mirrored frames
First Son sees Husband and Woman make love in his mind's eye.
Husband sees Woman and First Son make love in his mind's eye.
Second Son sees First Son in clear-eyed memory,
As Nurse sings reprise of "Orphan Boy"

NURSE. Orphan, orphan boy
Dream a thing or two
For there will be another
Who dreams a dream of you.

The gleaming house readies for slaughter. Woman is waiting. Husband walks in.

WOMAN. Late.

HUSBAND. What?

WOMAN. You're late.

HUSBAND. You've never minded before.

WOMAN. I'm here in this house. I wait. I watch the sea turn black.
I watch the sand curl up, and the gulls pick at the ground with their hideous beaks.

HUSBAND. What's this? A soliloquy?

WOMAN. I saw you.

HUSBAND. What are you talking about?

WOMAN. With her.

HUSBAND. I don't know who you mean.

WOMAN. Your whore.

HUSBAND. Are you following me?

WOMAN. I don't need to. You're out in the open. The whole world can see.

HUSBAND. . . . Does it disgust you?

WOMAN. My passion and my beauty are not sufficient for your needs?

HUSBAND. The veneer of artifice and civilization repels me.
You see, love without betrayal doesn't mean anything.
Without cruelty, there is no feast.
We all do what we need.

WOMAN. Really? And what is that?

HUSBAND. You've the boy, don't you?

WOMAN. My boy . . . he's a figment, a sweet thing, an innocent being.
That's all.
An apparition.

HUSBAND. A flesh-and-blood apparition.

WOMAN. Are you out of love with me?

HUSBAND. . . . Get some sleep.

WOMAN. Pacify her. Tranquilize her. Sedate her. Isn't that what you mean?

HUSBAND. We forge what we want out of what we have. I don't complain.

WOMAN. My passion is twice yours.

HUSBAND. You believe what you need to believe.

WOMAN. Don't silence me.

HUSBAND. I'm doing nothing of the kind.

WOMAN. You ignore me. You shut me out. Come to bed with me. Or would you rather have me cold-assed on the boardwalk like your good whore?

HUSBAND. A whore fuck is the purest fuck.

WOMAN. . . . Was she alive, then, your whore?

HUSBAND. Alive and warm as far as I could tell.

WOMAN. Was he?

Pause.

HUSBAND. How much did you see?

WOMAN. Answer me.

HUSBAND. He had flesh like a girl, if that's what you mean. Just like your boy. A somewhat transient thing. I gave, he received. He didn't really want me, but the rules were clear. There was no talk. Love's delusion didn't get in the way, and that made me love him all the more. In the manner in which I prefer.

WOMAN. Anonymously?

HUSBAND. The most personal act of intimacy engaged through the most impersonal circumstance. Yes. That is truth. The rest is lies.

WOMAN. Our lie?

HUSBAND. Yes. Yes. The lie of convenience: marriage, a fine house, money, social standing, power, privacy, at the expense of lust, sensation, and knowledge.

WOMAN. If you love me still, then love me as you would, and I'll return your harshness in kind.

HUSBAND. Shall I nail you, then? Shall I take you from behind? Which position would you like? Shall I crucify you like the unholy saint that you pretend to be? Would you like that, dear wife?

WOMAN. I'd like nothing more.

HUSBAND. What game is this?

WOMAN. A game of fury.

HUSBAND. Hell's fury . . .

WOMAN. Vengeance in my mouth.

HUSBAND. Trembling tongue, though.

WOMAN. This is the game of living, of life itself. The mischief is just beginning.

HUSBAND. Dirty . . .

WOMAN. Sublime

HUSBAND. Decaying

WOMAN. Beautiful

HUSBAND. Extreme.

WOMAN. I know no bounds, love. Know this about me.

HUSBAND. . . . . Until the boy . . .

WOMAN. Save your blame for another.

HUSBAND. We live in the darkest poverty of desire. And yet you want more.

WOMAN. Undo me. Yes.

HUSBAND. Harsh want.

WOMAN. A test of your true self.

HUSBAND. Very well then. This is as pure and honest as I'll ever be. Take off your clothes, strip away your finery. If this is a life-game, then let's play it. Let's exploit each other. I'm not taking anything, and you're not giving anything. The only barter here is flesh.

First Son appears.

FIRST SON. Don't touch her.

WOMAN. Get away from here, child. You've none of me. Not now.

FIRST SON. I've all of you. You promised me.

WOMAN. I didn't promise anything.

FIRST SON. What do you mean?

WOMAN. I never said . . .

FIRST SON. You wanted me from the first. You watched me sleep. I
remember.

"Soft eyelids," you said.

WOMAN. Dear, sweet boy . . .

FIRST SON. Stop treating me like a child!

HUSBAND. . . . Which one will you choose, dear? The tender skin, the
tired kisses,
The unconditional cuddle as would a likely son to a likely
mother?
Or my mirror, your true mirror,
which will never be in danger of ever becoming mired in
beauty?

WOMAN. . . . Get out.

FIRST SON. This is my house, too. You said you'd keep me.

HUSBAND. As a kept girl. Am I right? As a little plaything.

FIRST SON. Shut up.

HUSBAND. Boys will be boys.

WOMAN. I can't keep you, dear. Don't you see?
If you know what's best for you, if you care anything for me,
walk away now.
There's time.

FIRST SON. What words are those? You learnt them from some book
or something?

HUSBAND. They're words. As good as any.

FIRST SON. You've nothing to say to me.

HUSBAND. I don't know you.

FIRST SON. Love ceases, eh? Just like that?

WOMAN. I cut love out. Yes.

FIRST SON. You lie.

WOMAN. I always have.

FIRST SON. False woman?

HUSBAND. Falser than you think. I know her better than you. I've got the full view, son.

Do as she says. Walk away. Take a stroll. Feel the sand under your feet,

Feel its warmth; it will heal you.

FIRST SON. Go swimming?

HUSBAND. Yes. It's a good sport. Clears the mind.

FIRST SON. . . . Something tender, sweet . . .

WOMAN. Don't.

FIRST SON. Hold me. Please.

WOMAN. . . . Go.

FIRST SON. . . . Liar.

WOMAN. Believe what you need . . .

FIRST SON. I don't need anything.

First Son takes off the amber necklace, tossing it at her feet, and leaves.

HUSBAND. . . . The boy gone. Silence falls. No whispers here now. No figures behind the glass. It's just us.

WOMAN. What's left of us.

HUSBAND. Get used to it, dear. If you want to see me again. What I do is what I do.

He takes off his belt.

Wherever, whomever I seek . . .

He stands behind her, and places belt at her throat.

WOMAN. Get off me.

HUSBAND. It's what you want, how you want . . . pure extreme.

He takes her from behind by force. Close-up on Woman's face, transfigured.

17

Waves. The broadcast can be barely heard midst static.

VOICEOVER. Today . . .

in the murder . . .

the teen princess . . .

Said to be . . .

live . . .

TEEN PRINCESS (VOICEOVER). "And I just want to say that in my heart . . ."

VOICEOVER. This is live . . .

cruelty . . .

in other . . .

times.

Static.

First Son stands at road's edge ready for trade, and is met by Nurse.

NURSE. We're all disgraceful, obscene, and debased here.

That's the truth of our beings.

No sense looking up in this world. It's just sky. Nothing else up there.

No saints looking down on us, judging our deeds.

Look down, stay close to the ground.

Sex breaks the rational mind. You follow me?

FIRST SON. Maybe. Yeah.

NURSE. You're smart. I can see that. You've got some sense. Just waylaid, am I right?

Lost your place?

FIRST SON. Yes.

NURSE. "The little boy lost in the lonely fen,
Led by the wandering light . . ."[2]

FIRST SON. Thrown out, yeah. She'll have none of me.

NURSE. It's a pity. Fine boy like you.
Oh, I just look, that's all. I'm no one in this world. I keep low,
safe. Nothing hurts me . . . Heard the story?

FIRST SON. What?

NURSE. Over the waves.

FIRST SON. No.

NURSE. Got acquitted, she did.

FIRST SON. Who?

NURSE. A teen princess. Acquitted of murder. She killed her kid.
Choked him in revenge. Her man was cheating on her. Turns
out it was for love, not vengeance, that she did it. Said "Oh,
I'm sorry," like an apology is enough. Like simple words are
going to wipe the soul clean. Strange what people do, say . . .
I think she should've gotten the highest penalty.

FIRST SON. Hanging?

NURSE. Need a hanging every once in a while to clear the air, get
things moving again.

(*First Son starts to walk away.*)

Like you, right? Moving about.

FIRST SON. It's all screwy.

NURSE. What is?

FIRST SON. What I'm feeling.

NURSE. Inside?

FIRST SON. I want to go back to her. She was like my tether.
She brought things back to me, you see?
Things in my memory that I'd kept hidden away:
affection, kisses, peaceful things . . . Hurt, too, but hurt's all
right.

---

2 William Blake, "Little Boy Found", *Songs of Innocence and Experience* (1789)

I can take it. I'm strong, yeah.

Soil and garbage are nothing to me.

I breathe them in, 'cause they tell me what reality is. And I'm grateful.

NURSE. You're on the meat line now.

FIRST SON. And what of it? End all, I say. Finish me. That's what I'd like. Be ended of this world. Cast me out, feed me to the ocean. Love's gone from me.

NURSE. Crapped on. Haven't we been?

FIRST SON. Yes.

NURSE. Doomed from the start. That's us. Expecting goodness, getting none,

And getting by somehow . . .

Cut love out, I say. Cut one, get another.

We're all expendable here in this place. We all stand on the sand and piss on it.

FIRST SON. Yeah.

NURSE. And what we do, eh?

FIRST SON. I don't know.

NURSE. Make do, right? Like this pigeon I got. He's seen to the wise. He's got himself doing steady now.

FIRST SON. What'd you mean?

NURSE. On the boardwalk. Over there.

FIRST SON. I don't see anybody.

NURSE. Of course you do. Just look. Good look, son.

FIRST SON. The young one?

NURSE. Yeah. Joy's the name. Infant joy of mine.

FIRST SON. He's familiar somehow.

NURSE. Get a closer look, then.

FIRST SON. He's like the younger . . .

NURSE. Joy's young. I grant you that. A ripe one.

FIRST SON. He kissed me on the mouth.

NURSE. Know him already?

FIRST SON. His was a pure kiss.

NURSE. The best kind, eh?

FIRST SON. I thought I'd never see him again.

NURSE. Those that are familiar should be together.

FIRST SON. . . . Will he remember me?

NURSE. Infant Joy will know you. We all know our way back to love
from ignorance.
You recognize him, don't you?

FIRST SON. I remember him. Yes.

NURSE. That's good enough.

FIRST SON. . . . Can I get you something?

NURSE. From the store? You're a sweet thing.

FIRST SON. I'm not cheap.

NURSE. For my time and trouble, anything will do. I'm easy . . .
Just see to the younger.

FIRST SON. I will . . . What'll it be, then? Soda pop?

NURSE. Yeah . . . Cherry lime.

18

*On the boardwalk, Second Son offers himself; he waits for nothing and
everything.*

SECOND SON. This is how I'm seen
As a sacrificial body
Ready to be taken
Waiting to be torn.
I let them see me like this
'Cause this is what they want.
This is what they need.
I'm not a pure thing to them.
I'm an offering of love,

Which needs to be destroyed.
Right now.
Come on.
Do me in.
That's right.
That's what you're paying for, sweet:
The dead boy on your lap,
The dead boy on your altar.
This is the dead boy, live and complete
For your eternal pleasure,
And redemption.
Suffer through me,
Release yourself.
Count on the hope of this impossible exchange on the street,
To raise your position in society one hundred percent.
And once I am dead to you
I am worth ever so much more.
My market value skyrockets
Each time I am bent
Each time I am fucked
Each time I am . . .
Whatever you make me.
I am your son/daughter,
Father/mother
The before he, the girl she
The young thing
Waiting to be formed.
Get a look at my slim hips,
My long legs,
My fragile quivering lips
Aching for a kiss,
A real kiss
Uh-huh
Some sweet jazz, yeah.
I'll go mad if you don't come.
I'm mad already. Can't you see?

First Son in the convenience-store camera's eye with bottle of cherry lime soda in hand . . .

FIRST SON. This is the new me,
The brother sweet, the other son.
Hold me.
Don't waste any time.
This is precious.
This is how it's meant to be.
Romanticism is the world,
And I'm its empress.

SECOND SON. Box me.
Tear my flesh,
Flesh the boy now . . . Place my meat on your altar.

FIRST SON. And I'll smile.
I won't feel a thing.
There's nothing to feel when you've been left.
There's only every reason to be happy.
What are you afraid of, son?

SECOND SON. What are you waiting for?

FIRST SON. When will you come back for me, mother?

SECOND SON. I'm here. Take me.

Woman approaches. After a few gestures, and an exchange of hard smiles, Woman touches Second Son tenderly. She kisses his hands. He responds with an embrace.
A moment.
She leads Second Son away toward the beach. She picks up a conch shell. She strikes Second Son with it. A blow to the head. Second Son falls. Time shift.
The convenience-store camera watches Woman as she motions to First Son.
After a few moments of hesitation, she kisses him. He embraces her. A moment.
She walks away, he follows her. They head toward the sea. The Second Son is lying on the shoreline. He is still. First Son goes to

Second Son. He kneels over the body of Second Son, which remains still. Woman strikes First Son with the conch shell. A blow to the head. First Son falls upon Second Son's body. Their bodies are entwined. Woman watches the two boys for a long time. Waves.

19

The gleaming house is quiet. Woman stares at the sea. Husband stands, near her.

WOMAN. I held them in my arms
    Your lover, my lover, our boys.
    They were like children again somehow
    So willing
    So sweet
    All anger gone
    Each one indebted to my touch,
    Wanting so very much
    To belong to this world.
    And I made them believe it.
    I said, Yes, come with me. You are here now. Safe.
    I will protect you from all harm.
    My tears will purify you.
    They would believe anything,
    Innocent boys,
    Reckless in their ignorance.
    They took our love so tenderly.
    They were our amusement.
    We made of them what we wanted,
    Dear lovers, hard lovers,
    So very dear.
    How will you remember them?
    As a girl? Boy?
    Pliant daughter, bitter son?
    Figureless figures of vanishing origin.

How will they remember us
When they wake to their demise?
What memory will be left them
In their cruel abandonment?
What will follow this perfect sacrifice?
"Of one alone, one woman alone
Sent mad by Heaven.
O women's love,
So full of trouble,"
They will say.
And we'll honor them,
The nattering mouths,
The gawkers and gossip-mongers.
We'll give them something to look at, won't we?
We will be reborn.
We will escape death.
And we'll stay here in this clean, corrupt house
With only our fury to sustain us.
The whites of our eyes will be red,
Our tongues will breathe fire,
And our irises will burn.
And we'll return to our bed
Depleted of desire
Yet locked by our flesh
Which will not remember
A before or after
Only now, now, eternal.
Feeble lust governed us both
And it governs us still.
There is no guard but love itself,
Innocent of knowledge.
We have claimed our hateful hearts.
No forgiveness now.

Pause. Woman looks at her Husband. His head is down. She gestures toward the door, and they slowly walk further into the house.

Nurse is seen on the beach's edge with radio in hand. He sees the boys'
bodies. Silence.

NURSE. If this I see is true . . .

What greater woe

Now

For knowing

That what I have seen, and what I will see is forever marked

By love's selfish folly.

Infant joy of mine

Wrecked joy—deliverance sweet . . .

I look up, and admit Heaven.

For I am witness to all.

Listen now.

All will be found out:

The boys at sea, the elegant lady, the man's cruelty . . .

For in my eyes, in my mouth, lives truth.

Y'hear?

The radio is heard: static.

21

Time passes. The sound of waves. The boys are seen on the beach,
unmarked. They awaken slowly, and stare at the water.

SECOND SON. Was it like this?

FIRST SON. What?

SECOND SON. Swimming?

FIRST SON. Don't know.

SECOND SON. Don't you remember?

FIRST SON. I don't think I remember anything.

SECOND SON. Not even me?

FIRST SON. Of course I remember you. You're here.

SECOND SON. . . . I remember a kiss.

FIRST SON. What kind?

SECOND SON. A brother's kiss. Very sweet.

FIRST SON. When was this?

SECOND SON. Not long ago.

FIRST SON. A brother?

SECOND SON. Yes. A dear brother of mine.

FIRST SON. . . . What was he like?

SECOND SON. Taller. Older.

FIRST SON. Like me?

SECOND SON. He had tears in his eyes.

FIRST SON. How come?

SECOND SON. He was sorry. He held me. I was in his arms for a long time.

FIRST SON. And then?

SECOND SON. He kissed me.

FIRST SON. A kiss is important.

SECOND SON. Yes. But it's not everything.

Pause.

FIRST SON. Do you think she loved us?

SECOND SON. Who?

FIRST SON. Tall woman with fierce eyes.

SECOND SON. I don't know who you mean.

FIRST SON. She held us both. Don't you remember?

SECOND SON. You held me. That's all I know.

FIRST SON. . . . I'd like love in my life.

SECOND SON. Pure love?

FIRST SON. Stripped of everything.

SECOND SON. What would you do with it?

FIRST SON. Make something.

Pause.

SECOND SON. In olden times, there were animals . . .
    They came, and feasted on everything,
    For they were motherless and fatherless,
    And vanished to themselves.
    They ate the grapes, and bit the leaves,
    And chewed on the legs of insects.
    They gorged themselves with all manner of things:
    Plants and brains and hard stones, and fine claret
    To soothe their tired tongues.
    And when they were done feasting
    They killed, and not a goddamn did they give
    About anything.

FIRST SON. . . . You're older.

SECOND SON. I'm not.

FIRST SON. Are you sure?

SECOND SON. I'm the same. So are you.

Pause.

FIRST SON. Shall we go in?

SECOND SON. Now?

FIRST SON. The waves are coming up: beautiful, easy.

SECOND SON. . . . Let's wait. We have time.

    Second Son takes First Son's hand. They look at the water.
    Waves. Music is heard midst the waves: sweet jazz from a long time
    past.

The End.

CHARACTERS

DOWNCAST MARY	Clenched fists and straight-ahead eyes.
TROUBLED JOHN	Bone rail and tufts of hair.
ISRAFEL	Stiff boots and heavy hands.
PROVIDENCE	Sparrow-frail and a cracked voice.
MAN IN CORNFLOWER-BLUE COAT / UNDOCUMENTED MAN / HENRI GATIEN / CARNY PREACHER / MAN IN BLUE WORKCLOTHES	Ghosts in the rear view.

PLACES	Swatches of soil against bleached skies along the rail lines.

NOTE ON THE PLAY

This text may be performed with an interval after Part 1.

Original songs featured in the text may be performed a cappella.

SCRIPT HISTORY

This play received its premiere at the Kitchen Dog Theater in Dallas, Texas, and was subsequently presented at the National New Play Network Festival in Chicago, at Cleveland Public Theatre, and in updated, revised version at Salvage Vanguard Theatre in Austin, Texas.

This play was finalist for the 2001 PEN USA Award in Drama.

The play was published in *TheatreForum* 21 (Summer–Fall 2002) with an introduction by Matthew Maguire; and as an acting edition in www.playscripts.com.

FUGITIVE PIECES

A PLAY WITH SONGS

PART 1

SCENE 1

Dawn. The railroad tracks. Downcast Mary appears, singing . . .

Mercy

DOWNCAST MARY. Burn my dreams
  on a wayward sea.
  Let them drown.
  Oh mercy me.

  (*She stops by the edge of the tracks, and picks up a piece of glass that is on the ground, looks at it, and continues singing . . .*)

Ashen ghosts
on a pine bluff tree,
hanging still.
Oh sorrow be.

Oh mercy me.
Let down my dreams
on a rope of light,
in a raw smoke heap.

Oh mercy me.
Let down my dreams
on the twilight's vine,
in the river deep.

(*She holds the piece of glass up to the light.*)

Wayward boy,
won't you cut my need?
I got no dreams to carry me.

The sunlight bounces off the glass. The glass begins to burn in Downcast Mary's hand. Sharp flame. She opens her hand. A trickle of ash.

SCENE 2

A little after dawn. The railroad tracks. Downcast Mary has a foot on the rail. Troubled John is standing.

TROUBLED JOHN. Looking to jump?

DOWNCAST MARY. If I can cut it.

TROUBLED JOHN. The train's pretty fast.

DOWNCAST MARY. I'll take it slow.

He looks down the silence of the tracks, out toward the horizon, where the rails converge.

TROUBLED JOHN. I can't get used to this sun.

DOWNCAST MARY. The further west, the more bitter the sun.

TROUBLED JOHN. Damn claw in my belly.

DOWNCAST MARY. Breathe.

TROUBLED JOHN. Eh?

DOWNCAST MARY. Take in some air. It'll stop the hunger.

Troubled John starts to breathe in.

TROUBLED JOHN. My ribs will pop. I can feel them cracking.

DOWNCAST MARY. Slow breath. Let it fill you. Like this.

She breathes in through her nose slowly, and breathes out.

TROUBLED JOHN. Looks hard.

DOWNCAST MARY. I'm full.

TROUBLED JOHN. Green bean kind?

DOWNCAST MARY. Steak and hash.

TROUBLED JOHN. Yeah?

He breathes in through his nose slowly, and breathes out. He starts coughing.

DOWNCAST MARY. You shocked your stomach.

TROUBLED JOHN. Ain't that. I'm . . . sick-like.

DOWNCAST MARY. What do you mean?

TROUBLED JOHN. Dust in the lungs. Ever since I can count.

DOWNCAST MARY. Is it catching?

TROUBLED JOHN. Ain't no one died on me yet.

DOWNCAST MARY. . . . You should try sucking the air through your mouth next time.

It won't put so much pressure on your lungs.

TROUBLED JOHN. Through my mouth?

DOWNCAST MARY. Like this.

She breathes by sucking air through her mouth.

TROUBLED JOHN. That looks harder than the other.

DOWNCAST MARY. Gave Myrt another year.

TROUBLED JOHN. Who's Myrt?

DOWNCAST MARY. Orphan lady who smoked black cigarettes in a gin palace once.

TROUBLED JOHN. Kin of yours?

DOWNCAST MARY. No. Just a lady I met. . . . What's it feel like?

TROUBLED JOHN. Hmm?

DOWNCAST MARY. Belly. What's it feel like now after you've . . .?

TROUBLED JOHN. . . . Basket of black bread and cheese.

DOWNCAST MARY. Red wine in a glass.

TROUBLED JOHN. Cigarette on the lips.

DOWNCAST MARY. And a slap of guava jam.

TROUBLED JOHN. What's that?

DOWNCAST MARY. The Spanish eat it.

TROUBLED JOHN. You're Spanish?

DOWNCAST MARY. I don't know what I am . . .

But these cakes, these thin cakes filled with guava . . .

You only have to take one bite, and all the blood-red guava

spills over the cake's edges and onto your clothes like a squashed animal hitting dirt.

(*Troubled John bends over.*)

Are you all right?

TROUBLED JOHN. Too much food.

DOWNCAST MARY. You ain't et none.

TROUBLED JOHN. Talk's the same as eating. Everything seems bigger when you talk about it. Fills your belly twice-size.

DOWNCAST MARY. Hey. Don't retch. Not here.

TROUBLED JOHN. Why not?

DOWNCAST MARY. Runts come, they beat you dry for retching. Straighten up. Look out.

TROUBLED JOHN. Runts?

DOWNCAST MARY. Blue-coats.

TROUBLED JOHN. . . . Cops?

DOWNCAST MARY. Yeah.

TROUBLED JOHN. The cops won't come.

(*She kicks him.*)

Hey. I can straighten up just fine on my own.

He straightens up slowly, looks out.

DOWNCAST MARY. What are you looking at?

TROUBLED JOHN. Sky.

DOWNCAST MARY. What else?

TROUBLED JOHN. A man waving in a cornflower-blue coat. It looks like he's missing a hat.

DOWNCAST MARY. A runt.

TROUBLED JOHN. Just a wandering kind.

DOWNCAST MARY. Where's he at?

TROUBLED (*indicating, in the distance*). By the fence. See? Tied up.

DOWNCAST MARY. That's a scarecrow. Not a man.

TROUBLED JOHN. He's trying to move his arms. He's looking down.

DOWNCAST MARY. He's caught in a wire, moving in the breeze.

TROUBLED JOHN. How'd you know?

DOWNCAST MARY. I was born in a crossroads. I let the earth guide me.
That's a scarecrow, right-patched in cornflower-blue,
wire round his neck, twisting in the wind.
Figure he'll spend all day down and up again,
until the wire rips his head,
and there ain't nothing but straw and rags
climbing up to the heavens.

TROUBLED JOHN. Did you say a crossroads?

DOWNCAST MARY. Where I was born. A split in a road right in the middle of Kansas.

TROUBLED JOHN. You know where you're from.

DOWNCAST MARY. Don't you?

TROUBLED JOHN. I've been told everything from "Son, you were born in Missouri," to "You were born in New York."

DOWNCAST MARY. I wish I didn't know. I can't stand telling folks I'm from Kansas.

TROUBLED JOHN. Kansas is all right.

DOWNCAST MARY. Flatland. You're buried before you're born.

TROUBLED JOHN. . . . I used to tell people I was from France.

DOWNCAST MARY. France?

TROUBLED JOHN. Sounded like a good place to be from. All those songs, you know.
(*Sings*) "Non regrette rien. Non . . ."
Problem was, folks would start speaking to me in French
and I couldn't pick up anything of what they were saying,
so I had to stop telling them I was from France.
Beat.

DOWNCAST MARY. How are you feeling?

TROUBLED JOHN. Don't feel like retching no more.

DOWNCAST MARY. Clear of the runts.

TROUBLED JOHN. You don't like them much.

DOWNCAST MARY. They tag a soul just for walking, for not looking right.

TROUBLED JOHN. I had a brother. Step-kind. He was a cop. Blue-coat.
A "runt," like you call it.
He no more liked picking folks up,
than folks liked being picked,
except if it was someone who'd done a murder.
Steve liked taking the murderers down.
Said it was the Lord's work to do so.
But plain folks out doing nothing except, well . . .
Steve couldn't take it into his soul easy,
'cause he knew folks thought he was a "runt" for doing it,
when all he was doing was holding up the law
written in some book he'd had no part of.
As far as he could see, the only law there was was God's law,
and the earth book he worked for didn't have much to do with God,
except for the Commandments.
Earth book got those right.

DOWNCAST MARY. You're Bible man?

TROUBLED JOHN. No. Just grew up around it.

DOWNCAST MARY. Good. 'Cause if you were, I'd ask you to scoot.

TROUBLED JOHN. Don't you like the Bible?

DOWNCAST MARY. I like the Bible fine. Just don't like men preaching it.

TROUBLED JOHN. I wouldn't know how to do that. I just know what Steve taught me.
He'd read the Commandments out to me late at night.
And once he'd done so, he'd place his hand on my forehead and say
"Put these laws into your heart, and no trouble will come to you in this world."
And then he would turn over on the narrow bed

we shared against the cold, and shut his eyes to pray.
And as I felt his prayers turn into sleep,
blue puffs of breath escaping his body in a long rumble,
I knew Steve was a good man. No matter what hell all said.

DOWNCAST MARY. Did you ever see him work?

TROUBLED JOHN. I saw him beat a man once. The man deserved every
bit of the cruel mercy that came with the repeated blows of
Steve's hand.

DOWNCAST MARY. Was the man a murderer?

TROUBLED JOHN. He was a thief. "Same as." That's what Steve said.
"Thieves are the scavengers of the earth.
Got to beat the thieving out of them,
or they will overrun the land,
and leave us good folk with nothing but hellfire to walk
through."
I don't know if I'd put it like that,
but I know when Steve finished with him,
all I could see was the cage of that man's eyelids shaking like
God Almighty.
And Steve? He dragged the man off the broken road,
and carried him in his arms all the way to the station.
A pure act of kindness it was.

DOWNCAST MARY. After the man got beat.

TROUBLED JOHN. He was a thief.

DOWNCAST MARY. So are you.

TROUBLED JOHN. I'm not a thief.

DOWNCAST MARY. What do you live on?

TROUBLED JOHN. If Steve taught me anything . . .

DOWNCAST MARY. Where's he now?

TROUBLED JOHN. I don't know. We were wards of the state. One house
one year, another house . . . couple hundred unnamed cities
by the time I was twelve. Once he became a cop, we were split
up, lost track . . . It's getting cold, isn't it?

DOWNCAST MARY. Wind hits the skin like metal in the morning.

TROUBLED JOHN. My stomach's ripped.

DOWNCAST MARY. Breathe.

(*He breathes through his mouth. A long cough, spits into his jacket.*)
Is that blood?

TROUBLED JOHN. Dust. (*Holds up scuffed lapel*) See?

DOWNCAST MARY. . . . So, you're thinking you'll run into Steve?

TROUBLED JOHN. I'd like to see him, but it's not like I'm out hunting . . .

DOWNCAST MARY. I bet you wouldn't mind it one bit if Steve took a stick to your hide and beat you clean, 'cause he'd just be offering you the Lord's mercy, isn't that right?

TROUBLED JOHN. Why would Steve . . .?

DOWNCAST MARY. If you were to steal something.

TROUBLED JOHN. I'm not a thief.

DOWNCAST MARY. But if you were.

TROUBLED JOHN. If I was, and he caught me? He'd have the law on his side. He'd have to beat me clean.

DOWNCAST MARY. . . . You know how much I stole? First time?
A can of beans.
I thought like you: "Stealing's wrong. God's law."
But I'd been fire-walking for a good ten days . . .

TROUBLED JOHN. Fire-walking?

DOWNCAST MARY. Walking without stop, burning my soles, running.

TROUBLED JOHN. Oh.

DOWNCAST MARY. I was dead hungry.
I thought "If I get picked up, at least it'd be some kind of sanctuary."
So, I walk into this dime market that was lit like Christmas
so there was no way a blue-coat could miss it.
And I take a can of French-cut green beans, and slide it into my bag
and I think "All right, all right," but there's nobody.
I walk out of that store and there's not a sound.
So, I turn into this little side yard,

an ash-brown patch of grass,
and start to bust open the can,
when a runt comes down and breaks my back,
pushes my face between his legs until I can't breathe,
and I hear the sounds of the can hitting the ground,
French-cut green beans snaking across the grass,
and I'm bleeding.
Next I know I'm in a blind place,
my back feels like sharp metal's been put into it,
and I haven't stopped being hungry.
Runt puts me on quinine for a week.
"This bird is quarantined," he said.
"She's suffering from malaria.
Pay no heed to what she says. She's got a head full of dreams.
Dreams and inventions. Cruel sort of disease."
Quinine stuck to my throat.
Every time I asked for water, all I got was a lime the size of a
bull penny: flat and round.
And King Runt would come into me every night,
four and five times. See, he was a Bible man. He didn't like
thieves.
When I got let out, I couldn't walk without falling to my knees.
Runt wrote down on some paper I had a "chemical deficiency,"
and there wasn't a doctor that could cure me.
He made me sign the paper with my teeth.
"Bit by an unlettered bird," he wrote,
"an unlettered daughter of the Kansas plains."
And then a spurred boot hit my rear
and landed me onto a blank street,
where every grain of light and dark
seemed to be reaching toward my eye.
I started to walk, but I was bleeding inside.
The blank street turned into a rough footpath.
The twilight's murmur hit my brow.
I could hear voices call out:
"How many dead? How many dead?"

A light fell on me. Skin-and-bone.
I looked up. And there were a hundred stars
hung in the sky like loose flowers on snow.
And I swore from that day on that they'd be my sanctuary.
And yes, I'd be a thief,
but I wouldn't take a can of beans,
I'd just take, and take, and take.
I'd out-thieve all the runts.
I'd dare them to catch me.
'Cause I had the protection of the stars.
Only a constellation could cage me.

Troubled John begins to laugh.

TROUBLED JOHN. I ain't heard a spook-tale like that in weeks.

DOWNCAST MARY. You don't believe me?

She slips down her grey jacket, the thin dress she wears exposes her scarred back. He grows quiet.

TROUBLED JOHN. Your back . . .

DOWNCAST MARY. And between my legs. Go on. Touch me. I don't feel anything anymore.

TROUBLED JOHN. . . . Shouldn't have.

DOWNCAST MARY. What?

TROUBLED JOHN. You shouldn't have stole. You wouldn't have . . . got beat.

DOWNCAST MARY. Son of a bitch.

TROUBLED JOHN. It's God's law.

DOWNCAST MARY. Is it God's law to break someone's back? Break their back and then fuck them wide like butcher's beef?

(She hits him.)

Fucking step-bastard step-runt

He restrains her.

TROUBLED JOHN. I believe you. All right? You hear me? I'm not a runt. I'm not a goddamn runt.

Beat. He releases her.

DOWNCAST MARY. You said it like you meant it.

TROUBLED JOHN. Huh?

DOWNCAST MARY. "Runt." Like you wasn't trying to defend your step-brother.

TROUBLED JOHN. You got a name?

DOWNCAST MARY. "Downcast."

TROUBLED JOHN. What?

DOWNCAST MARY. It's what people call me: "Downcast."

TROUBLED JOHN. You got a real name?

DOWNCAST MARY. "Mary." But don't nobody call me that.

TROUBLED JOHN. I'll call you. (*Indicating train*) This one's a lickety-split. Are you ready?

DOWNCAST MARY. What about you?

TROUBLED JOHN. Eh?

DOWNCAST MARY. Your name . . . ?

TROUBLED JOHN. John.

Train is louder, nearer.

DOWNCAST MARY. What?

TROUBLED JOHN (*indicating train*). Jump!

Train speeds past. A line of smoke. An electrical fizz. Downcast Mary and Troubled John have disappeared.

SCENE 3

The Ballad of the Strung-Up Man

A glazed sky. Ancient sun beats down on Man in Cornflower-Blue Coat. He is tied to a fence with wire. A piece of paper with illegible words is pinned onto his open chest. A crushed bowler on the ground near him. He sings . . .

MAN IN CORNFLOWER-BLUE COAT. Bring down the hours.
Bring down the days.
The tied-up man
wants to cover his head.

A bloodless rain
will fall on the grave
of the man strung up
for no reason.

Bring down the hours.
Bring down the days.
The tied-up man
wants to lift his arms.

A needle bent
in the hollow brain
of the man strung up
for no reason.

What evil have I done, Lord?
What evil have I done?
A voice called out
in the cold dawn
of a life gone by
for no reason.

Lights fade.

SCENE 4

*Night. Open freight car on the train. Troubled John and Downcast
Mary are leaning against each other.*

TROUBLED JOHN. I can't close my eyes. They're stuck open. Like that
damn scarecrow by the road. Steve would read to me. Would
always send me to sleep.

DOWNCAST MARY. I ain't Steve.

TROUBLED JOHN. One of the houses we stayed in had newspaper all
over the walls.
When I couldn't sleep, Steve would read bits of stories to me
off the walls:
"In a Kentucky minefield today . . . an Italian ship was spotted
off the coast of . . . Montana. While in China . . ."

The jumble of stories and places would stir in my head
until I couldn't think of anything.
And Steve would say "Go sleep, John. Go sleep."
Just like that without the "to" in the middle. My eyes closed in
an instant.
. . . I can hear it.

DOWNCAST MARY. What?

TROUBLED JOHN. The rain.

(*Troubled John sticks his head out the open train.*)
It stings.

DOWNCAST MARY. You stick your head out like that in the rain, of
course it's going to sting.

TROUBLED JOHN. I wanted to feel it.

DOWNCAST MARY. It could be poison.

TROUBLED JOHN. What are you talking about?

DOWNCAST MARY. Some rain's poison. Full of chemicals and disease.
It ain't always clear water from heaven. . . . I like fire. When I
was a kid, I would think of fire to make me sleep. Flames up
and down the blue walls by my bed, and I'd go right under.

TROUBLED JOHN. . . . I got rain in my ear.

DOWNCAST MARY. Shake it out.

TROUBLED JOHN. It's too far in. I can't hear anything. I can't . . . I can't
hear.

*Downcast Mary turns his head to the right, then tilts it to one side,
shakes his head gently.*

DOWNCAST MARY. You hear me now?

TROUBLED JOHN. Yeah.

DOWNCAST MARY. I swear. If a strong wind comes through here, you'll
blow straight-away. How'd you make it this far anyway?

Troubled John looks out . . .

TROUBLED JOHN. Waist-high grass.

DOWNCAST MARY. Illinois.

TROUBLED JOHN. How'd you know?

DOWNCAST MARY. See that great finger of land? Only Illinois has that.

TROUBLED JOHN. How do you remember places? All I remember are things.

DOWNCAST MARY. I take pictures in my brain. (*Looks out.*) A mass of wildflowers on black soil. See?

TROUBLED JOHN. Yes.

DOWNCAST MARY. You try it.

TROUBLED JOHN. I don't know what to look at.

DOWNCAST MARY. Look at anything.

TROUBLED JOHN. . . . Quail on an oak branch.

DOWNCAST MARY. Yeah?

TROUBLED JOHN. Slanted moon through trees.

DOWNCAST MARY. What else?

TROUBLED JOHN. Everything's going too fast.

DOWNCAST MARY. It's like taking a picture. Just look.

TROUBLED JOHN. . . . A little girl's dress clinging to a fence. Looks like it's been there some time.

DOWNCAST MARY. A little girl . . .

TROUBLED JOHN. A dress. With red checks. What's wrong?

DOWNCAST MARY. Nothing.

TROUBLED JOHN. Didn't I do all right?

DOWNCAST MARY. You did fine. It's Illinois.

TROUBLED JOHN. . . . Hey. You know any movies? Black and white, or in color.
I bet if you told me a movie, I'd go to sleep.
Doesn't have to be a new one. It could be one of those they show in drive-ins.

DOWNCAST MARY. What?

TROUBLED JOHN. You've never been to a drive-in?

DOWNCAST MARY. No.

TROUBLED JOHN. The whole movie is yours. You see, it's not only way up on the screen but on the grass, the cars, the weeds. You could be driving on a highway, and catch Elizabeth Taylor's face right off the side of the road, have her violet eyes light your way.

DOWNCAST MARY. That's creepy.

TROUBLED JOHN. It's great, 'cause it's part of you. The movie is living in the same space you are. With birds shitting and dirty shoes hanging on the clothesline.

DOWNCAST MARY. They're too big for me.

TROUBLED JOHN. Movies?

DOWNCAST MARY. I don't like the idea of 20-foot people walking around.

TROUBLED JOHN. . . . Train's starting to clip.

DOWNCAST MARY. Leaving Illinois.

TROUBLED JOHN (*shouts*). Bye, Illinois.

DOWNCAST MARY. You're crazy.

TROUBLED JOHN. There's no harm in shouting. What? Cops? There are no cops around here.

DOWNCAST MARY. You can't be too sure.

TROUBLED JOHN. You can't live like that. Scared all the time.

DOWNCAST MARY. I'm not scared.

TROUBLED JOHN. You know, Steve used to . . .

DOWNCAST MARY. Fuck Steve. I can't hear about him right now. I can't.

Pause.

TROUBLED JOHN. Can I touch your back?

DOWNCAST MARY. Your eyes still . . .?

TROUBLED JOHN. Yes.

DOWNCAST MARY. . . . Go sleep.

Downcast Mary slips down her jacket, exposing her back. Troubled John traces the scars on her back with his hand. In the distance, faint, the sound of a little girl laughing.

Day. Open freight car on the train. Troubled John is sleeping in Downcast Mary's arms. She nudges him.

DOWNCAST MARY. It's light.

TROUBLED JOHN. Why'd you let me shut my eyes?

DOWNCAST MARY. You were tired.

TROUBLED JOHN. I can't think straight now.

DOWNCAST MARY. You'll be all right.

Downcast Mary slips on her jacket, and rises.

TROUBLED JOHN. Where are you going?

DOWNCAST MARY. I saw a man. Slipped himself onto another car. He was waving a loaf of bread around.

TROUBLED JOHN. What am I supposed to do, huh? What if you don't come back?

DOWNCAST MARY. Look at the sky. Take a picture.

Downcast Mary jumps out of the car.

TROUBLED JOHN. Mary?

Lights fade.

SCENE 6

Open freight car on the train. Troubled John and Downcast Mary are seated, sharing a piece of black bread. Israfel, who has been carrying frail Providence on his back for what clearly has been a considerable time, sets her down on the floor of the freight car. Israfel wears an oversized coat under which are assorted layers of clothes, and boots. Providence wears a floral print dress, and lace-up oxfords with stacked heels. An empty spice threaded with a thin cord can hangs from her neck.

ISRAFEL. Forty hours of light is what we need
so we can beat down the laughing god, and the laughing girl
which is his mistress.
Never been as end-overed as I am now.
Been carrying Providence, my mother here, for a good fifty miles.
Couldn't find us a soul who'd hand us a nickel.

IMAGE 3.1 **Troubled John (Judson Jones) and Downcast Mary (Lee Eddy) share nourishment.**

Fugitive Pieces, directed by Jason Neulander at Salvage Vanguard Theatre, Austin, Texas (2002).

Photograph by Salvage Vanguard Theatre press office.

PROVIDENCE. . . . Ra.

ISRAFEL. That's all she says these days: "Ra." Makes for a good act. I stand her up by a pole or something like, and just tell her to make her sound over and over. You'd be surprised how much money folks throw in her (*indicates spice can*) can. Old woman like this, well, old enough, 'cause she had me young; we practically raised each other, can get folks bawling and shooting dimes quicker than any carny act I've seen.

PROVIDENCE. Ra . . .

ISRAFEL. But fifty miles and nothing. Under the spell of a laughing god. Hand me a crust of bread?

DOWNCAST MARY. This is all we got.

TROUBLED JOHN. Here.

Troubled John breaks a crust and hands it to Israfel, who hands it to Providence, who eats as if she won't have another chance for a long time.

DOWNCAST MARY (*to Troubled John*). Why the hell did you do that?

TROUBLED JOHN. She's damn hungry.

DOWNCAST MARY. You got a bleeding stomach. That's worse than hunger.

PROVIDENCE. Ra. Ra. . . . Ra. Ra.

DOWNCAST MARY. What does she want now?

ISRAFEL. I reckon she wants all of it.

PROVIDENCE. Ra . . .

Troubled John takes the bread from Downcast Mary's hands and offers it to Providence, who grabs t with her teeth and eats.

DOWNCAST MARY. What about us?

TROUBLED JOHN. We'll get by.

DOWNCAST MARY. You weren't saying that last night. Clutching your stomach and shit.

ISRAFEL (*to Troubled John*). You're sick?

TROUBLED JOHN. At night sometimes . . .

ISRAFEL. At night?

TROUBLED JOHN. Everything glimmers and fades.

ISRAFEL. . . . You're a kind man.

DOWNCAST MARY. He's a wretch.

ISRAFEL. Most folks would do nothing. Why, that piece of bread will last in her stomach for days. Days upon days. You see, Providence don't eat much anymore.
Her stomach can't take. She just picks. Like a bird.

PROVIDENCE. Ra . . .

DOWNCAST MARY. She don't swallow like one.

ISRAFEL. She picks a crust, scarfs it down. A couple of days later, she picks another.

She wasn't always like that. But ever since she stopped talking right . . . (*To Troubled John*) Name's Israfel. You?

TROUBLED JOHN. John.

ISRAFEL. John Akin?

TROUBLED JOHN. No.

ISRAFEL. I knew a John Akin. I ran into him in Arkansas. Little bit of a town called Helena. You heard of it?

TROUBLED JOHN and DOWNCAST MARY. No.

ISRAFEL. Speck of a town: one-room shacks, green patches of grass,

Old man making bottle-neck guitars out of scrap,

out of nothing, and playing them like a dream.

John Akin was hiding there. The bulls were after him.

TROUBLED JOHN. Bulls?

ISRAFEL. Blue suits.

TROUBLED JOHN. . . . Cops?

ISRAFEL. Yeah.

DOWNCAST MARY. Runts.

ISRAFEL. "Nobody'd think to find me in Helena," he said.

And things were peace-quiet for a while,

But John, he couldn't stand silence for too long.

He had to slit some fool's throat.

"I don't like the way that man looked at me," he said.

And he skipped town in the wink of an eye.

(*Sings*) "John Akin fought like a hound.

Would leave a man drowning in blood

Without so much as a turn-around."

TROUBLED JOHN. Well, I don't fight.

ISRAFEL. I wouldn't hold you to a name.

But you sure do put me in mind of John Akin.

He kept his eyes bowed down. Like you. Straight at the ground.

"Looking for pennies?" folks would call out. "Looking for

knives," he'd come back.

What'd you say they call you again?

DOWNCAST MARY. Folks call me "Downcast."

ISRAFEL. Eh?

DOWNCAST MARY. And I don't even keep my eyes bowed down.

TROUBLED JOHN. . . . "Troubled."

ISRAFEL. Trouble?

TROUBLED JOHN. "Troubled."

ISRAFEL. Why do they call you that?

TROUBLED JOHN. Fuck do I know. You think I like having people call me something for no reason, like I got something written on me that says "fucked-up"?

There's nothing wrong with me. It's everyone else in the world that's fucked.

PROVIDENCE. Ra . . .

ISRAFEL. You like the bread, Ma?

The train stops abruptly. A flat roar. A skeletal clang.

TROUBLED JOHN. What the hell . . .?

PROVIDENCE. Ra.

ISRAFEL. It's just the train, Ma. We'll be all right.

TROUBLED JOHN. What the hell is it? Huh?

ISRAFEL. I don't know, John. The train stopped. You want to jump out and take a look-see?

TROUBLED JOHN. We're supposed to be moving. Not stuck in some . . .

DOWNCAST MARY (*looking out*). Pale bark. Must be Ohio.

ISRAFEL. I thought we were going to Utah.

DOWNCAST MARY. Why would you want to go to Utah?

ISRAFEL. All those Mormons. Are you kidding? Providence and I could run us a fine racket over there.

TROUBLED JOHN. Fucking hell. Fucking hell. Fucking hell.

ISRAFEL. Are you all right, soldier?

TROUBLED JOHN. I don't like . . . not moving.

DOWNCAST MARY (*looking out*). Looks like they're carrying someone out. Putting a sheet over him.

ISRAFEL. Dead man on the tracks. This hasn't happened to us in a long time. Remember, Providence?

PROVIDENCE. Ra.

ISRAFEL. Must have been in Illinois somewhere. Damn train stopped for hours.

TROUBLED JOHN. Fucking hell.

ISRAFEL (*continuing*). Bulls all around, investigating . . .
Providence and I walked up to the diner car,
sat us down on plush vinyl, and had ourselves a fine half-pound
of rib-eye steak.

PROVIDENCE. Ra.

ISRAFEL. And corned beef hash. That's right. That was one hell of
a day.
Praise to God for having that man kill himself on those tracks
and letting us eat.

TROUBLED JOHN. Shut.

ISRAFEL. What'd I say?

DOWNCAST MARY (*looking out*). They're dumping the man.

ISRAFEL. An undocumented son of a bitch.

DOWNCAST MARY. They've tossed him into the ravine.

ISRAFEL. Can't do much against the wrath of man.

The train begins to move again: an escalating hum.

TROUBLED JOHN. "Israfel." What kind of name is that?

ISRAFEL. It's a Bible name. Old Testament, I believe.

TROUBLED JOHN. I don't recall such a name.

ISRAFEL. You writ the Bible now?

TROUBLED JOHN. My stepbrother would read it to me.

ISRAFEL. He a preacher?

TROUBLED JOHN. Cop.

ISRAFEL. A bull?

TROUBLED JOHN. His name's Steve. You may have heard of him.

ISRAFEL. Steve? Can't say that I have. But then I don't make much time to talk to bulls.

DOWNCAST MARY. They make your skin itch?

ISRAFEL. Something like that.

TROUBLED JOHN. . . . Well, "Israfel" ain't a Bible name.

ISRAFEL. It was Providence who gave it me, You'd have to ask her where it came from.

PROVIDENCE. Ra . . .

ISRAFEL. Could be a long time . . .

DOWNCAST MARY. Feels nice, though. In the mouth. "Is-ra-fel."
You can really wrap your tongue around a name like that.

ISRAFEL. That you can.

DOWNCAST MARY. You can stretch it out and wiggle it: Iss-ra-fel. Issss-ra-fel.

ISRAFEL. You can do anything you like.

DOWNCAST MARY. Issssss-ra-fel.

TROUBLED JOHN. Bitch.

DOWNCAST MARY. What'd you say?

TROUBLED JOHN. Someone just died on these tracks, and you're wiggling your ass?

DOWNCAST MARY. I wiggle when I want.

TROUBLED JOHN. Damn whore.
I bet you flung yourself on your knees and begged that King Runt to break you wide,
you little thief.

Downcast Mary punches Troubled John.

DOWNCAST MARY. Come on, Bible boy. Say it again.

PROVIDENCE. Ra . . .

DOWNCAST MARY. Say what you said again and I will—

TROUBLED JOHN. Once I called Steve about a hundred things.
"Gutfuck . . ." I didn't even know what I was saying.

DOWNCAST MARY. What?

TROUBLED JOHN. No thought in my head.

Downcast Mary draws close to Troubled John, gently kisses him.

DOWNCAST MARY. You should put something on that. It'll start bruising.

ISRAFEL. How about a stone?

Israfel pulls out a slightly jagged piece of limestone from his coat pocket.

DOWNCAST MARY. Put your cheek against this, John.

Troubled John puts the limestone against his cheek.

TROUBLED JOHN. Ice.

DOWNCAST MARY. Do you good.

ISRAFEL. Where'd you learn to hit like that? You got a mean hand.

DOWNCAST MARY. When I was little, I would hit the back of the house with my bare hands. Over and over. Until my knuckles bled. Fist against wood. Against bone.
Sometimes I would spend whole nights with my fists clenched, I would wake up in the morning hitting, smacking air.
It would take me a good half-day to unclench my fists.

PROVIDENCE. Ra . . .

Providence rocks a bit.

ISRAFEL. The bread go down all right, Ma?
You wouldn't have any liquid on you, would you?

DOWNCAST MARY. No. That's all right. She'll just swallow a bit. Won't you, Ma?
Bunch up some saliva. Like I do when I spit.
I know it don't taste good.
But it's better to get something in you, than nothing.
(*Providence laughs quietly. Troubled John sets the limestone down.*)
You feel all better?

TROUBLED JOHN. I'm fine.

Troubled John hands the limestone back to Israfel.

DOWNCAST MARY. Ain't swollen a bit.

TROUBLED JOHN. Don't touch me.

Beat.

DOWNCAST MARY. How long has Providence been like that?

ISRAFEL. What do you mean?

DOWNCAST MARY. Making that sound. Acting, you know . . .

ISRAFEL. I've been walking fifty miles. I need a rest.

Israfel turns away from Downcast Mary and Troubled John, closes his eyes. The darkness of the day comes through the open car of the train.

TROUBLED JOHN. I think sometimes I'll come to a place that's not even
a bit of itself,
but a whole combination of places put together,
like a town made up of all the towns in the world.

ISRAFEL. Like an amusement park?

TROUBLED JOHN. No. Just a place that's become, through time,
a place where all the bits of the world have come together:
a stack of Irish hay next to a New York City building,
a burst of Chinese poppies in the middle of a Kentucky
minefield . . .

DOWNCAST MARY. Like the newspapers all over your walls.

TROUBLED JOHN. Yes.

ISRAFEL. What newspapers are you talking about?

TROUBLED JOHN. Except this time it'd be real:
Arabian horses running next to German cars,
Italian ships resting on the hills of Montana,
The sound of French phonographs playing 78 rpm.

ISRAFEL. French? I like that.

TROUBLED JOHN (*continuing*). While a Hollywood screen twenty feet
tall
moves back and forth through the gravity field of the frontier,
illuminating the holes of the earth
with huge, flaming stars in black, white, and color,

who to measure themselves against the world,
burst through the screen with their painted ivory teeth
and irradiate the frontier with a ferocious kiss.

DOWNCAST MARY. At the drive-in.

TROUBLED JOHN. Yes.

ISRAFEL. And you're saying all this would be in one place?

TROUBLED JOHN. Down a road, a couple hundred miles somewhere.

ISRAFEL. Kissing stars, eh?

TROUBLED JOHN. Come down from the screen. Flesh-and-bone shadows.

ISRAFEL. I always had me a thing for Natalie Wood. Remember her?

TROUBLED JOHN. And in this place, there'd be a child.

ISRAFEL. Oh no, I'm talking about when she was older, making real movies.

TROUBLED JOHN (*continuing*). A child with a Brownie camera in his hand
given to him by a man he once called "father."
A child who takes pictures of a solar eclipse
with his small, eager eyes looking straight at the sun.
And nothing happens to him. Nothing.

DOWNCAST MARY. The sun don't hurt his eyes?

TROUBLED JOHN. No. His eyes grow large,
and the small of his camera un-spools plates of hieroglyphs.

DOWNCAST MARY. Hieroglyphs?

TROUBLED JOHN. Hard rock pictures: part Egyptian, part Indian, part no one knows.
The French songs fade.
The child stops staring at the sun.
And all the bits of the world
that have come together in this place
made up of scraps of places
Stir in silence against the mist.
There is a scream.

The child can't hear anything.
He's lost his hearing. Like sometimes happens in dreams.
He can only see flames
turn into smoke the color of silver
like when the projector dies and the screen goes dark.
The child lets the camera fall from his hands.
He sits with the Brownie camera, broken, in front of him,
and glides his hand over the plates of hieroglyphs.
"I was born in Missouri," he says,
"I was born in New York. I was . . ."
His hand stops on a half-formed hieroglyph.
He kisses it with his unpracticed lips,
and the half-formed shape burns itself onto his skin,
and he is left with a mark that runs down his tongue
and rests on his chin.
And so he will always be known
as the child marked by the sun, by its very eclipse,
who is from a place made up of other places,
who walks around
with a trace of twenty-foot Hollywood silver in his veins,
and the eye of a broken-down Brownie camera in his heart.

ISRAFEL. . . . Is that why they call you "Troubled"?

TROUBLED JOHN. What?

ISRAFEL. They got to call you something thinking like that, looking
like that.
Isn't that a mark on your chin? A sickle-shaped scar?
Half-moon is what.
John Akin burned his boy on the chin, so the story went.

TROUBLED JOHN. I don't know what you're . . .

ISRAFEL. Then he took a picture of his bastard son with an old camera
and smashed him over the head with it.
The boy was kicked out into the world
with his head messed up, and his half-remembered father's
mean-ness inside his skin.
Who was your mother, son?

DOWNCAST MARY. He don't know.

ISRAFEL. Whore's son. Mother died in an opium haze: Chinese poppies dancing in her brain.

TROUBLED JOHN. No.

ISRAFEL. So, John Akin finds himself with a dead whore, and a bastard child who's inherited his mother's madness. What's John Akin to do but burn the boy and kick him out into the world?

TROUBLED JOHN. Shut.

ISRAFEL. You're operating with a blown mind, son. The only thing that can set you right is to beat the craziness out of you.

Israfel takes the limestone out of his pocket.

DOWNCAST MARY. You should rest.

ISRAFEL. What?

DOWNCAST MARY. Rest your head.

ISRAFEL. My head's fine. It's his goddamn head that's a mess, talking about phantom fathers and goddamn hieroglyphs. Fucking plague shit.

Israfel strikes Troubled John in the eye with the limestone.

PROVIDENCE. Ra . . .

TROUBLED JOHN. I can't see anything.

ISRAFEL. It's a rotten world, son. There's nothing to see.

DOWNCAST MARY. He's damn bleeding. Fucking runt.

Downcast Mary goes to hit him. Israfel knocks her down with one move.

ISRAFEL. I know all about mean hands, Mary.

(*Downcast Mary goes to rise. Israfel places the heel of his boot on her stomach, digs in.*)

Stay down. It'll do you good.
Breathe. That's right. Suck that air through your mouth.

TROUBLED JOHN. . . . Mary?

After a moment, he releases his boot slowly.

DOWNCAST MARY. I'm here, John.

TROUBLED JOHN. I can't . . .

DOWNCAST MARY. I know.

Troubled John starts coughing. A racking cough that won't stop.

ISRAFEL. Shut up.

DOWNCAST MARY. He's got dust in the lungs.

ISRAFEL. Fucking mad sick . . .

DOWNCAST MARY. Ain't catching. Isn't that right, John?

Troubled John starts coughing up a mixture of dust and phlegm.

ISRAFEL. Providence? Let's go. It's all infected here.

(*Providence is very still.*)

Providence?

(*Israfel rips the spice can off Providence's neck, pulls her to him, shaking her with his heavy hands.*)

Speak. Ra . . . Providence?

Troubled John's coughing grows more severe. He is now convulsively twitching.

DOWNCAST MARY. John?

ISRAFEL. Ra. Ra.

DOWNCAST MARY. Go sleep now. Go sleep.

Troubled John kicks Downcast Mary away, continues convulsively twitching. Dust and phlegm are now caught in his throat. Odd, choking sounds.

ISRAFEL. Ra. Ra.

DOWNCAST MARY. John . . .?

(*Troubled John continues twitching. Jerk-like spasms. Occasional sound. Israfel continues to call out "Ra" while pressing Providence's still body against him. Downcast Mary walks toward the edge of the open car, looks onto fields of raw grass, liquid mud, and battered arteries of land. She sings to herself, as she stands on the open car's edge . . .)*

Mercy (reprise)

Burn my dreams
on a wayward sea.
Let them drown.
Oh mercy me.
Open arms
on a pale bark tree.
Wings of blood.
Oh sorrow be.

Oh mercy me . . .

Downcast Mary casts herself off the edge of the car, and disappears in the roar of the train. Troubled John stills. Israfel grows quiet. Providence lets out a yell from the inside of Israfel's chest, against which she is tightly pressed. Israfel trembles. Providence's yell turns into a persistent cough, which makes Israfel pull away from her, and spin out of the car. Blackout.

SCENE 7

Lament of the Undocumented Man

Undocumented Man stands in the ravine. He sings . . .

UNDOCUMENTED MAN. Good night, sweet baby child,
on wings of water go I.
Set me down
in your cold, dark mouth.
Hush
while the train goes by.

Good night, good night, sweet laughing girl,
I'm caught in your arms tonight.
No words can break this dying world.

Hush
while the train goes by.

Made two hundred dollars, and wounded bones
left on the rail to dry.
Spit on the wind, and the dollars gone . . .
My body flung over the side.

Hello, hello, sweet angel child,
I'm down on my knees tonight.
Somebody please call my name.
Not a soul I can see in this light.

Somebody please call my name.
A green card I was going to buy.

Lights fade.

PART 2

SCENE 8

A red sun. A field. Troubled John is lying on the ground, his head at an odd angle. Providence is curled up on the grass, her legs against her chest. She watches him.
A bird flies overhead. Troubled John stirs. Providence lifts her arms slowly toward the sky. Troubled John looks up.

TROUBLED JOHN. It's light.

   Lights fade.

SCENE 9

At the rim of the highway, Troubled John and Providence stand. Coarse grass at their feet. The faint sound of a carnival in the distance. Troubled John wears a sign around his neck that reads "Sermons $1."

TROUBLED JOHN (*calling out*). And the Lord God said . . .

Christ. What did He say?

I can't preach if I can't get a word of Scripture into my head.

And God knows I don't got money to pitch a tent,

not like those carny folk back there

with their weeping Jesuses and stigmata shows.

You made a sound for that bastard Israfel.

Why won't you make one for me? Eh, Providence? I treat you good.

Where the hell is Mary? I come to, and she's gone.

. . . Did you see something? Providence?

You're a spiteful bitch.

What did Israfel do to you? He burn your tongue?

(*Providence points to a lone spot in the distance.*)

What? Someone coming this way?

(*Calling out*) And the angels came down from heaven and said

"Damned soul, let me put you out of your pain.

Thou shalt not covet, bear, or steal nothing from nobody,

Or you will be shamed. You will live in Shame's house.

(*Henri Gatien appears. He wears a fur-lined coat and a hat adorned with bird claws.*)

And that's a cursed thing because Shame is the devil's harlot."

But you, sir. You!

HENRI. Yes?

TROUBLED JOHN. You look like someone who wouldn't know Shame if she walked through your door.

HENRI. I'm afraid I wouldn't.

TROUBLED JOHN. That's what I thought. I said to Providence here, "Providence, this is a good man. A fine man. I'll venture to say he's seen a bit of the world."

HENRI. Providence?

TROUBLED JOHN. She'd be all alone in the world if it wasn't for me, and the Almighty's grace.

HENRI. Don't preach to me, son.

TROUBLED JOHN. What?

HENRI. I don't want to hear your preaching.

TROUBLED JOHN. I don't got to preach.

(*Troubled John slips off sign from around his neck, throws it to the ground.*)

I could haul something for you. I got plenty of strength in my arms.

HENRI. How old is she?

TROUBLED JOHN. Hmm?

HENRI. Providence.

TROUBLED JOHN. I'd ask, but she don't talk.

HENRI. Is she mute?

TROUBLED JOHN. She makes a sound sometimes. Hasn't made it in a damn while.

HENRI. You keep her well. Look at her legs. They're still strong.

TROUBLED JOHN. We've been walking.

HENRI. Up from Ohio?

TROUBLED JOHN. How'd you know that?

HENRI. The smell.

TROUBLED JOHN. I didn't know Ohio had a—

HENRI. Everywhere does. Where do you think I'm from? Go on. Have a sniff. I'll give you a dollar.

(*Troubled John approaches Henri and sniffs.*)

Very good.

TROUBLED JOHN. My lungs are shot, but I can still use my nose.

HENRI. So, where am I from?

TROUBLED JOHN. . . . New Hampshire.

HENRI. Canada.

TROUBLED JOHN. Shit.

HENRI. Henri Gatien from Canada. And you?

TROUBLED JOHN. What was that?

HENRI. Henri Gatien.

TROUBLED JOHN. John.

HENRI. John Akin?

TROUBLED JOHN. No.

HENRI. My mistake.

TROUBLED JOHN. And everybody else's. I don't know what I got to do to get this damn hex off me.

HENRI. A hex can just go away. Like spit crackled in the air.

TROUBLED JOHN. Crackled?

HENRI. When it's freeze-eye cold.

TROUBLED JOHN. You're from Canada, eh?

HENRI. Between Nictaux and Paradise. Acadie. You know it?

TROUBLED JOHN. That like French and that?

HENRI. *Tout bien, mon ami*.

TROUBLED JOHN. I used to tell people I was from France.

HENRI. I'm not—

TROUBLED JOHN. All those great songs. And wine. Hey. You know that song?

HENRI. Eh?

TROUBLED JOHN. There's this song I used to hear on this phonograph that come all the way from France in a sleek box, real elegant. "Non, regrette . . ."

Henri continues singing line from Vaucier-Dumont's "Non, Je Ne Regrette Rien."

HENRI. "Non, je ne regrette rien . . ."

TROUBLED JOHN. You know it?

Henri sings from another part of the song . . .

HENRI. "Avec me souvenir . . . Me chagrin, me plaisir . . ."

TROUBLED JOHN. I didn't think I'd find anybody who'd come across that song.

HENRI. It's Piaf. Speck of a bird. Not unlike your Providence here. "Little Sparrow," they called her. (*To Providence*) Eh, *mon petit*?

TROUBLED JOHN. You're lucky you're French.

HENRI. *Merde* French.

TROUBLED JOHN. I thought you—

HENRI. I'm Acadian. Acadie. "Where it is plentiful." *Bon*? Nova Scotia. *Comprends*?

TROUBLED JOHN. I could've sworn New Hampshire.

HENRI. You figured one snow smells like another, eh?

TROUBLED JOHN. I figured nothing.

HENRI. You're stupid, eh?

TROUBLED JOHN. Yes.

HENRI. I'll give you the dollar.

TROUBLED JOHN. But I didn't . . .

HENRI. I'll give it you.

    Henri pulls out a one-dollar bill from inside the brim of his hat.

TROUBLED JOHN. You're rich?

HENRI. I ply a trade.

TROUBLED JOHN. What do you do?

HENRI. Fur.

TROUBLED JOHN. There's money in that?

HENRI. There can be. You want the dollar or not?

TROUBLED JOHN. Thanks.

HENRI. Not everyone would think of New Hampshire.

TROUBLED JOHN. . . . Hey. You want to hear a sermon?

HENRI. I don't like Scripture.

    (*Looking at Providence*) How old did you say she was?

TROUBLED JOHN. I don't like Scripture myself. It gives me a headache.

HENRI. Does it now?

TROUBLED JOHN. Buzzing in my head. Makes me . . .

HENRI. Providence, look at me. That's right, *mon petit.* (*Providence smiles.*) Such fine teeth.

TROUBLED JOHN. I like the Commandments, though. The sound of them. "Thou shalt . . ."

HENRI. What's wrong with your eye? A little sunk, eh? Was it cut?

TROUBLED JOHN. It twitches sometimes. It's nothing.

HENRI (*punches him lightly in the stomach*). Fire in the belly.

TROUBLED JOHN. What?

HENRI. You're strong.

Troubled John coughs a bit.

TROUBLED JOHN. Steve is stronger.

HENRI. Eh?

TROUBLED JOHN. My step-brother. You heard of him? He's a blue-coat. Bull. Runt. Cop.

HENRI. A *flic*?

TROUBLED JOHN. What?

HENRI. A *flic*. *Agent de police*.

TROUBLED JOHN. *Flic*. Yeah. Steve would read me the Commandments. Did I say that already? It's getting hard to follow them all the time. It's getting hard to find God. Where the hell is He, right?

PROVIDENCE. Ra.

HENRI. What was that?

TROUBLED JOHN. What?

HENRI. That sound she just made?

TROUBLED JOHN. I don't know. I didn't . . .

PROVIDENCE. Ra.

HENRI. *C'est un miracle*.

TROUBLED JOHN. That's just a sound. It don't mean . . .

PROVIDENCE. Ra.

HENRI. Glorious.

PROVIDENCE. Ra . . .

HENRI. *Formidable*.

TROUBLED JOHN. That's what I thought. I thought, this is a fine man, a man of means . . .

HENRI. I'll pay you one hundred dollars to fuck her. With sound. One hundred. Right now. . . . Two hundred. She'll do it, John. Isn't that right, bird?

PROVIDENCE. . . . Ra.

HENRI. My *petit moineau*. Two hundred. In a "blink," as they say. (*Henri grabs Troubled John by the throat, choking him.*) What's it going to be, John?

TROUBLED JOHN. . . . Yes.

HENRI. *Bon*.

(*Henri releases Troubled John. Troubled John coughs, recovers his breath.*)

Now, take off your pants, and Providence, *cheri*, lift up your dress. Ask the Good Lord and He shall give.

TROUBLED JOHN. Son of a . . .

Troubled John lunges at Henri. Henri punches him hard in the stomach.

HENRI. This is a gift from heaven, *mon ami*. Take it. *Allons!*

Henri pushes Troubled John toward Providence.

TROUBLED JOHN. . . . I'm sorry.

PROVIDENCE. Ra.

Providence lifts her dress. Troubled John slips Providence's underpants down and undoes his trousers.

HENRI. *Tout suite*.

Troubled John penetrates Providence.

PROVIDENCE. Ra.

HENRI. That's right. And pray, John. Pray.

TROUBLED JOHN. ". . . Our Father . . ."

Henri pulls out a Brownie camera from inside his coat.

PROVIDENCE. Ra.

TROUBLED JOHN. Fucking hell . . .

The flash of the camera as Henri takes a photograph of Troubled John and Providence. Blackout.

SCENE 10

Providence is on the ground. Her dress is torn.

PROVIDENCE. Ra. Ro-bin. Last I saw.
 Wings. Robin. Flap, flap.
 Bird. In air.
 Ground. Saw egg on ground.
 Smelled funny. Blue. Like Easter.
 I looked. Look. And a hand pulls,
 "Go. This way. Bird."
 Israfel. Boots on tar. Red sun . . .
 I remember. I remember sound.
 Sickle on one side of the grate.
 And Israfel with elbow
 slammed in the gut of a crying wound.
 Hand. Fist on back.
 Then quiet.
 Everything quiet. Like church.
 Everything broken.
 No wings.

 Providence rises, smoothes her dress. She walks away slowly.

SCENE 11

Troubled John is revealed among the parched weeds that skirt the rim of the highway. He breathes by sucking air through his mouth, and breathes out. He bends, as if to vomit. Downcast Mary appears, bouncing a red cellophane strip from a cigarette pack against the light. She wears a new dress and jacket.

DOWNCAST MARY. Don't retch. Not here.

TROUBLED JOHN. Huh?

DOWNCAST MARY. Runts come, beat you dry for retching.

TROUBLED JOHN. Mary?

DOWNCAST MARY. What are you doing, John?

TROUBLED JOHN. What's that you got? In your hand?

DOWNCAST MARY. Cellophane. Been living on cigarettes the last couple of days.

TROUBLED JOHN. Steal them?

DOWNCAST MARY. A pack in Louisville, another in Bluefield, another by the carny show back there . . . Red strip can make a helluva flare when you hold it up against the sun.

TROUBLED JOHN. Damn whore.

DOWNCAST MARY. What?

TROUBLED JOHN. You look clean.

DOWNCAST MARY. Fell down river. Had to get me a new set of clothes.

TROUBLED JOHN. Shiny.

Troubled John goes to her.

DOWNCAST MARY. What are you doing?

TROUBLED JOHN. Fuck you. Split you open.

Downcast Mary hits him.

TROUBLED JOHN. Nothing but hit me all the time. Let's see how much John can take.

DOWNCAST MARY. No.

TROUBLED JOHN. Give me. Whatever you got. I don't got all day, girl.

DOWNCAST MARY. What happened to you?

TROUBLED JOHN. Fucking gypping me all the time.

DOWNCAST MARY. I don't got nothing, John.

TROUBLED JOHN. I made two hundred dollars. In a blink. Pop. Pop. Pop. Not a cent.

DOWNCAST MARY. You're shaking.

TROUBLED JOHN. Can't stop.

DOWNCAST MARY. Come here. (*She takes off her jacket.*)

TROUBLED JOHN. What are you doing?

DOWNCAST MARY. You're cold. (*She places jacket on him.*)

TROUBLED JOHN. This jacket is like pins.

DOWNCAST MARY. You don't want it?

TROUBLED JOHN. How much you want for it?

DOWNCAST MARY. Nothing.

TROUBLED JOHN. Everybody wants something. They want so much they string folks up like scarecrows for it, dump men off tracks. Pop, pop, pop. Fucking hot . . .

Troubled John throws off jacket. Downcast Mary picks it up, slips it on. He lets out a long, choking cough. She pulls out a slim vial from pocket, offers it to him.

DOWNCAST MARY. Here.

TROUBLED JOHN. What's that?

DOWNCAST MARY. For your lungs.

TROUBLED JOHN. Poison?

DOWNCAST MARY. It's like wine. Red wine in a glass.

TROUBLED JOHN. Cigarette on the lips?

DOWNCAST MARY. And a slap of guava jam.

TROUBLED JOHN. . . . Mary?

DOWNCAST MARY. Yes.

TROUBLED JOHN. I knew you weren't dead. I knew you were lost, like a star floating outside the drive-in screen, but not dead.

DOWNCAST MARY (*indicating vial*). Go on. It'll stop everything for a while.

He downs the vial.

TROUBLED JOHN. New dress, huh? Flowers . . . How'd you find me, huh?

DOWNCAST MARY. I wasn't looking.

TROUBLED JOHN. Out of nowhere, Mary.

(*He collapses onto her. After a moment, she sings softly . . .*)
"Morphine"

DOWNCAST MARY. Morphine. Take me in your dreams. Sweet, sweet morphine . . .

Downcast Mary picks up a piece of glass that is on the ground, looks at it, begins to carve a name onto her forehead with the glass. Lights fade.

SCENE 12

Walking the Weeping Jesus

Carny Preacher in tinted glasses drags a makeshift cart, on which stands a statue of a weeping Jesus, down the road. The cart is adorned with red ribbons. He sings . . .

CARNY PREACHER. When I die, I want you to bury me
  sweet, sweet morphine.
  When I die, I want you to bury me
  sweet, sweet morphine.

  Straight to hell we go, boys.
  Straight to hell we go.
  By the light of the moon
  we're drowned below.
  Straight to hell we go.

  Weeping Jesus, won't you save my soul?
  Hand me a bucket of gold.
  Show me how the glory road
  lies under morphine's glow.

  Straight to hell we go, boys.
  Straight to hell we go.
  Lights fade.

SCENE 13

Telegraph wires cut through the sky. Troubled John carries a thin plastic bag overflowing with assorted junk food, and miscellaneous dime-store toys. He dumps the contents of the bag onto the ground.

TROUBLED JOHN. Take. Take. Take . . . And take.
  Lights fade.

Where the rails converge. Troubled John is eating a Red Vine licorice twist from a bag. Downcast Mary watches him.

DOWNCAST MARY. You're going to get sick if you keep eating like that.

TROUBLED JOHN. I like to eat.

DOWNCAST MARY. You're going to get us killed.

TROUBLED JOHN. What'd I do?

DOWNCAST MARY. You steal all the time. Stuff we don't even need. Wind-up ducks.

TROUBLED JOHN. I hadn't seen one in a while. Not since I was a kid.

DOWNCAST MARY. Broke down in five minutes.

TROUBLED JOHN. Made in China.

DOWNCAST MARY. Jacks, yo-yos, pencil sharpeners, rock candy.

TROUBLED JOHN. We made it through the Carolinas on rock candy.

DOWNCAST MARY. And that fucking peanut brittle. Messed up your teeth.

TROUBLED JOHN. I'll get them fixed.

DOWNCAST MARY. With what?

TROUBLED JOHN. I'll work for a bit. I can lift things.

DOWNCAST MARY. You can't even sign your name.

TROUBLED JOHN. What the hell are you talking about?

DOWNCAST MARY. I've seen you looking at the signs on the road.

TROUBLED JOHN. 'Cause I couldn't read that billboard? Is that why?

DOWNCAST MARY. Letters as big as me.

TROUBLED JOHN. I couldn't make sense of it, but I could read it. You're going to tell me you know what "Have Not. Will Go. Next Five Miles" means?

DOWNCAST MARY. . . . You're a lousy thief.

TROUBLED JOHN (*indicating her forehead*). Why'd you have to carve my name?

DOWNCAST MARY. I thought you'd like it.

TROUBLED JOHN. It makes my lips itch.

DOWNCAST MARY. Don't kiss me.

TROUBLED JOHN. Damn, wish I could rub it out.

DOWNCAST MARY. I could put a Band-Aid over it.

(*Troubled John pulls another Red Vine out of the bag, eats.*)

You're going to choke on that thing.

TROUBLED JOHN. You want one?

DOWNCAST MARY. . . . You shouldn't steal.

TROUBLED JOHN. What?

DOWNCAST MARY. It's wrong.

TROUBLED JOHN. You get me more morphine, all right? Crystal, powder, liquid . . . you get it.

DOWNCAST MARY. It makes you retch.

TROUBLED JOHN. Ain't nobody caught us, have they? Nobody's come round and picked us up for retching.

DOWNCAST MARY. God looks down.

TROUBLED JOHN. Yeah? And what does He see? Fucking bird-claw man, Providence by the side of the road . . .

DOWNCAST MARY. That was the devil's doing.

TROUBLED JOHN. You've got religion bad, don't you?

DOWNCAST MARY. Some things aren't right. You spend your life making yourself think they are, but they're not.

TROUBLED JOHN. Like stealing?

DOWNCAST MARY. Yeah. Or wishing ill on people, wanting them dead, beating someone up for a loaf of bread.

TROUBLED JOHN. You beat that guy—?

DOWNCAST MARY. On the train. Yeah. He wouldn't give it to me. I had to beat him up.

I stuffed his handkerchief in his mouth, so he wouldn't say anything.

TROUBLED JOHN. You choked him?

DOWNCAST MARY. He turned purple, that's all. You think I'm going to let somebody die on me, give cops a reason to throw me under lock?

TROUBLED JOHN. Cops?

DOWNCAST MARY. God looks down, John. He looks down. Wind-up ducks, yo-yos, ain't worth crap. You can't go into every dime-store on the road and walk out with a bag top-full of—

TROUBLED JOHN. What do you want me to do?

DOWNCAST MARY. When I dropped down river, and ended up living on cigarettes
from the tail end of Ohio straight through Kentucky and into Virginia,
I thought I'd die my lungs were so burned up.
Thought I'd end up stretched out on a long white table somewhere
with my new clothes on, and there wouldn't be a soul who'd weep for me,
'cause who'd know I was there? My folks in Kansas?
I was handed down to an aunt who handed me down to a cousin
who handed me down to a complete stranger who didn't know what to do with me.
"Go to the movies," he'd say, when he knew there wasn't a single movie theater in town, "Leave me be."
I would hit the back wall of the house so hard the whole house would shake.
The stranger would come around and strap me with this long belt he had and say to me,
"You got to be put somewhere."
And he'd throw me down on the linoleum, turn on the gas, and shut the kitchen door
tight. And I'd dream of fire, with the end-buckle digging into my skin.
I'd suck air through my mouth. Slowly. And I'd breathe.
And when he got tired of listening to me breathe,
he'd open the door quietly and unstrap me.

So, there's no one, you see?

If I'm on a long white table, there's no one who's going to weep for me,

except God.

And I thought to myself "I've been fooling myself against God.

I've twisted the whole world around

'cause of one stranger and a King Runt, and that ain't right."

And just as I'm thinking this, this old woman comes up to me.

She's got a wiry face and a parched blue dress, and she says,

"Child, you need some milk. I can see your bones breaking from here."

She starts to unbutton her dress.

Her breasts are young, bursting with milk.

And in the middle of a town square

with my lungs filled with nicotine

and my head spinning with memory,

I drink from her. I take her milk.

And when I'm done, she puts her hand on my forehead,

right across your name, and she smiles.

I think, "I don't know what the Bible says.

But I know this: what this old woman has done is pure grace."

I'd never felt that.

TROUBLED JOHN. So, you want me to stop stealing 'cause some bitch comes up to you and offers you tit?

DOWNCAST MARY. You haven't prayed but once. Not since we left Virginia.

TROUBLED JOHN. Why should I pray? 'Cause some kick-ass strapped you up? Go on. Step out on that rail with your fists clenched, Downcast.

DOWNCAST MARY. Quiet.

TROUBLED JOHN. Hit me, Mary. That's what you're good at.

Downcast Mary slaps Troubled John. He slaps her back. She slaps him again. Beat.

Troubled John slaps her. She touches her face.

She slaps him again. He looks away. Beat.

She touches her forehead, clenches her fists.
She moves a few paces to the left.
She tackles him to the ground.
They wrestle for some time. Beat.
Troubled John rises. From the ground, she grabs his ankle.
He walks, dragging her, five steps to the left. He stops.
Downcast Mary rises. She smoothes her clothes.
He coughs slightly. She touches her forehead.
He looks at her, smiles.
Downcast Mary moves toward him. One step.
Troubled John collapses. She looks out. Lights fade.

SCENE 15

Shell of a billboard. Downcast Mary carries Troubled John on her back.

DOWNCAST MARY. I had me a vision:
   black petals on the Super 8 sign down the road.
   I thought, "There's God. Smelling of fire.
   Dreaming up trouble in the red Georgia clay."
   Black petals cast down on everything:
   clinging to the scoop of the "8" in Super 8,
   hugging the back of the sign,
   lining the metal edge of the cold rail
   that used to be a conduit for trains at one time
   long past now.
   You don't have to look too close to see God in everything.
   You just have to look.
   I'm not talking about a weeping Jesus
   put up by a carny preacher in green sunglasses in some beat-
   back tent.
   I'm talking about:
   black petals out of nowhere, skin-and-bone light,
   copperhead stars looking down on you in the freezing cold
   when you think there are no more kind eyes.

And then you feel them staring at you from a great height, touching down on your shoulder, and you think "All right now. All right."

Lights fade.

SCENE 16

Vacant industrial lot. A remnant of a factory. Troubled John is trying to scratch an itch he can't reach. Downcast Mary is looking at the ground.

DOWNCAST MARY. Nothing but wires on this lot. What'd you think was this place?

Israfel appears from behind the remnant of the factory. He wears trousers and nothing else. His torso is lacerated—odd markings and wounds. A section of his head has been shaved.

ISRAFEL. Brown field. Used to be a cotton mill. Nothing but brown fields around here: graveyards of factories.

TROUBLED JOHN. Israfel?

ISRAFEL. John Akin's son? (*sings*) "John Akin fought like a hound. Would leave a man drowning in blood, without so much as a turn-around."

TROUBLED JOHN. You don't let up, do you?

DOWNCAST MARY. What are you doing here, Iss? I thought you'd be in Utah.

ISRAFEL. Ain't nothing in Utah except salt. Salt and rock. Damn Mormons won't give their money to nobody.

DOWNCAST MARY. How about Providence?

ISRAFEL. She run off with some naked son of a bitch.

TROUBLED JOHN. What?

ISRAFEL. Man comes up to me, selling pictures. "I got prime fur," he says. And he's true to his word. He's got all kinds. "This one will do you," he says. (*He pulls a photo strip from trouser pocket.*) Turns out to be Providence, with her mouth open, arms flapping like a bird, and some thin buck riding her like . . . See? It looks like she's shouting. Ra . . .

TROUBLED JOHN. Stop.

ISRAFEL. It's just a sound.

Israfel puts photo strip back in trouser pocket.

DOWNCAST MARY. She could come back to you.

ISRAFEL. She's dead. Under a tree. Looking up at the sky.

TROUBLED JOHN. You're wrong.

ISRAFEL. I saw her. With my own eyes . . . You look good, Mary. Is that a new dress?

DOWNCAST MARY. Yes.

ISRAFEL. Shame about your forehead.

DOWNCAST MARY. You look a wreck.

ISRAFEL. First it was the whiskey men, then the Bible thumpers, then the goddamn Nazis. They shaved off my hair, the Nazis did. (*Shows skull.*) That's my number. They burned it into my skull. That way if I run into another one of them, they know not to burn me again.

DOWNCAST MARY. Does it hurt?

ISRAFEL. Itches sometimes.

TROUBLED JOHN. I know all about that.

ISRAFEL. What are you on?

DOWNCAST MARY. Morphine.

ISRAFEL. I lived on morphine when I was in the army. Got me through all sorts of shit.

TROUBLED JOHN. I ain't coughed in weeks.

ISRAFEL. Ready for the pictures, eh? High up on the screen?

TROUBLED JOHN. Damn picture show.

ISRAFEL. We could go up.

TROUBLED JOHN. We could walk right into that drive-in, straight through the grid behind the screen.

ISRAFEL. And it'd be peaceful, wouldn't it? Like Natalie Wood's smile.

TROUBLED JOHN. Or Elizabeth Taylor's eyes.

ISRAFEL. Except at night.

TROUBLED JOHN. Yeah. It still gets bad at night. Sometimes Mary's got to hold me for hours.

DOWNCAST MARY. You don't got to tell him everything.

ISRAFEL. He's confiding in me, Mary. That's a sign of friendship.

TROUBLED JOHN. Then we go down to a canal or something, and get some water on our skin.

ISRAFEL. Is that right?

TROUBLED JOHN. She's got goodness in her, Iss. I wish I had that.

Troubled John closes his eyes. He is still.

DOWNCAST MARY. Open your eyes, John. Wake.

TROUBLED JOHN (*stirs*). What?

DOWNCAST MARY. You closed your eyes.

TROUBLED JOHN. I was dreaming.

DOWNCAST MARY. We got no time for that.

ISRAFEL. Good woman, eh?

DOWNCAST MARY. I haven't forgotten your boot on my belly.

ISRAFEL. What's that?

DOWNCAST MARY. On the train.

ISRAFEL. What happened to forgiveness, Mary? Don't you believe in that?

DOWNCAST MARY. I ain't about to forgive you.

ISRAFEL. What would the Bible say about that?

DOWNCAST MARY. Leave us be.

ISRAFEL. You want me to leave, John?

TROUBLED JOHN. What?

ISRAFEL. See? He wants to talk.

TROUBLED JOHN. It's been kind of quiet for a while.

ISRAFEL. You got some morphine left, John?

TROUBLED JOHN. In my veins. I'm hungry all the time.

ISRAFEL. You eat?

TROUBLED JOHN. Licorice. It lasts for days.

ISRAFEL. You think Providence would like some? Licorice, Pop-Tarts, pink-and-white candy?

TROUBLED JOHN. I thought you said she was . . .

ISRAFEL. Got fucked dead. Ra . . . Ra . . . Don't you think I recognize you, buck? I've had your damn picture in my brain for weeks. Ra . . . Ra . . .

DOWNCAST MARY. Shut.

ISRAFEL. It's time somebody rode you, buck. Break you in . . .

As Israfel goes to him, Troubled John grabs a wire form the ground and wraps it around Israfel's neck.

DOWNCAST MARY. John? John.

TROUBLED JOHN. Not one more word, Steve. Not one . . .

Troubled John chokes Israfel. Blackout.

SCENE 17

Cradlesong

The remnant of the factory is burning. Israfel is on the ground. Providnece appears through the flames. She sings . . .

PROVIDENCE. Straw man, straw man, lift your head.
Lift your head to me.
Robin flying over there
looking for a spot of green.

Providence takes Israfel in her arms. Lights fade.

SCENE 18

Blazing neon sign. Parking meter on a lot. A drive-in screen. Man in Blue Workclothes leans on the meter, eating a guava cake. Downcast Mary and Troubled John approach him.

MAN IN BLUE WORKCLOTHES. You want to see a movie? You got to go into town.

DOWNCAST MARY. The sign up the road said "Florida's best drive-in."

MAN IN BLUE WORKCLOTHES. They're turning this place into an amusement park now. They're going to fill it with the whole world: Italian ships, Arabian horses and the like.

DOWNCAST MARY. What are you doing here?

MAN IN BLUE WORKCLOTHES. I tend the grounds. I look after the land. I watch it. Until the park gets built.

DOWNCAST MARY. That a guava cake?

MAN IN BLUE WORKCLOTHES. Want one? (*Man in Blue Workclothes pulls a guava cake out of inside jacket pocket.*) I hide them in here. My wife don't want me eating them all the time. Says I'll get fat. But they're good, you know.

DOWNCAST MARY. Yeah.

Downcast Mary takes guava cake and hands it to Troubled John, who eats as if he hasn't in a long time.

MAN IN BLUE WORKCLOTHES. Got a look in his eye.

DOWNCAST MARY. He's never tasted one before. It's good, isn't it, John?

MAN IN BLUE WORKCLOTHES. He don't talk?

DOWNCAST MARY. He hasn't said anything for a while.

MAN IN BLUE WORKCLOTHES. Lost your speech, son?

DOWNCAST MARY. Don't do that.

MAN IN BLUE WORKCLOTHES. What?

DOWNCAST MARY. He don't like people coming up to him like that.

MAN IN BLUE WORKCLOTHES. Sorry. Something about his eye, though.

DOWNCAST MARY. It twitches sometimes.

MAN IN BLUE WORKCLOTHES. Puts me in mind . . .

Troubled John finishes eating, tugs at Downcast Mary.

DOWNCAST MARY. What? You want another?

MAN IN BLUE WORKCLOTHES. That was all I got.

DOWNCAST MARY. He don't got no more, John. Stop. Stop tugging.

MAN IN BLUE WORKCLOTHES. He liked it, huh? You know, the shop ain't but a couple miles down.

You could ask the lady there, Carmen, she might give you some guava cakes. If you ask her right.

DOWNCAST MARY. . . . Never seen one.

MAN IN BLUE WORKCLOTHES. What?

DOWNCAST MARY. Drive-in.

MAN IN BLUE WORKCLOTHES. You're shitting me?

DOWNCAST MARY. No.

MAN IN BLUE WORKCLOTHES. You want to take a look?

DOWNCAST MARY. It's big.

MAN IN BLUE WORKCLOTHES. The screen? Go on. Walk up to it. I won't tell nobody. I walk up to it myself sometimes. Pretend I'm in the movies. Like I'm Steve McQueen.

TROUBLED JOHN. . . . Steve?

MAN IN BLUE WORKCLOTHES. Flippin' cars like I was in that ol' movie *The Getaway*, screwing all the Commandments . . .

TROUBLED JOHN. . . . Steve.

DOWNCAST MARY. Come on, John. Come on.

(*Downcast Mary takes Troubled John by the hand. They walk up to the screen.*)

What do you think, John? Is this the best damn drive-in you ever saw? Look at the screen. We could walk into it right now. Straight into Elizabeth Taylor's eyes.

(*Troubled John begins to laugh.*)

Go on. Take a picture. Picture in the brain.

The screen turns into a field of red poppies. Troubled John and Downcast Mary walk into it. All goes dark except for the neon sign blazing.

The End.

CHARACTERS

CHORUS	Witnesses to slaughter, messenger-guides of the shattered terrain (could be played by one or two voices).
MINERVA	Young woman orphaned by war, making her way, her memory is contained in song(s).
BETTE / FERRY-YARD GUARD	Woman hardened by time, spirit guide, and survivor of ruin.
GHOST CHILD	A willful apparition (played by Bette).
SOLDIER KECK	Young man at odds with himself, complicit in crime, vulnerable and armored at the same time.
SOLDIER FURST / PIMP	Brutish and violent by nature, a ruthless profiteer.
SOLDIER PINT / GUARD / DISPLACED ONE	Alternately guileless and guileful young man, ghost voice of his former self.

SETTING	Ruined country stitched together from the pages of tabloid newspapers, quick, massive bombs, and piles of human bones. Detainment camps where living songs of the forgotten past are sung from a beggar's mouth.

SYNOPSIS	Scenes from war and after. Slaughter songs for broken times. A love story and vaudeville of the far and near country. A young woman walks the fields. A young man trails her. The ghost voices of the fallen rise up in ballads, hymns, blues and swing as if torn from roots of mad sorrow.
SCRIPT HISTORY	This text originally began its life as a song for a cappella voices (words by Caridad Svich, music by O-Lan Jones) entitled "Appalachia Song" written for ASK Theater Projects/Nautilus Composer-Librettist Studio. The initial song served as catalyst for this full-length play with songs, which was written with support from the Radcliffe Institute for Advanced Study at Harvard University. The play initially received a reading at New Dramatists in New York City with a cast comprised of Chris Wells, Heidi Schreck, Alfredo Narciso, Kristi Casey, Alexandra Oliver, and Jeffrey Frace.

An alternate, separate performing version of this text also exists as a stand-alone 40-minute song suite/chamber piece for three voices entitled *Slaughter Songs* which was developed as part of producer Arielle Tepper's music–theater program "Working Sessions" at New Dramatists, New York City. Composer Miranda Zent set the lyrics for this version. This revised version received a mini-workshop at Salvage Vanguard Theatre in Austin, Texas as part of SVT READS under the direction of Jenny Larson with a cast comprising Kathy Catmull, Jason Hays, Jude Hickey, Jeff Mills, Elizabeth Wakehouse, Adriene Mishler, and Adam Sultan; Colin Denby Swanson served as dramaturg; and music was composed by Adam Sultan. This play premiered at Salvage Vanguard Theatre in October 2006 under Jenny Larson's direction.

Out of earshot, Out of the breath of so many left . . .
A vowel is torn from its root throat

A PLAY WITH SLAUGHTER SONGS

PART 1

SCENE 1

Quiet time. Minerva is seen in an eerie yet gentle light. She has emerged from the waves of many, now gone.

MINERVA. They came in waves.
    I saw them.
    I was witness.
    To boys, men, women . . .
    They came in waves.
    They were a flood.

    They come through me.
    Come straight through.
    I said Hey.
    Don't nobody listen.
    I said Come on, now. Spare me . . .?
    They moved on.

    Flood come, war come,
    All hell rain down
    Til' there was nothing I could do
    But let my voice out
    like a thrush.

    (*Spoken-sung*) Hum, yelp, howl, and yodel.
    Let the ghosts run.
    (*Spoken*) They came in waves.
    Then in bits.
    Then nothing.

    . . .

No one knows nothing now.
We just spit, and shit, and pray.
We try to pray. But it don't work none.
I'm witness. I know.

I was born in this place.
I was born in this place.
Fired with dust.
I was born with my hands in red earth, and blue mud.
Nothing gleaming here, no Chrysler shiny.
Everything shit flat
and blind plenty.

Chorus appears, faintly, in the distance, singing section from "No Hosanna"

CHORUS (*sung*). Grace is fallen carbon acid
All the way from gray chute butter

MINERVA (*sings softly, to herself*) with CHORUS. No hosanna, no hosanna

CHORUS (*sung*). All the way to swill ice water
Down down down down
No hosanna.

MINERVA. (*spoken*) Ain't no story here. Ain't nothing fantastic.
Just blunder and shame.

SCENE 2

On the wide, scorched field, Minerva is met by Bette. Bette carries a bucket of water.

BETTE. Girl, whatcha doin' out here? Lookin' to get shot?

MINERVA. No.

BETTE. Then come on now. Come with me.

MINERVA. I don't know you.

BETTE. I'm Bette. That's all you gotta know.

MINERVA. Got water there?

BETTE. Yeah.

MINERVA. Give me.

BETTE. This is foul water, girl. What you want with foul water? Lookin' to get sick?

MINERVA. No.

BETTE. Look sick to me.

MINERVA. You don't look no better.

BETTE. I look fine. Do fine. I make do, right?

MINERVA. What you do?

BETTE. Take care of the likes of you.

MINERVA. Bull.

BETTE. You don't want me to?

MINERVA. Where you from?

BETTE. Here.

MINERVA. Don't look it.

BETTE. This is a big place. All sorts *here*, girl. Come on, you want water? I'll get you some.

MINERVA. Foul?

BETTE. No. Good water.

MINERVA. There ain't none left.

BETTE. There's a bit.

MINERVA. Where?

BETTE. I tell you, you do me in.

MINERVA. I wouldn't.

BETTE. I know your kind.

MINERVA. I'm not like that. Not like all them other . . . I look out, I watch out, keep under ground, if I have to.

BETTE. Is that right?

MINERVA. I've hid under for a while. Yeah.
Buried myself in dirt so as to not get caught. Soldier come by once, he dug me up.
He was a mad one, wrecked one, all fury.

He had part of his arm blown off. Scabs and scars all over. Felt
sorry for him. I did. Thought he could use a prayer or some
sign of Heaven. But he wouldn't listen.
He just wanted to dig up, have his way and move on.
I let him, right? He was a mad one. Wrecked boy. I give him
a dirt smile.
He didn't know what . . .
He shot himself. Right in front of me.
I buried him. I put him in the ground where I'd been,
covered him up in dirt and leaves.
If anybody ask? I never seen him. You see?
I bury everything. I bury, and do good. That's what I'm like.
No hosanna. No hosanna here.

BETTE. . . . You're a mess of a girl.

MINERVA. I'm not.

BETTE. Girly girl, that's what you are.

MINERVA. I am not.

BETTE. Prove it, then.

MINERVA. What you mean?

BETTE (*indicates bucket*). Bury yourself in it.

MINERVA. That's foul.

BETTE. What's a little foul water in this mess of a place? You scared?

    (*Minerva puts her head in the bucket of water.*)

    That's enough now. I said, that's enough.

    Minerva rises.

MINERVA. Water was good. Wasn't foul at all.

BETTE. Shh.

MINERVA. We'll take care of each other, won't we?

BETTE. We'll do what we can. Come on now, dry yourself. (*Offers rag.*) Wipe your face. You can't walk around like that.

MINERVA. Yes, ma'am.

BETTE. And don't call me that. I'm Bette. Just Bette. That's all.

MINERVA. Yes, Bette.

Minerva kisses Bette lightly.

BETTE. Why'd you do that?

MINERVA. Wanted to.

BETTE. There'll be none of that. No room for that here.

MINERVA. Just a little kiss . . .

BETTE. Hush now.

MINERVA. Yes, ma'am.

BETTE. And quit.

MINERVA. Yes.

Pause.

BETTE. . . . Look at you.

MINERVA. What?

BETTE. You're all . . . shiny.

MINERVA. I'm Minerva.

BETTE. What?

MINERVA. That's my name. I haven't told anyone in a long while.

BETTE. Shh.

MINERVA. What?

BETTE. Runners . . . y'hear?

MINERVA. Up in the hills . . .

BETTE. Come on.

Minerva and Bette run away.

SCENE 3

No Hosanna (1)

Up in the hills, the Chorus is seen singing.

CHORUS. (*Verse 1*) A dull stare like a green knife
　　　Rain on a long hot road
　　　Forty churches rise in the dust
　　　On the breath
　　　Of an ill-spent morning.

(*Verse 2*) The woman stands with her back to the wall
Her eyes fixed in a hollow.
In the green-gray of an unrepentant life
Oh let my heart run out.

(*Chorus*) Nothing to sing for anymore
Nothing to believe in anymore
All's gone down in a wash of tears
All's gone down

(*2nd chorus*) Grace is fallen carbon acid
All the way from gray chute butter
No hosanna, no hosanna
Pray to God send down down down
No hosanna
Down down down down
No hosanna.

SCENE 4

Evening. The sound of rain. Minerva and Bette are hiding in a makeshift shed.

MINERVA. Where are they now?

BETTE. Don't know.

MINERVA. Felt close by.

BETTE. Not yet.

MINERVA. How many they shot this time?

BETTE. Counted ten.

MINERVA. Ten shots. One woman.

BETTE. Could've been just ten shots. Ten people.

MINERVA. Didn't seem like. Crying voice seemed the same.

BETTE. What do you care, anyway? Ain't got us.

MINERVA. Not yet.

BETTE. Quit with that talk. Just quit. That's cursed talk. And ain't no
   one put a hex on me. Y'hear?

MINERVA. Yes, ma'am.

BETTE. And quit with that, too. I ain't but two years older than you.

MINERVA. You know more than me, though.

BETTE. We know the same: pain and death. Same all over. No different . . . What?

MINERVA. You put a smile on me.

BETTE. Leave that now.

MINERVA. Make me wanna fill my arms up with you.

BETTE. Hush now.

MINERVA. You always say that.

BETTE. Yeah? And how we done? We're alive, right?

MINERVA. Yeah.

BETTE. So, best to hush. Be quiet.

Silence. Minerva puts her hand on Bette's shoulder. Bette rests her hand on Minerva's. They stay like this for a while, then Bette kisses Minerva's hand. Minerva draws closer in. Bette puts her fingers to Minerva's lips indicating "silence." Minerva caresses Bette's fingers. Their bodies tremble with laughter, but there is no sound. Suddenly, a shot is heard. They break away gently, on the alert.

MINERVA. Closer now.

BETTE. Felt like.

MINERVA. Must be scoping . . . just shooting to shoot . . .

BETTE. Heavy feet.

MINERVA. Loud on the leaves.

BETTE. Steps . . .

MINERVA. Not here.

BETTE. By the other . . . the other house.

MINERVA. We should run.

BETTE. Not now.

MINERVA. They'll find us here.

BETTE. I'll wave to them.

IMAGE 4.1 **Bette (Katherine Catmull) comforts Minerva (Elizabeth Wakehouse).**
Thrush, directed by Jenny Larson at Salvage Vanguard Theatre, Austin, Texas (2006).

Photograph by Chris O' Shea (*Courtesy Salvage Vanguard Theatre press office*).

MINERVA. What?

BETTE. Go out and wave. Distract them.

MINERVA. You're talkin' crazy.

BETTE. It'll make them stop. You want them to keep killing?

MINERVA. Don't go out there.

BETTE. I know what to do. (*Takes out old lipstick, puts it on.*)

MINERVA. Where'd you get that?

BETTE. Old house.

MINERVA. It's nice.

BETTE. It's old. Like everything else around here. Old, rotten, falling apart . . .

How do I look? Do I look like something?

MINERVA. Is this what you do?

BETTE. What'd you mean?

MINERVA. Whore around?

BETTE. I do what I do, right? Ain't nothing else. 'Cept scraps and what. Running and selling water, and running and selling again, and running and selling until you find—what? Old pack of cigarettes somewhere or a piece of candy to chew on til' you can't chew no more 'cause nothing tastes like anything . . . and in the end, what? They'll fuck us all the same. Like they've all done, and keep doing. If I stop them now, that's one less dead.

MINERVA. They'll kill you. They don't give a fuck.

BETTE. Shh.

MINERVA. I'll go out, then.

BETTE. You'll do nothing of the kind.

MINERVA. Why? You don't think I can wave and make myself a pretty thing?

BETTE. I didn't say that.

MINERVA. I can give him a show. Be an all-out girly girl. Come here, boys. Put me in your magazine.

BETTE. . . . Minerva.

MINERVA. What?

BETTE. . . . Just stay close. They won't find us if we're just close . . . like we're already dead.

Bette lies down. After a moment, Minerva lies next to Bette. They lie still with their eyes closed.

SCENE 5

Chorus is seen, in the distance, surveying the wide, scorched field, singing a section of "No Hosanna."

CHORUS (*Intro*). Back bent at prayer
    An angel on the line
    Clapboard houses in the dusk
    Sin in the blue mud

In the rolling hills
In the burnt sheaves of corn.

Chorus fades as the soldier boys with twisted hair and hollow eyes are seen. They have been walking for miles.

SOLDIER FURST. Fuck.

SOLDIER KECK. Yeah.

SOLDIER PINT. Fuck . . . Furst? Hey, Furst.

SOLDIER FURST. What say you, Pint?

SOLDIER PINT. What kind of name is Furst?

SOLDIER FURST. Old name. Long line. Haven't you heard, Pint?

SOLDIER PINT. Can't say . . . can't say I have.

SOLDIER FURST. You ask stupid things.

SOLDIER PINT. Just thinking. Right?

SOLDIER FURST. Thinking's a waste. Ain't that right, Keck?

SOLDIER KECK. Stop thinking.

SOLDIER FURST. Yeah.

SOLDIER KECK. Make it stop.

SOLDIER FURST. Uh-huh.

SOLDIER KECK. . . . Fuck.

SOLDIER PINT. Yeah.

SOLDIER KECK. I cry all the time.
I don't remember my family.
I don't remember where I was born.
Everything's two of everything.
Fields of smoke, broken pipelines . . .
I used to live somewhere near here: river down . . .

SOLDIER PINT. I dream of the beach. Acapulco . . .
Beaches are far away.
Everything is like the movies.

SOLDIER FURST. . . . Fuck.

SOLDIER KECK. Yeah.

SOLDIER PINT. Fuck.

SOLDIER FURST. Duty's what.

SOLDIER KECK. Duty's crap.

SOLDIER FURST. Duty's what makes us. Yeah?

SOLDIER PINT. Duty's all we got.

> *The soldier boys approach the shed where the women are still. They beat the door with their fists and palms. The women run away. The boys watch them.*

SCENE 6

Minerva quietly hums to herself a song from her memory. Bette approaches with two buckets of water.

BETTE. Girly girl, are you being a girly girl?

MINERVA. No, ma'am.

BETTE. Pull your socks up and face the field. It's time to hand out the water from the well. There's mad thirst and only one well for these many miles . . .

MINERVA. Yes, ma'am.

BETTE. They'll be a-comin', and it'll be us with the water and them with the stares.

And we'll have to act like we like serving; like we like giving things away.

We'll have to smile.

MINERVA. Like this?

BETTE. Bigger than that. Like the whole world fits in our mouth.

MINERVA. Don't know I can do that.

BETTE. You do. You've done. That's all there is . . .

MINERVA. I don't like you, Bette.

BETTE. Don't have to like. Not one of us put here on this soil to like each other.

MINERVA. . . . Pail's heavy.

BETTE. It's got water in it.

MINERVA. Won't last.

BETTE. Not meant to.

MINERVA. I wonder what they'll be like today.

BETTE. Today like always. Thirsty ones.

MINERVA. I wonder what their eyes will be like.

BETTE. What do you care about someone's eyes, Minerva?

MINERVA. I got to look at them.

BETTE. You look past them. That's what you're supposed to do. Haven't you learnt anything by now?

MINERVA. Yes, ma'am.

BETTE. And quit with that.

MINERVA. What?

BETTE. "Ma'am."

MINERVA. . . . The water smells.

BETTE. It ain't good, that's why. It's contaminated.

MINERVA. And we're going to give it to them anyway?

BETTE. There's nothing else.

MINERVA. . . . You put lipstick on, Bette?

BETTE. No.

MINERVA. Your lips are bright coral.

BETTE. Hush.

MINERVA. They are.

BETTE. They're natural. Everything about me is natural, all right?

MINERVA. . . . I'm going to kiss you later. I'm going to put you in my mouth and have me the world.

BETTE. Hush now.

MINERVA. I can say things.

BETTE. Not so loud.

MINERVA. You're afraid?

BETTE. . . . They're coming up against the horizon.

MINERVA. My arms hurt.

BETTE. It'll be over soon.

They smile their fixed smiles to meet the soldier boys.

SCENE 7

No Hosanna (2)

The Chorus sings as soldier boys Furst, Pint and Keck approach Minerva and Bette. Furst and Pint go forward and have their rough way with Minerva and Bette, respectively.

CHORUS. (*Verse 1*) A warm smile like a cracked bowl
    Snow on a shot-out trail
    Forty shadows walk through the coal
    On the wing of a hell-sent evening

    (*Keck stops in the path and turns away, paralyzed by shame and guilt.*)

    (*Verse 2*) The soldier stands with his head to his chest
    His eyes shut with the memory
    Of a red day from a misbegotten time
    Oh let my heart run out.

    (*Furst and Pint drag Minerva and Bette away with them to another part of the field, unseen.*)

    (*Chorus*) Nothing to sing for anymore
    Nothing to believe in anymore
    All's gone down
    In a rain of blood
    All's gone down.

    Keck runs.

In another part of the field, the women are seen. They lie apart from each other.

MINERVA. Gone . . .?

BETTE. Yeah.

MINERVA. I hear them.

BETTE. They're gone.

MINERVA. How do you know?

BETTE. Just know.

MINERVA. Are you bleeding?

BETTE. Inside.

MINERVA. He stuck his rifle in. I wanted to . . . make a sound.

BETTE. Best not to.

MINERVA. I know.

BETTE. Best be silent. You know what happens to a loose tongue.

MINERVA. I know, but song got caught in my throat. Old song. It wouldn't let go of me.

BETTE. It ran through your head?

MINERVA. Over and over. I couldn't stop hearing it. . . . Rifle dug . . . awful hurt . . .

BETTE. They do what they do. They leave. Most men are not murderers.

MINERVA. Some.

BETTE. Some who've been broken. Some who've always been. But not all.

MINERVA. I might have recognized one.

BETTE. Yeah?

MINERVA. He seemed familiar. From school maybe. Long ago.

BETTE. We got to get washed. They'll be more a-comin'.

MINERVA. Do you pray for them? I try to pray, but I don't think I should anymore.

BETTE. Try to get up. Come on. Try to get yourself moving.

MINERVA. My body's nothing. It means nothing. So, it don't matter what . . .

BETTE. Keep that song in your head.

MINERVA. Huh?

BETTE. Old song you were thinking about.

MINERVA (*half-sung*). Hum, yelp, howl, and yodel.

BETTE. That's right.

MINERVA (*half-sung*). Let the ghost run

BETTE. Come on.

MINERVA (*half-sung*). Come a time.
Cleansing time.
Let the ghosts run . . .

Soldier Keck watches them from a distance. He seeks a quiet shell of forgiveness.

SCENE 9

Incognito Blues

As the women leave to yet another part of the field, the Chorus sings its mordant blues.

CHORUS. We are all whores
By men who have become savage.
We take matters into our own hands.
To feed our dying ones . . .
We're all the same, you see? Made for slaughter, aren't we?
Hey hey, you say.
Fuck you, I say.
Fuck us all.
Howling boy, I cry. Burn me. Put me out.
And you burn. Hah. You stick light on my flesh.
And I close my eyes.

We bleed.
We are crushed.

We fall silent.
But we rise.
And keep walking.
Somehow,
Incognito.
Incognita . . .

SCENE 10

The women have fallen into each other in the open field. Silence.

MINERVA. . . . Noise . . .

BETTE. Runners?

MINERVA. Like an animal.

BETTE. A hungry thing.

MINERVA. Could've been a bird.

BETTE. Birds, dogs, rabbits . . . they're all hungry, famished. You got to watch them or they'll feed on you.

MINERVA. Wouldn't mind a bird. Just to have in my hand. Feathers on my skin. Soft-like.

BETTE. Are you turning?

MINERVA. What do you mean?

BETTE. Talking 'bout feathers. Turning inward, inside. That's first sign of being mad-like. You got to watch yourself. Or you'll be of no use. Mad ones don't last. They just go mad. Ripe for slaughter.

MINERVA. Bird in my hand. That's all. The thought of it comforts.

BETTE. Sick of comfort.

MINERVA. What you want, then?

BETTE. To be rid of you, to be rid of this place.

MINERVA. What'd you mean?

BETTE. You get me thinking 'bout things, thinking 'bout the past. . . . You touch, and awaken me.

MINERVA. I thought you liked . . .

BETTE. Calloused hands on my skin, muddy legs, cracked mouth? No. We're not meant to be a-drowned in kisses. Neither of us. You see? Not after what they've done.
And what they'll do. 'Cause you know they will. Poor boys come through here sun-up to nightfall. They come with their thirst and we give. Without feeling. Without so much as a blood-cry. And they leave, and we cover ourselves, and wait to heal while the air beats down black. But you don't let up.

MINERVA. I'm sorry.

BETTE. Vomit words don't mean spit. I should cut you is what. An act of cleansing. Fresh start. Fresh out of here.

MINERVA. But we're all we got.

BETTE. "We?" We are nothing, girl.

MINERVA. What?

BETTE. Give here. Give wrist.

MINERVA. No.

BETTE. I'm stronger than you.

MINERVA. I'll fight back.

BETTE. You won't. You love me too much. Isn't that right, girl? You love me.

MINERVA. I never used that word.

BETTE. Is that word too big for you? (*Sung*) Love, love . . .

MINERVA. Stop.

BETTE (*continues singing*). As a summer's glove. Oh, love, what have you done to me? (*Bette cuts Minerva with a makeshift knife.*) (*Spoken*) No tears, child. No words. Forget me.

Bette runs away. The Chorus observes.

CHORUS (*spoken*). And the soldier who has been watching makes himself seen.
He motions to the Heavens and does not wait for a sign.
He simply walks toward the bleeding girl
And lifts her up
Against reason, against all better judgment,

Not knowing what will become of him or her,
But simply o'ertaken by a lost sense of mercy.
And he carries her away in his tired arms
Toward a clearing.

SCENE 11

The Soldier's Waltz

Soldier Keck sings a healing waltz to Minerva.

SOLDIER KECK. Like this
rest now
you'll be fine
now that bleeding's stopped.
I know that much.

I used to live round here.
I used to walk down river.
I used to find things:

Treasures long time ago. When I was a child.
This place is different now,
but I remember things:
Prayers said. Hosannas to the sky.
Prayers like sparklers in a box.
Now things blow up like old movies.
I'm all changed.
No dreams.

(*Spoken*) Rest now. 'S good to rest.
She cut you, didn't she? I saw her. I watched. Yeah.
I do nothing. That's my job. Do nothing and kill when I
have to.
What you think that is? Waking out of the sky?
Animal. Yeah. Soon to be extinct.
But it'll torture us first. Sure thing.
It'll rip out our fingernails and gnaw on us.

(Minerva awakens in a fury, clawing and hitting Keck with wordless cries.)

(Under Minerva's cries) Hey. Let go of me. Let go.
I don't know you, right? I don't know anyone.
I just take pictures in my head: snap. Yeah. Hot. Yeah. Like a fucking carnival, see?
Let go! Let go of me!
Minerva stops. Slight pause.

MINERVA. . . . witness.

SOLDIER KECK. What'd you say?

MINERVA. I seen them all. I seen everything. Waves . . . .

SOLDIER KECK. What're you talking about?

MINERVA. Flood of them all about
and then nothing but
words raining,
voices let out,
shouts falling from on high with nowhere to land.
Ground's broken, you see? It can't take
so the shouts gotta go back up and hang in the sky, and wait.
I try to lift my voice
not to change things, but just to . . .
Have it be part of the air, you know . . .
But it don't do no good.
Nothing does any good.
All them back there . . . all them boys . . . all of them shooting
and laughing it up,
digging their rifles in, pressing their mouths up close,
their voices are loud.
And their sounds don't just hang in the air, but get stuck
so that you can't even breathe sometimes 'cause they're so loud.
You think Bette done wrong to hurt me?
I was the one who had to get rid of her, or we'd both be
drowned in some mess of a thing,
In some weird knot of feeling. No. She done right by me. She
was kind.

If you think you saved me from something, you didn't.
You just picked me up, that's all. Anyone could've done.

SOLDIER KECK. I could've left you. On the ground. Forgotten. I've left plenty. One more body ain't nothing to me.

MINERVA. Then why'd you pick me up? Right and wrong, is that what you think about? (*As if quoting from heard memory*) Them that watch and do nothing are just as wrong as them that do.

SOLDIER KECK. What'd you say?

MINERVA. I saw you. Standing, head down, doing nothing way back there.
You think just 'cause you did nothing, you're a good man,
A good soldier boy? You're the same as all them . . .

SOLDIER KECK. . . . . I should've left you for dead.

MINERVA. You should have.

SOLDIER KECK. I'm no use to nobody.

MINERVA. Got that right.

SOLDIER KECK. I'll leave then. I'll leave. Fuck this.

MINERVA. . . . Go on, then.

SOLDIER KECK. . . . Don't know which way.

MINERVA. I ain't no guide.

SOLDIER KECK. . . . I'll go this way, then. (*He walks away for a bit, then stops.*) . . . Keck.

MINERVA. What?

SOLDIER KECK. My name. I thought you should know . . . Kicking Keck. That's what they call me.

MINERVA. Keck?

SOLDIER KECK. Yeah. Fuck. It sounds good when you say it.

MINERVA. Keck.

SOLDIER KECK. Like home.

MINERVA. I ain't your home.

SOLDIER KECK. Didn't say you—just meant—just felt good to hear you say it.
. . . Give me yours?

MINERVA. What?

SOLDIER KECK. Your name.

MINERVA. What for?

SOLDIER KECK. Need something . . . To go on.

MINERVA. . . . Minerva.

SOLDIER KECK. That's a nice name.

MINERVA. It's what I was given. Don't know nothing else.

> *Pause.*

SOLDIER KECK. I'm sorry, Minerva.

MINERVA. Hmm?

SOLDIER KECK. For not . . . back there . . . for not . . . I'm sorry . . . You rest up, find cover, you'll be all right. (*He walks away.*)

MINERVA. You got anything to eat?

SOLDIER KECK. . . . Chocolate bar. It's old, though.

MINERVA. I'll take it.

> (*Soldier Keck hands her a chocolate bar that's been in his pocket for a long time.*)

Looks funny. Hard. What're you carrying this thing around for?

SOLDIER KECK. I don't know. Last pangs.

MINERVA. Last what?

SOLDIER KECK. Look, if you don't want it . . .

MINERVA (*reading label on wrapper*). Comet. Never heard of it.

SOLDIER KECK. It's a brand.

MINERVA. Good brand?

SOLDIER KECK. I don't know.

MINERVA. Comet. Shooting star.

SOLDIER KECK. You like that, eh? . . . Look, if Furst or Pint show up, you didn't see me, right?

MINERVA. Furst and Pint?

SOLDIER KECK. I wasn't here.

MINERVA. You were never here.

> *He exits. Minerva looks at chocolate bar. She is about to unwrap it, but then decides against it, and puts it in her pocket instead.*

SCENE 12

Soldier Furst approaches Minerva.

SOLDIER FURST. Seen him?

MINERVA. What?

SOLDIER FURST. Soldier. He walks around with his head down, with the weight of the goddamn world on his fucking head.

MINERVA. Don't know. Lots of people come through . . .

SOLDIER FURST. Goes by Keck.

MINERVA. Keck?

SOLDIER FURST. Miserable sonofabitch. Lost in mind. Know what I mean?

MINERVA. Yes.

SOLDIER FURST. I bet you do. You look a little lost in mind yourself.

MINERVA. I'm all right.

SOLDIER FURST. Yeah?

MINERVA. I'm fine. Just fine, sir.

SOLDIER FURST. If you see him, you have him report to me, understand? Sergeant Furst.

MINERVA. Furst.

SOLDIER FURST. That's an order. You hear me?

MINERVA. Yes, sir.

SOLDIER FURST. I run things now. I'm in charge. I keep the peace. Understand?

MINERVA. Yes, sir. Sergeant Furst.

SOLDIER FURST. That's right. Now, move it!

IMAGE 4.2 **Minerva (Elizabeth Wakehouse).**

Thrush, directed by Jenny Larson at Salvage Vanguard Theatre, Austin, Texas (2006).

Photograph by Chris O' Shea (Courtesy Salvage Vanguard Theatre press office).

Minerva runs away. Soldier Furst stands at attention, guarding the empty field that belongs to no one.

SCENE 13

Spirit Walk

Minerva walks the length of the horizon toward the new border. She sings a lullaby to keep herself going.

MINERVA. The girl moves
    On tired legs

Against the country gutted
Across hot pools of squalor . . .

The tall cry of the yodeling girl
All breath bent and yearning
Who brings the daily bread
Who marks this journey?

Care not the Heavens
What use is rest
In this daily, daily?

The girl runs across the clearing
straight to the border
No voice
declaring

SCENE 14

To cross the new border . . .

BETTE. The line is here.

SOLDIER KECK (NOW) DISGUISED. No, the line is here.

MINERVA. I say the line is here.

BETTE. Christ, child, if the line is here then we'll never cross this
border.

MINERVA. Bette? Is that you? Hey. I'm talking to you.

BETTE. I heard.

MINERVA. Aren't you going to speak to me?

BETTE. I don't know you.

MINERVA. What you mean?

BETTE. Don't know anybody. I'm just in line, see? I'm waiting my turn.
Breath.

MINERVA. You left me bleeding, but I'm all right.

BETTE. You're all right? That's good. We're all fucking all right. How
are you, son?

SOLDIER KECK DISGUISED. Fine. Just fine.

MINERVA. What are you doing here?

SOLDIER KECK DISGUISED. What?

MINERVA. Aren't you—?

SOLDIER KECK DISGUISED. No.

MINERVA. Oh.

SOLDIER KECK DISGUISED. I'm no one.

MINERVA. I'm no one too.

BETTE. We're all fucking nobodies. Isn't that right?

SOLDIER KECK DISGUISED. Yes.

MINERVA. Where does this road go?

BETTE. Other side.

MINERVA. You know what I mean.

BETTE. They speak the same language over there.

MINERVA. They do?

BETTE. Ain't one word different.

MINERVA. Crossing to the same, then.

SOLDIER KECK DISGUISED. Not the same. City life.

MINERVA. Yeah?

SOLDIER KECK DISGUISED. Sewage in the streets, vendors selling cigarettes and soda, all kinds of traffic.

MINERVA. You've been?

SOLDIER KECK DISGUISED. Heard. That's all.

MINERVA. Jobs and houses.

SOLDIER KECK DISGUISED. What?

MINERVA. They got jobs and houses over there, I bet.

BETTE. You want a job and a house? Is that what you want?

MINERVA. I'd like a house. Yeah. Job. Sure. Don't you want a house, Bette?

BETTE. Quit with that. That's not my name. That's not who I am. You got me mixed up with someone else. Okay?

MINERVA. I don't have to know you. I don't have to know anyone. I can pretend just like everybody else that I am alone in the world, alone with my story, and ain't nobody a part of it.

BETTE. That's right.

MINERVA. . . . You don't want a house, then? Your own roof?

BETTE. I don't want to own anything. And I don't want to be owned. That's all I want.

Breath.

MINERVA. They set up this crossing yesterday. New path.
I saw them. There was a long-ass line of people waiting to cross. They didn't know where they were going but they were moving headlong just the same.

SOLDIER KECK DISGUISED. How long did they have to wait?

MINERVA. I don't got a watch. I just saw them. They waited a long time.
The guard was new at his job. I could tell. Just by the way he looked at them, eyed them down. He didn't have practice. Not for checking people through he didn't. There he is.

SOLDIER KECK DISGUISED. What?

MINERVA. Guard.

SOLDIER KECK DISGUISED. I'll go first.

BETTE. What?

SOLDIER KECK DISGUISED. To get things moving.

BETTE. What about me? I've been standing here as long as you.

MINERVA. So have I.

SOLDIER KECK DISGUISED. I'll be quick.

BETTE. How do you know?

SOLDIER KECK DISGUISED. I'm good at these things.

MINERVA. You go from one place to another all the time, don't you?

SOLDIER KECK DISGUISED. Yeah.

BETTE. Gives you no more right than anybody else.

SOLDIER KECK DISGUISED. Gives me as much right as I want.

SOLDIER PINT AS A GUARD. Okay okay okay okay okay okay. Form a line. A straight line. If you don't make a straight line, you go back. That's right. A good, straight line. Perfect geometry. The only thing we got is order. And keep straight. Clear eyes. Straight at me. No looking ahead to some other place. There is no other place until you cross. You get me? That's right. And step forward. I said, step forward. What do you have, soldier?

SOLDIER KECK DISGUISED. I'm not a soldier, sir.

SOLDIER PINT AS A GUARD. What are you telling me?

SOLDIER KECK DISGUISED. I ain't a soldier.

SOLDIER PINT AS A GUARD. What are you, then?

MINERVA. He's displaced.

SOLDIER PINT AS A GUARD. Am I talking to you? Am I?

MINERVA. No.

SOLDIER PINT AS A GUARD. Then shut up. What are you, son?

SOLDIER KECK DISGUISED. Lost.

SOLDIER PINT AS A GUARD. Lost how? Lost what? Family, country, what?

SOLDIER KECK DISGUISED. Everything.

SOLDIER PINT AS A GUARD. Is that a fact?

SOLDIER KECK DISGUISED. Yes, sir.

SOLDIER PINT (NOW) AS A GUARD. You're good with the words, aren't you? "Yes, sir. No, sir." Real good with the words.

SOLDIER KECK DISGUISED. Just leave me be.

SOLDIER PINT AS A GUARD. Pity, eh? That what you want? I get suck detail, and you want pity? . . . I'm talking to you, soldier.

SOLDIER KECK DISGUISED. I'm not—

SOLDIER PINT AS A GUARD. I know. I know. I'm just toying with you. I do that. Gotta do something in this job. Right? You mind if I hit you? Just a little, you know . . . (*punches Keck in the stomach*) You don't mind, do you? I mean, you're not a soldier anymore, right? So, you don't mind anything. You're like all them here.

BETTE. What you say?

SOLDIER PINT AS A GUARD. I'm not talking to you, peaches. You'll have your turn. Like all the rest in this godforsaken world. So, tell me, young man, what is it you lost, huh? You say you lost something, right? What mountain of shit you lost to get here?

SOLDIER KECK DISGUISED. You want a story? I'll give you a story.

SOLDIER PINT AS A GUARD. What do I want with a story? I got no use for stories. They fill up my head. And they're all the same in the end: husbands beaten and tortured, wives left behind, left to make their way, move a step and they're killed, fathers murdered, aunts raped, days spent without water and nothing to eat, worlds caving in and nowhere else to go. I've heard every story there is. And there's no end to them. They keep being told, and I keep hearing them, but I stopped listening a long time ago. You can lose your mind from listening to something. Stories get inside you, right? You start to question things. I don't want to question my life, who I am, what I do. I am a God-fearing man and that's the truth. I believe in freedom, and I believe in protecting freedom for all. I am firm in mind. But I got no patience for listening. I got plenty of stomach. I can take any story, right? No matter how horrible, how disgusting, lurid and the like. A man told me his cousin sewed his eyes and mouth shut to make a statement against the world. I said to him, what kind of statement's that? There's the evil that men do and the evil that just is. There's enough evil to go around. You want to make a statement? Do something else. Do things to have an effect. Screw stories. They do nothing.

SOLDIER KECK DISGUISED. What do you want, then?

SOLDIER PINT AS A GUARD. . . . . I could do with a song.

SOLDIER KECK DISGUISED. A song? I don't know any songs.

SOLDIER PINT AS A GUARD. Well, you ain't crossing until I get one.

BETTE. What kind of fucking guard are you?

SOLDIER PINT AS A GUARD. Hey. I make the rules. Right? This is a sweet rule, a kind rule. 'Cause I aspire to be a kind benevolent leader one day. You got a song, soldier?

SOLDIER KECK DISGUISED. I told you. I ain't a—

SOLDIER PINT AS A GUARD. That's right. I forgot. Well? No song? Then back you go. Go on. I got no time to waste, son—

SOLDIER KECK DISGUISED (*sings*). . . . Lost . . .

SOLDIER PINT AS A GUARD. What was that?

SOLDIER KECK DISGUISED (*sings*). Lost . . .

MINERVA. . . . Like a restless sparrow.

SOLDIER PINT AS A GUARD. No help for him. No images. No signs. Fact songs. That's what I like. Go on, young man. Nice and loud.

SOLDIER KECK DISGUISED (*sung*). Lost my family, lost my wife . . .

SOLDIER PINT AS A GUARD. Louder. Louder.

SOLDIER KECK DISGUISED (*sung*). Lost all memory . . . Don't know what's become of my life.

SOLDIER PINT AS A GUARD. Plain sentiments. I like that. Plain speech. That's the public idiom. That's what people understand. Go on.

SOLDIER KECK DISGUISED (*sung*). Lost friends,
And strangers near and far.
Lost who I was . . .
Can't taste.

SOLDIER PINT AS A GUARD. What's that?

SOLDIER KECK DISGUISED (*sung*). Can't taste things.
I see things. What ain't there.
And some days I vomit all the time.
Wasted lost. Who I was . . .
Pause.

SOLDIER PINT AS A GUARD. That's your song? That is one weird song. I don't know I can sing to that. How'd it go again? (*Sings*) "Wasted lost. Who I was."
Weird song. Weird fucking song. Fact song, though. Yeah. I'll give you that. It's got a measure of fact. What you got, then?

SOLDIER KECK DISGUISED. Eh?

SOLDIER PINT AS A GUARD. What tangible thing are you going to give me for my loot box, for my treasure bin?

SOLDIER KECK DISGUISED. Huh?

BETTE. He means a bon bon.

SOLDIER KECK DISGUISED. What?

BETTE. Carrot, candy, sweetie . . . you know . . . a fucking bribe.

SOLDIER PINT AS A GUARD. You got some tongue on you, peaches. If you keep on like that . . . I'm going to have to . . .

SOLDIER KECK DISGUISED. Pen.

SOLDIER PINT AS A GUARD. Huh?

SOLDIER KECK DISGUISED. Bic pen. That's what I got.

SOLDIER PINT AS A GUARD. Real Bic?

(*Keck shows Bic pen to Pint as a Guard.*)

Looks authentic. What's that smell?

SOLDIER KECK DISGUISED. Nothing.

SOLDIER PINT AS A GUARD. Smells of the earth. Stinks of blood. Where'd you get this pen?

SOLDIER KECK DISGUISED. Took it.

SOLDIER PINT AS A GUARD. Off a body? Is that what you've done? Come on, soldier, confess.

SOLDIER KECK DISGUISED. I told you. I ain't a—

SOLDIER PINT AS A GUARD. You took this Bic pen off a dead body. You spotted it from a ways, right? Like a hawk. You swooped down and took it. Ruthless sonofabitch.

SOLDIER KECK DISGUISED. Yes.

SOLDIER PINT AS A GUARD. Well done. I applaud actions like that. You see, this man knows something about recovery, about moving a society forward. You're going to do fine, son. You cross this line, and you're definitely on your way.

SOLDIER KECK DISGUISED. I can cross, then?

SOLDIER PINT AS A GUARD. Got anything else?

SOLDIER KECK DISGUISED. No, sir.

SOLDIER PINT AS A GUARD. That's right. You just got what you give me. You understand the rules, son. You've got your schooling down proper. Move on, then.

(*Keck crosses the border.*)

  . . . Next.

BETTE (*sung*). Full moon in my belly, that's what I got. Full, and glorious moon.

SOLDIER PINT AS A GUARD. What's that?

BETTE. Song.

SOLDIER PINT AS A GUARD. Who told you I wanted a song?

BETTE. You just said-

SOLDIER PINT AS A GUARD. From him. From him I wanted a song. I don't want one from you. You got a high voice, peaches. What do I want with a high voice in my ear?

BETTE. My voice ain't high.

SOLDIER PINT AS A GUARD. Pitch. Pitch. I hear it. I don't want that.

BETTE. What do you want, then?

SOLDIER PINT AS A GUARD. What are you asking me questions for, eh? I ask the questions here. That's my job. That's what I get paid for.

MINERVA. You get paid?

SOLDIER PINT AS A GUARD. Rifle butt. How that feel, huh? You like that? Answer me. I want the right answer. What's the right answer? Eh? I'm talking to you, peaches.

BETTE. Yes.

SOLDIER PINT AS A GUARD. Hear that? "Yes." She knows the right answer. "Yes."

BETTE. Yes, sir.

SOLDIER PINT AS A GUARD. Yes, sir. That's right. Don't move—no flinching, twitching, none of that . . . That's right. Good mouse. Good mouse wretch trying to get across the wiggly line of this border.

MINERVA. Yes, sir.

SOLDIER PINT AS A GUARD. Well done. . . . What are you looking at?

BETTE. He's walking awful slow.

SOLDIER PINT AS A GUARD. What do you care? He's crossed already. He's done with. No need of him. No minding him. Now, what do you got?

BETTE. Camels.

SOLDIER PINT AS A GUARD. Camel Lights?

BETTE. Yes.

SOLDIER PINT AS A GUARD. Camel Lights are no good. Go back.

BETTE. What are you talking about? Camel Lights are rare here. Rare item. Choice goods.

SOLDIER PINT AS A GUARD. Sorry.

BETTE. You let him go with a Bic.

SOLDIER PINT AS A GUARD. Bic pens have value. Bic's a fine brand, been in the market a long time. You see that pile over there? That's a whole mess of Bics. I get good trade on them. Camel Lights? I get nothing. Sorry.

BETTE. . . . Screw this.

SOLDIER PINT AS A GUARD. What are you doing?

BETTE. I'm getting out of here, out of this country.

SOLDIER PINT AS A GUARD. You are in defiance of the law, ma'am.

BETTE. Law? What law? The laws change every day here.

Bette runs across the border. Soldier Pint shoots Bette.

MINERVA. Bette? Bette?

SOLDIER PINT AS A GUARD. Don't mind her.

MINERVA. Bette! Bette!

SOLDIER PINT AS A GUARD. Stop your wailing, meat. She's gone. She's over with.

MINERVA. Sonofmotherfucking cock—

SOLDIER PINT AS A GUARD. Hold that tongue. Hold it. Open your mouth, Open your mouth, and hold your tongue . . . You want to cross, meat? Do you? Or you do you want to end up like her?

MINERVA. . . . Cross.

SOLDIER PINT AS A GUARD. That's the right answer. You're learning the rules round here real quick. And quit with the tears. Crying's a messy thing. I hate crying. Pure fucking waste thing to do . . . Okay. Okay. Okay now. . . . Juicy morsel. Come on.

MINERVA. What?

SOLDIER PINT AS A GUARD. I want a juicy morsel. Fucking tongue kiss, girl. Come on. Initiate. . . . Now.

MINERVA. Like this?

SOLDIER PINT AS A GUARD. What you—? Dancing now? Giving me a show? Like in the movies?

MINERVA. Yes, sir.

SOLDIER PINT AS A GUARD. Good fucking meat, you are. Good fucking meat.

Pity we don't got any music, huh? That way I would know what you were dancing to.

MINERVA. It's a secret.

SOLDIER PINT AS A GUARD. Between us, huh? That's sweet. I haven't had nothing sweet in a long time. That's a fact. (*She kisses him.*) . . . What—?

MINERVA. Razor kiss. Just for you.

She runs away. He is left with a bleeding tongue. Chorus appears, sings in high, lonesome mode.

Haunting Time

CHORUS. (*Verse 1*) *Along the highroad*

Foul country ragged
This made I
I say
This made none.

(*Verse 2*) Limp am I
Cursed wretch.
Still bleeding, I see,
For that which is left.

(*Chorus*) Here.
In fat clouds
In cool darkness
I make you mine
I make you mine.

In rain and death
I make you mine
'Tis haunting time.
'Tis haunting.

(*Verse 3*) Say, what's your crime, sir?
Why, nothing, says I.
Nothing at all
Save for peace.
Remember?

(*Verse 4*) And I hold you again
In mind.
Look here. This is ruin.
Go on now. Look.

*In slightly altered time, Soldier Pint and Bette rise a little and join
the Chorus in song.*

SOLDIER PINT AS GUARD, BETTE, and CHORUS. My smile is warm
My back surrendered.
I haven't breathed like this for a long time.
In rain and death
I make you mine.
'Tis haunting time.
'Tis haunting.

In rain and death
I make you mine.
'Tis haunting time.
'Tis haunting.

SCENE 15

Further up the new road, Minerva moves on. She sings to herself.

MINERVA. Hum, yelp, howl, and yodel.
>Let the ghost run.
>Come a time,
>Cleansing time
>Let the ghosts run.

SOLDIER KECK (*revealed on roadside with bag of chips in hand*). You all right?

MINERVA. What you doing . . .?

SOLDIER KECK. Nothing. Just here. Kicking about. Been nothing for miles. No one round.

MINERVA. Been a while. Yeah.

SOLDIER KECK. Like the city's . . . not even there. Hear it, though, right? Sometimes. A noise or something.

MINERVA. Birds crying . . .

SOLDIER KECK. Or a truck turning over. Yeah. Hear all sorts of things. See stuff, too.

MINERVA. What'd you mean?

SOLDIER KECK. A couple miles back there I swear I could see bits of my family down the road.

MINERVA. Your family?

SOLDIER KECK. Like they were right there. Looking at me. Fuck. I had to stop. Just stop for a while, get my mind sorted ou. . . . You want a chip?

MINERVA. No.

SOLDIER KECK. They're lime tortilla.

MINERVA. I'm fine.

>*She moves on.*

SOLDIER KECK. Anybody ask around about me?

MINERVA. I wouldn't tell.

SOLDIER KECK. Somebody asked, then.

MINERVA. People ask things, don't mean nothing.

SOLDIER KECK. They'll kill me. They'll put a fucking hole in me. I've seen them do it. To this other guy that got lost in mind? They strung him up like he was one of them cows at the butcher's . . . It's best in twos.

MINERVA. What?

SOLDIER KECK. Best to travel in twos. It's safer.

MINERVA. Like Noah's ark?

SOLDIER KECK. We could cover each other, protect each other.

MINERVA. . . . . I'm no good in twos. I couldn't protect Bette. Guard killed her, right?

SOLDIER KECK. . . . . I'm sorry.

Pause.

MINERVA. Everything looks the same.

SOLDIER KECK. Flat. Yeah.

MINERVA. Flat, wide, and endless.

SOLDIER KECK. Hot, too.

MINERVA. Don't know I like this place.

SOLDIER KECK. We're here, right?

MINERVA. . . . . Don't know I can . . .

SOLDIER KECK. What?

MINERVA. Legs are giving out. Hurt all over. Hurt so much I'm past hurt . . . Shit. I'm crying. I'm not supposed to cry. Bette always said to be quiet. That's how you get by.

SOLDIER KECK. You can get by by shouting too.

MINERVA. Yeah?

SOLDIER KECK. When I was moving through the fields back there, sometimes I'd shout so loud just to feel I was really. Wanna try?

MINERVA. . . . . I'm so hungry.

SOLDIER KECK. Have a chip.

MINERVA. Can't.

SOLDIER KECK. One chip. What's it gonna hurt?

MINERVA. I'll get sick.

SOLDIER KECK. Take a little bite. Ease yourself into it.

MINERVA (*she does so*). . . . Hot.

SOLDIER KECK. Yeah.

MINERVA. Good, though.

SOLDIER KECK. I told you.

MINERVA. . . . I could stay out here forever.

SOLDIER KECK. Gotta get a move on. It'll be dark soon.

MINERVA. . . . Keck.

SOLDIER KECK. You can't be calling me that. Not until we're . . . long out of here.

MINERVA. What do I call you, then?

SOLDIER KECK. Bobby's fine.

MINERVA. Bobby . . .

SOLDIER KECK. Yeah.

> *After a little while, Minerva falls asleep. Time passes. Keck sings to keep himself awake.*

Soldier's Song

> I had knowledge in the palm of my hand.
> I used to know a prayer.
> I had me a rosary on my chest
> Given to me by Aunt Mary.
> She had blue fluorescent eyes.
> Said I used to . . .
> Yeah.
> Things.
> Yeah.
> Said I used to . . .
>
> I had a sparkler in a cardboard box.
> It burned.

And I eased myself into prayer
Like a good one, a good son.
I believed in the gospel.
I don't know what now.
Thirst.
Yeah.
Thirst.
Uh-huh . . .
Lights fade.

SCENE 16

The new road is a long stretch of nothing. Minerva and Keck keep going.

SOLDIER KECK. Lights now. Easy.

MINERVA. Stop someplace soon.

SOLDIER KECK. Just a little bit more. Up ahead now. See?

MINERVA. You was singing. Last night. I heard you.

SOLDIER KECK. Wasn't me.

MINERVA. Sounded like you. Your voice.

SOLDIER KECK. I don't sing. Never have.

MINERVA. Except for that guard back there.

SOLDIER KECK. . . . Yeah.

MINERVA. I liked your voice. It sounded different. Like you were a child.

SOLDIER KECK. I wish I was.

MINERVA. I don't remember anything about my childhood.

SOLDIER KECK. Must remember something.

MINERVA. Feathers sometimes. Birds and things. Scraps of songs. But no one. Not a real person that I can put a picture to.

SOLDIER KECK. . . . What's that over there?

MINERVA. A campground of some kind.

SOLDIER KECK. Stinks. Even from here.

MINERVA. Edge, though. Edges of towns always stink.

SOLDIER KECK. Where'd you get that?

MINERVA. That's what people say, isn't it?

SOLDIER KECK. Weird thing to say.

MINERVA. Why's that?

SOLDIER KECK. I'm from an edge, right? Place I was born—it was on
the edge of town. You see me stinking?

MINERVA. . . . Yes.

SOLDIER KECK. All right. Fine. Go ahead, laugh all you want to . . .

MINERVA. You really stink.

SOLDIER KECK. Well, so do you.

MINERVA. I know. We're both a fucking mess. Can you imagine when
they see us in the city?

SOLDIER KECK. They're gonna . . . steer clear . . .

MINERVA. Look out. Here are them . . . .

They laugh until they are almost in tears.

SOLDIER KECK. Fucking messed up, we are . . . Fucking crazy.

MINERVA. Yeah.

Laughter resumes for a moment, then subsides. Pause.

SOLDIER KECK. It's like it's on fire.

MINERVA. What?

SOLDIER KECK. City. Nothing but lights.

SCENE 17

A City Song

CHORUS (*spoken-sung*). The city burns. It glows and quivers.
The soldier and the woman see garbage spilling off sidewalks
Hundreds of burned cars, and jeeps
Piles of brick
And the rotting carcasses of dogs.
Tons of debris flood their field of vision.
Untold rounds of ammunition

lie in wait.
The soldier no longer a soldier,
and the woman
Find themselves
detained.

SCENE 18

A camp lies beneath an immense steel roof. Minerva and Keck enter the camp filled with the many, and the forgotten ghosts of the broken terrain.

MINERVA. Smells.

SOLDIER KECK. Yeah.

MINERVA. Piss and dog meat.

SOLDIER KECK. Dead dogs, wild dogs . . . all sorts it seems . . .

MINERVA. What place is this?

SOLDIER KECK. Place we wait, till they call us, right? That's what the guard said.

MINERVA. Fuck can't get anywhere. I'm sick of it.

SOLDIER KECK. We'll be all right.

MINERVA. You keep saying that, but I don't see it. I don't see nothing right here. Miles and fucking miles. And what? . . . I was better off with Bette.

SOLDIER KECK. Look, the guard said a couple of days. Couple of days and we're out of here.

SOLDIER PINT (NOW) AS DISPLACED ONE (*appearing*). Couple of years maybe.

MINERVA. What'd you mean?

SOLDIER PINT DISPLACED. Ain't seen anyone get out of here. Not in a while.

SOLDIER KECK. How long you been?

SOLDIER PINT DISPLACED. I don't know. I don't keep track anymore, soldier.

SOLDIER KECK. I'm not a soldier.

SOLDIER PINT DISPLACED. What are you, then?

SOLDIER KECK. Nothing.

SOLDIER PINT DISPLACED. Is that a fact? I'm nothing too. We're all nothing.
Isn't that right, meat? Hey. I'm talking to you.

MINERVA. I heard.

SOLDIER PINT DISPLACED. Yeah. We're all meat here. This is the cemetery of the living. Right here. Goddamn cemetery. Regular fucking show.

GHOST CHILD (*appearing, half-sung*). Smell the dead. See the dead.
Watch the children play with razors on the ground.

MINERVA. Bette?

GHOST CHILD (*half-sung*). Screw the dead. Nail the dead.
Watch the children put the razors in their mouths.

MINERVA. Is that you? Bette?

GHOST CHILD. What name you say?

MINERVA. Bette.

GHOST CHILD. Weird name. Cracked name. Don't know that name.

MINERVA. You got her voice.

GHOST CHILD. Yeah? I sound like all the dead.

SOLDIER PINT DISPLACED. I tell you, the moment we walked into this place, we died. Quick. No time to waste. Just wasting and fucking time. You get me? Hey. Where you going, soldier?

SOLDIER KECK. I'm not a soldier, okay? I am not a fucking soldier. Can you get that through your head, you fucking asshole?

SOLDIER PINT DISPLACED. Hey. I'm just talking. It's not like you gotta get all whacked out of proportion, son. Where are you going?

SOLDIER KECK. To get some water . . .

GHOST CHILD. Water's foul. Foul, dirty water. Used water.

SOLDIER KECK. What?

SOLDIER PINT DISPLACED. That's what we got. Used water. Recycled shit from the crapholes. And if you want some, you got to form a line. A straight line. Stretching all the way from here to the end of the camp. You'll be waiting for days, son, before you get any.

SOLDIER KECK. What crap place is this . . .?

SOLDIER PINT DISPLACED. Crap home. Crap shithole. Crap way station. It's all there is, son. You spend your life running, and look where you end up? Same as all the rest. Ain't that a fucking peach?

SOLDIER KECK. Shut up.

SOLDIER PINT DISPLACED. I'm just talking.

SOLDIER KECK. Talking shit.

SOLDIER PINT DISPLACED. Oh, you think you're better than me? Ain't no one here better than anyone else. Unless they got goods to trade with. Prime goods. You got goods?

SOLDIER KECK. No.

SOLDIER PINT DISPLACED. Then hop on the merry-go-round, son. Chain yourself to the wheel. This one's gonna be a long ride.

GHOST CHILD. Here. Take a razor. Play like all the rest of them, like all the little children.

MINERVA. Don't you remember me?

GHOST CHILD. I don't remember nobody.

SOLDIER KECK. Well, I'm thirsty now. I don't care 'bout a line. I'm cutting in.

SOLDIER PINT DISPLACED. You'll get strangled.

SOLDIER KECK. I'll risk it.

GHOST CHILD. Here. Take this. It's water from the washbasin. I collect it. Every day a drop or two. See?

SOLDIER KECK. It's foul.

GHOST CHILD. Foul foul like an asshole's owl.

SOLDIER KECK. I'll go to sleep, then.

SOLDIER PINT DISPLACED. Hey. Hey. You sleep outside.

SOLDIER KECK. But there are cubicles over there. I see them.

SOLDIER PINT DISPLACED. If you don't got trade goods, you don't get a cubicle.

MINERVA. So what? We just . . . sleep out here? . . . can't even see the sky.

SOLDIER PINT DISPLACED. Hey. They're not my rules. See that guy over there with the long coat and short hair?

MINERVA. Yeah.

SOLDIER PINT DISPLACED. They're his rules. He kinda runs this place. You get me? He's got a whole system, a goddamn network. I'm just . . . what? . . . foot soldier, messenger boy. That's me. I got no say here. We're the same, you see? I scam for goods just like you. No different.

SOLDIER KECK. And what's he do?

SOLDIER PINT DISPLACED. He gets people through, gets them wherever they want to go. Like a travel agency.

GHOST CHILD. Connections in all countries. All the countries in the world.

SOLDIER KECK. Is that right?

SOLDIER PINT DISPLACED. I wouldn't lie.

MINERVA. So, how do you get him to do that?

SOLDIER PINT DISPLACED. Do what?

MINERVA. Get you places.

GHOST CHILD. Prayers. Signs. Hosannas to the sky.

MINERVA. I ain't praying to him.

SOLDIER PINT DISPLACED. He takes cash, too. He doesn't discriminate. Course, most people don't got nothing, so there's this voucher system he's got set up. He's a smart one, he is. He's figured it all out. A one-dollar pen you used to be able to buy in any old dime store is equivalent to fifty dollars here. Blankets? Blankets are worth hundreds of dollars. One person has five, he wants twenty, twenty is equivalent to five hundred dollars, five hundred and some change gets you inside a container and overseas.

SOLDIER KECK. Where do you get them?

SOLDIER PINT DISPLACED. What?

SOLDIER KECK. Blankets.

GHOST CHILD. Blankets are gone. No more blankets for nobody.

SOLDIER KECK. Fucking joke.

SOLDIER PINT DISPLACED. It's ring-around-the-pony here. You get what you can. There was this one guy who got himself a hold of twenty-five blankets. He got out of here in no time. Me? I've killed what? A couple dozen? Ain't do me no good. Some asshole come and take all my blankets from me in the shithole. Just as I was taking a crap. What are you looking at?

MINERVA. Nothing.

SOLDIER PINT DISPLACED. That's right. Nothing. A whole mess of nothing, girl.

The sound of a loud buzzer.

MINERVA. What's that?

GHOST CHILD (*half-sung*). Time for the daily drill. Time for the daily spill.

SOLDIER KECK. Line-up?

SOLDIER PINT DISPLACED. It's a way to keep order, try to count who's left. Come on. We gotta get in line. Over here. So they can see us.

(*They line up. Soldier Furst as Pimp steals into view.*)

. . . Fucking pimp. Long-coat man.

MINERVA. That him there?

SOLDIER PINT DISPLACED. Coming this way. Yeah.

SOLDIER FURST (NOW) AS PIMP (*appears*). Happy morning.

SOLDIER PINT DISPLACED and GHOST CHILD. Happy morning.

SOLDIER FURST AS PIMP. You two just get put in here? I'm talking to you.

MINERVA and SOLDIER KECK. Yes, sir.

SOLDIER FURST AS PIMP. Like little lovebirds, eh?

MINERVA. No. No. We're not . . .

SOLDIER FURST AS PIMP. What's that?

SOLDIER KECK. We're not together.

SOLDIER FURST AS PIMP. No?

MINERVA. No. We're just . . .

SOLDIER KECK. . . . passing through.

SOLDIER FURST AS PIMP. Like everybody else who's stuck here, eh, soldier?

SOLDIER KECK. I'm not . . .

SOLDIER FURST AS PIMP. Born a soldier, die a soldier, son. Isn't that right?

SOLDIER PINT DISPLACED and GHOST CHILD. Fuck. Yeah.

SOLDIER FURST PIMP. That's right.

MINERVA. So, how much you want?

SOLDIER FURST AS PIMP. What's that?

MINERVA. If we want to leave, get out, how much do you want?

SOLDIER FURST AS PIMP. She's direct.

MINERVA. I don't like to waste time.

SOLDIER FURST AS PIMP. Time's all we got here, dear. Nothing but fucking time.

SOLDIER PINT DISPLACED and GHOST CHILD. Yes, sir. Fuck. Yeah.

SOLDIER FURST AS PIMP. That's right.

MINERVA. But if a person wants to go . . . you . . . help, right?

SOLDIER FURST AS PIMP. Depends on where they want to go. How do you want to travel, dear? By land or by sea?

MINERVA. What's cheaper?

GHOST CHILD. Land.

MINERVA. Land, then.

SOLDIER FURST AS PIMP. She knows what she wants. I like that. That's a good quality. How old are you, girl?

MINERVA. I could be your sister.

SOLDIER FURST AS PIMP. Or cousin, eh? We could be kin. Right?

MINERVA. One happy family.

SOLDIER FURST AS PIMP. That's what I like to hear. Happy thoughts. Happy.

SOLDIER PINT DISPLACED and GHOST CHILD. Happy. Happy.

SOLDIER FURST AS PIMP. Shut.

SOLDIER PINT DISPLACED and GHOST CHILD. Yes, sir.

MINERVA. How much, then?

SOLDIER FURST AS PIMP. I don't like to discuss prices. Not like this. In the open air. In mixed company. It's vulgar. And I'm not a vulgar man. My cubicle is over there. You come visit tonight, we'll discuss your options of getting out of here and seeing the world.

SOLDIER KECK. What about me?

SOLDIER FURST AS PIMP. Do you have a blanket?

SOLDIER KECK. No.

SOLDIER FURST AS PIMP. Two hundred blankets and we can talk.

SOLDIER PINT DISPLACED. Why aren't they calling out our names? They should be calling out our names. That's the drill. They call out our names. They call out our names. What are they waiting for? What the hell are they waiting for?

GHOST CHILD. They're waiting for us to forget. To forget we're here.

Loud buzzer is heard. They all stand to attention. Time shift. They sing in full-out showbiz, swing mode.

In Slaughter

SOLDIER FURST AS PIMP (*with swagger*). This is how bone
Meets flesh
This is how human turns
Beast
With a cut of the palm
With a switch of the pine
Blood yields to appetite

MINERVA and CHORUS (*light, breezy*). Consider me slaughtered
Fresh on the fields

Consider my ruin
Make me a deal;
Whatever you want
I will deliver.

SOLDIER PINT DISPLACED (*crooning, in solo mode*). No better mercy you
will find
Consider my fortune
It is sublime.
For in slaughter
Only in slaughter
Am I your perfect martyr.

GHOST CHILD (*torchy*). Use me.
Use me as you will
Revel in my glory
Put up a shrine
See how the world dances on a dime
Over and over
(*all with Ghost Child*) And over and over,
And
Oh . . .

MINERVA and CHORUS (*light, breezy*). How quick the world likens death
to valor
Silly death, sad death
Useless slaughter
Rend me innocent

SOLDIER KECK (*taking the spotlight*). Tear up my shrine
No use have I
For courage
(*all with Soldier Keck*) No use have I
At all.

*Song ends. They smile fixed smiles and bow to an imaginary audience.
Time shift. A roll call of first names is heard, through an old
microphone (this is done by the Chorus). Everyone scatters. The names
are from different countries: African names, Balkan names,
Caribbean names, Asian names, Chinese names, English names, etc.*

Night. Soldier Furst as Pimp's cubicle. Maps of different destinations across the world adorn the walls of the cubicle. He sits at his desk, drinking vodka. He looks spent. Minerva stands in the doorway, waits for a moment, then . . .

MINERVA. You in?

> *Soldier Furst as Pimp adopts a calculated, salesman-cum-gameshow host air. This is his routine.*

SOLDIER FURST AS PIMP. Well, if isn't family . . . Come in. Come in. Sit down. Make yourself at home.

MINERVA. Thanks.

SOLDIER FURST AS PIMP. Sorry for the mess. I was just . . . I wasn't expecting . . .

MINERVA. That's all right.

SOLDIER FURST AS PIMP (*calling to hidden room, breaking salesman mode*). Honey, hour's over now. Come on. Get yourself cleaned up. I've got company.

MINERVA. What's that?

SOLDIER FURST AS PIMP (*returning to mode*). Nothing. Just a friend. Can I get you anything? Moravian cookies, Canadian syrup, Danish ham, Polish vodka, Spanish cider. I've got all sorts of delicacies.

MINERVA. No, thanks.

SOLDIER FURST AS PIMP. Don't spite me. Come on. How 'bout some Spanish cider? Eh? It'll warm you up.

MINERVA. All right.

SOLDIER FURST AS PIMP. Good. That's what I like to hear. Now, I'll just get some glasses and . . . we'll serve you right up. (*Calling to hidden room, breaking salesman mode*) Honey, get a move on now.

SOLDIER PINT DISPLACED (*from within*). I can't get them off.

SOLDIER FURST AS PIMP (*returning to mode*). I'm sorry about this. I'm really sorry. Would you mind if I take care of this for a moment?

MINERVA. Not at all.

SOLDIER FURST AS PIMP. Thank you. (*Soldier Furst as Pimp goes into the hidden room; speaks from within throughout in non-salesman mode*) What the fuck did I tell you, eh? Time's up. It's over, you fucking shit. Anything extra is not part of the plan. Understand?

SOLDIER PINT DISPLACED (*from within*). I just can't . . .

SOLDIER FURST AS PIMP (*from within*). Fucking useless meat. There. You're fine now?

SOLDIER PINT DISPLACED (*from within*). Yes, sir.

SOLDIER FURST AS PIMP (*from within*). Lick my ass. Come on. Lick it.

SOLDIER PINT DISPLACED (*from within*). . . . Yes, sir.

SOLDIER FURST AS PIMP (*from within*). . . . Now, get out. Get a move on, meat.

SOLDIER PINT DISPLACED. (*from within*). Yes, sir. Thank you, sir.

Soldier Pint Displaced appears from hidden room, half-dressed, with remaining clothes in hand. He has many small cuts on his torso. He sees Minerva sitting in the main room.

SOLDIER PINT DISPLACED. Good cider, huh?

MINERVA. Yes.

SOLDIER PINT DISPLACED. You mind if I—?

MINERVA. No.

Soldier Pint Displaced drinks some cider. Soldier Furst as Pimp appears.

SOLDIER FURST AS PIMP. Did I tell you you could drink that? Fucking shit, I am talking to you. Did I?

SOLDIER PINT DISPLACED. No, sir. Sorry, sir.

SOLDIER FURST AS PIMP. Fucking useless.

SOLDIER PINT DISPLACED. Yes, sir. I come by tomorrow, sir?

SOLDIER FURST AS PIMP. What's your plan say?

SOLDIER PINT DISPLACED. It says . . . tomorrow.

SOLDIER FURST AS PIMP. Then you know what to do. Don't you?

SOLDIER PINT DISPLACED. Yes, sir. Good night, sir.

SOLDIER FURST AS PIMP. Good night.

Soldier Pint Displaced exits. Soldier Furst as Pimp resumes his salesman mode again.

I'm sorry about that. Hazards of the job, I'm afraid. The cider all right?

MINERVA. Yes.

SOLDIER FURST AS PIMP. It's Spanish cider. Top of the line. Won't do any better. So, what is it you want, huh?

MINERVA. Well, you said I could talk to you . . . about figuring out something. To get out.

SOLDIER FURST AS PIMP. Oh. Yes. Of course. (*On a roll*) Well, I got three plans I can offer you. There's Plan A, Plan B, and Plan C. You with me? Plan A is the blanket plan. Five hundred blankets gets you a ticket out and a van and unspecified passage to whatever's available.

MINERVA. I thought you said two hundred.

SOLDIER FURST AS PIMP. No. Five hundred. That's Plan A. Then there's Plan B which is the electronics-appliances-and-miscellaneous-household-goods plan, which grants you a ticket out, van, and then a car or boat to a clear destination.

MINERVA. And this plan B is—?

SOLDIER FURST AS PIMP. Just what it says. You got radios, toasters, Walkmans, pens . . . we tally it up, and you get out. Of course, everything's gotta be in good working condition. I don't take irregulars of any kind. I can't do anything with them.

(*Ghost Child appears in the doorway.*)

Whatcha doin there, lovely?

GHOST CHILD. Appointment.

SOLDIER FURST AS PIMP. Right on time too. Can you wait out a while, lovely? I'm with a client now.

GHOST CHILD. Come back in an hour? An hour like flour?

SOLDIER FURST AS PIMP. No, lovely. Just wait out. Right out there.

GHOST CHILD (*goes out*). Right out here?

SOLDIER FURST AS PIMP. And I'll be with you in a bit.

GHOST CHILD. Yes, sir.

SOLDIER FURST AS PIMP. She's one of my best clients.

MINERVA. Is that so?

SOLDIER FURST AS PIMP. Put in thousand dollars' worth already. In a month, she'll be home free. Wherever she wants to go.

MINERVA. And what plan's she on?

SOLDIER FURST AS PIMP. Plan C. That's a special plan. I don't offer it to everybody. 'Cause, well, not everybody qualifies for Plan C.

MINERVA. Do I qualify?

SOLDIER FURST AS PIMP. You might.

MINERVA. What would I have to do?

SOLDIER FURST AS PIMP. You'll do anything, won't you?

MINERVA. We all do what we do.

SOLDIER FURST AS PIMP. Absolutely. No judgment here, dear. Not from me.

MINERVA. So, what's plan C?

SOLDIER FURST AS PIMP. Simple, really. It's about as honest as you can get. You come here. Three times a day. Go into my room there (*refers to hidden room*). Take off your clothes, and do whatever I ask on the condition that you keep a smile on your face at all times.

MINERVA. Like this?

SOLDIER FURST AS PIMP. A little more genuine. I don't like fake smiles.

MINERVA. Like this?

SOLDIER FURST AS PIMP. That's better.

MINERVA. And then what?

SOLDIER FURST AS PIMP. Then we do what we do. Happy as can be. Plan C is all about happiness and pleasure. Some people get through Plan C in a month. Others, well, it takes a little more time. And others, they mix it up: a bit of B and C, a bit of A and B.

MINERVA. And you keep track?

SOLDIER FURST AS PIMP. I've a book. Everything's written down. Absolutely. Everything's recorded. See? Every transaction.

MINERVA. I see. And safe passage is—?

SOLDIER FURST AS PIMP. Guaranteed. I set it all up. No worry there. So, which one will it be? Plan A, Plan B or Plan C? Can't make up your mind? . . . Honey, this offer is good for today and today only. If you want to talk tomorrow, I'll be busy. Understand? I won't have time for you. This is the way it works here. It's either now or never again. How 'bout we go with Plan C and see how it takes? In a month's time, you'd be up and out of here. No questions asked. You have my word.

GHOST CHILD (*from outside*). Can I come in now?

SOLDIER FURST AS PIMP. Give me a minute.

MINERVA. . . . . Okay.

SOLDIER FURST AS PIMP. Yeah?

MINERVA. Okay.

SOLDIER FURST AS PIMP. You've made the right decision, girl. I'd do the same in your shoes. Absolutely the same. (*Calling out to Ghost Child*) Come in now, my lovely.

Minerva walks out as Ghost Child walks in. Their paths cross. They look at each other for a moment. Minerva walks away. Ghost Child and Soldier Furst as Pimp go into the hidden room.

SCENE 20

The camp at night. Minerva is awake. From another part of the camp, Keck rushes in blood-stained with two blankets in hand.

SOLDIER KECK. I did it. Didn't I tell you? Two blankets. He didn't know what hit him. Whack. I was on him and ain't nobody mess with me. I'm at good at this. I'm real good at this. I'm gonna get two hundred blankets in a goddamn week. You'll see.

MINERVA. What'd you do to him?

SOLDIER KECK. What do you care? I got the blankets.

MINERVA. So now somebody is going to kill you for them?

SOLDIER KECK. They won't.

MINERVA. How do you know?

SOLDIER KECK. I'm protected.

MINERVA. Shining star?

SOLDIER KECK. That's right. Fucking Comet.

MINERVA. Give 'em here.

SOLDIER KECK. You cold?

MINERVA. . . . They stink of him.

SOLDIER KECK. I'll get them washed.

MINERVA. You're hopeless.

SOLDIER KECK. I am not.

MINERVA. You ain't done one thing right.

SOLDIER KECK. You wanna go out there, then? You wanna chase somebody down for a couple of blankets? Go right ahead.

MINERVA. There was a woman with her breast cut off. And a soldier smoking a cigarette.

SOLDIER KECK. What're you talking?

MINERVA. She had her eyes closed.
She didn't want to see anymore.
She'd done her seeing.
The soldier just kept smoking. His work was done.
And when he was through smoking,
He burned the woman.
Everywhere except her face.
He spared her face.
She kept her eyes closed.
She was half-dead already.

And he kept on.

He was bored, you see? So he just kept on and on.

He didn't know nothing else.

And I hid. I pretended I was a ghost.

SOLDIER KECK. You're not.

MINERVA. I feel like one.

SOLDIER KECK. I killed this guy for both of us, right? To get us out of here. It's not the same as . . .

MINERVA. That soldier, and what I remember and keep remembering? Nothing's the same and everything's the same. One kill is the same as another. Cold night, cold earth, blood in the air, and a steel roof for our sky. And no way to get out unless we got special privileges, or we damn well kill everyone to get out. Fuck all, I say. Fuck them all to hell for what they've done and keep doing.

SOLDIER KECK. You go see him? Is that what this is about? You go see that fucking pimp?

MINERVA. I do what I do. Same as you.

SOLDIER KECK. Not the same.

MINERVA. Plan A, Plan B, Plan C . . .

SOLDIER KECK. What'd you mean?

MINERVA. He's got you running around for two hundred blankets when he wants five.

SOLDIER KECK. Five hundred?

MINERVA. Unless you mix it up. Get yourself a fucking appliance.

SOLDIER KECK. Is that what he tell you?

MINERVA. And we'll just keep on and on, until someone kills us for what we got.

SOLDIER KECK. What kind of appliance?

SOLDIER PINT DISPLACED (*appearing*). Walkmans, toasters, egg-beaters, electric rolling pins, three-speed blenders, two-speed mixers, portable TVs, calculators, VCRs, DVD players, heating pads, sonic feather dusters, electric blankets, handheld vacuums, cool touch irons, large-scale fans, Hoky sweepers, brass lamps, percolators, bun warmers, alarm clocks, waffle irons, easy griddles, popcorn poppers . . .

Soldier Pint walks away continuing his list.

MINERVA. We'll be like him soon.

SOLDIER KECK. We'll be all right.

MINERVA. Stop saying that. We are not all right. We haven't been all right. There ain't no right here.

SOLDIER KECK. Shh.

MINERVA. Am I too loud for you?

SOLDIER KECK. Just be quiet, okay? Get some sleep.

MINERVA. Sleep. Yeah. Sleep it all away. Bury myself in sleep.

Pause.

SOLDIER KECK. . . . You want a blanket?

MINERVA. I don't want anything.

Soldier Keck walks away to another side of the camp. After a while, Minerva begins to sing to herself a song she has invented. It is a song without words. Time shift. Bette appears in an evening gown.

BETTE. Girly girl, are you being a girly girl?

MINERVA. Bette? Is that you?

BETTE. How you been, girl?

MINERVA. Look at you. Fancy dress. Where are you off to?

BETTE. Three-quarter moon has lit the river, haven't you heard? I'm off to a party.

MINERVA. Take me with you.

BETTE. You got to have been invited. This is an exclusive party. I can't just take anyone.

MINERVA. Why do you spite me all the time?

BETTE. 'Cause you're ruin: talking of ruin, singing of ruin, living in ruin. You've no part of a meritocracy.

MINERVA. You speak strange.

BETTE. I speak how I speak. You never listened to me.

MINERVA. All this time I've been thinking about you on the road, shot down like that, like an animal.

BETTE. That wasn't me.

MINERVA. I recognized you.

BETTE. Your eyes deceive. I'm here. See? I'm all right. I've made out just fine. I've figured out how to survive.

MINERVA. Let me kiss you.

BETTE. You're still in love with me.

MINERVA. Yes.

BETTE. Foolish girl. How are you going to survive in this world?

MINERVA. By being like you.

BETTE. Just like me?

MINERVA. Yes, ma'am.

BETTE. Quit with that. I'm no more than two years older than you.

MINERVA. Your lips are bright coral.

BETTE. My lips are red wine. Go on. Drink, child.

MINERVA. You won't mind?

BETTE. Go on.

Minerva kisses Bette.

What's wrong, girl? You got a sorry face on you.

MINERVA. I forgot what it was like.

BETTE. What's that?

MINERVA. Gentle things.

BETTE. Hey now. Don't cry. Tears don't do any good. You want to dance a bit?

MINERVA. What about your party?

BETTE. It can wait. Come on, take my hand.

MINERVA. I never was a good dancer.

BETTE. It's just about twirling and things, knowing how to move through space.

MINERVA. Yeah?

BETTE. Like this.

MINERVA. That's good.

BETTE. You try.

MINERVA. What about—?

BETTE. I told you. Nobody minds anything here. Go on.

MINERVA (*she dances*). Like this?

BETTE. You're getting the hang of it.

MINERVA. Yeah?

BETTE. Like fireworks crackling in the sky.

MINERVA. What?

BETTE. Pure electric motion.

Minerva dances and dances and dances. Bette disappears.

SCENE 21

The pimp's station.

SOLDIER FURST AS PIMP. I told you, until you give me five hundred, I can't do anything for you.

SOLDIER KECK. You said two hundred.

SOLDIER FURST AS PIMP. A slip of the tongue.

SOLDIER KECK. Yeah? Then how 'bout a Walkman?

SOLDIER FURST AS PIMP. It has to be in working condition. Is it in working condition?

SOLDIER KECK. Perfect.

SOLDIER FURST AS PIMP. Show. Come on, son. I haven't got all night. I've other business to take care of.

SOLDIER KECK. Here.

SOLDIER FURST AS PIMP. It has a speck of blood on it.

SOLDIER KECK. It's a Walkman. You take Walkmans, right? Prime goods.

SOLDIER FURST AS PIMP. I take what I take.

SOLDIER KECK. So, we're agreed. I leave tomorrow. On a boat. You get me on a boat, yeah?

SOLDIER FURST AS PIMP. I can get you on a van maybe. I can't promise a boat. Besides, I don't know if this is working yet, do I?

SOLDIER KECK. Play.

SOLDIER FURST AS PIMP. You're in a hurry, soldier.

SOLDIER KECK. I'm not a soldier.

SOLDIER FURST AS PIMP. Could've sworn.

SOLDIER KECK. I'm not.

SOLDIER FURST AS PIMP (*puts headphones on*, *listens*). . . . Bay City Rollers? Fucking crap.

SOLDIER KECK. It's what was in there.

SOLDIER FURST AS PIMP. I can't take this.

SOLDIER KECK. You said if it was working. You promised.

SOLDIER FURST AS PIMP. I didn't promise anything.

SOLDIER KECK. You said if it was working. You promised. I heard you. You said if it was working. You said if it was working we were agreed and I'd get on a boat in the morning.

SOLDIER FURST AS PIMP. It's a shame to see a man lose his senses. It really is.

SOLDIER KECK. You promised me.

SOLDIER FURST AS PIMP. I promised nothing.

SOLDIER KECK. Give me back the Walkman, then.

SOLDIER FURST AS PIMP. What for? You want to listen to some old music?

SOLDIER KECK. You don't want it.

SOLDIER FURST AS PIMP. I didn't say I didn't want it. I said the music was crap.

SOLDIER KECK. But you won't give me passage for it.

SOLDIER FURST AS PIMP. No.

SOLDIER KECK. What do I have to do, eh? What else do I fucking have to do for you, sir? Endless roll call, and drills, and no decent food, and shit water to drink and bathe, and dead dogs all over, and I've stolen blankets, and killed people . . . so many people . . . Everything, right? With a promise in mind. The promise of leaving this place, this end-world place that nobody thinks about, nobody wants to hear about; dead place, right? And I bring you a fucking Walkman, a fucking brand-name item you could sell on the street, you could trade with whatever, whomever, and what the fuck do I get? Eh? Fucking nothing. Fucking asshole.

SOLDIER FURST AS PIMP. Hey. Don't get all squiffy now.

SOLDIER KECK. Squiffy? I ain't squiffy. You think I'm squiffy? Not like you, eh? Fucking vodka queen.

SOLDIER FURST AS PIMP. All right now.

SOLDIER KECK. Placating me, are you? Placating the lost man?

SOLDIER FURST AS PIMP. I'll take it. All right?

SOLDIER KECK. . . . The Walkman? Five hundred dollars equivalency and boat across?

SOLDIER FURST AS PIMP. Yes.

SOLDIER KECK. . . . Fucking all right, then. Fucking great. You're a generous fucker.

SOLDIER FURST AS PIMP. I am, Keck.

SOLDIER KECK. What?

SOLDIER FURST AS PIMP. Keck. Isn't that your name?

SOLDIER KECK. No. No. I'm Bobby.

SOLDIER FIRST AS PIMP. Is that a fact?

SOLDIER KECK. Yes, sir. You can look it up.

SOLDIER FURST AS PIMP. Bobby, eh?

SOLDIER KECK. A boat to Wales, sir. I just want to get a boat to Wales.

SOLDIER FURST AS PIMP. Wherever you'd like, soldier.

Furst shoots Keck in the leg.

SOLDIER KECK. What the—?

SOLDIER FURST AS PIMP. You think I'd forget you? I've had you in mind for a long time, you piece of shit.

SOLDIER KECK. . . . I'm sorry . . .

SOLDIER FURST AS PIMP. Sorry. Yeah. We're all sorry here, son. Except some of us are sorrier than others. (*Towards hidden room*) Isn't that right, hon(ey)? You in there?

SOLDIER PINT DISPLACED (*from within*). Yes, sir. Right here, sir.

SOLDIER FURST AS PIMP. You wait there for me. Nice and tight. I'll be right with you.

SOLDIER PINT DISPLACED (*from within*). Yes, sir.

SOLDIER FURST AS PIMP. And no moving, you fucking piece of shit.

SOLDIER PINT DISPLACED (*from within*). No sir. I can't, sir. Not a bit.

SOLDIER FURST AS PIMP. And don't make a sound. Just quiet now. All's quiet. All's at peace . . . We're going to go nice and slow here, soldier.

SOLDIER KECK. Please, sir.

SOLDIER FURST AS PIMP. One shot.

(*shoots him in the arm.*)

And another . . .

Furst is about to shoot him again, when Minerva appears.

MINERVA. You in?

SOLDIER FURST AS PIMP (*adopting salesman mode slightly*). Ah, my family . . . come in, come in.

MINERVA. Yes, sir.

SOLDIER FURST AS PIMP. Sit down. Don't mind him. He's nothing. I'll be through with him in a minute. You like music? I got some music on.

MINERVA. Music? Sure. Music's fine.

SOLDIER FURST AS PIMP. I'll let you listen. It's classic stuff. Would you like that?

Be happy. Come on. No sad faces here.

MINERVA. No, sir.

SOLDIER FURST AS PIMP. That's right. A nice, warm smile. Come here. Listen. (*Minerva goes to him. She adopts a strong sexual stance.*) Hey, what are you doing? Take it easy. (*She begins to get rough with him, a little overwhelming.*) Hey. What are you—?

MINERVA. Fucking had it.

Minerva strangles him with the cord of the Walkman headphones. The chorus to the Bay City Rollers' song "Saturday Night" blares.

SCENE 22

On the other side of the fence, outside the camp, Minerva and Keck try to move on.

MINERVA. Come on.

SOLDIER KECK. . . . I can't . . .

MINERVA. Just a bit more. Before the lights hit us.

SOLDIER KECK. Everything hurts.

MINERVA. Hush.

SOLDIER KECK. I just want to go home. I want to go home.

MINERVA. Ain't no home. Ain't nothing. Come on.

SOLDIER KECK. No.

MINERVA. I can't leave you here. I won't.

SOLDIER KECK. Why not?

MINERVA. . . . We got nothing else, nothing else 'cept to keep going.

Minerva carries him. They move through the dark fields.

SCENE 23

Quick Daughter

CHORUS (*sung*). (*Verse 1*) Swift comes the fire
　　　Out the mouth
　　　Soft words in a blue flame.

Quick is the daughter of the earth's unrest
She walks through the silver
And makes her escape.

(*Chorus*) Quick daughter, where have you gone?
Across the border to find a home.
Across the border with a broken tongue.

(*Verse 2*) Slow comes the water
Out the mouth
Hard words in a clear rush.

Slow is the daughter of the earth's unrest
She walks through the amber
A wounded thrush.

(*Chorus*) Quick daughter, where have you gone?
Across the border to find a home.
Across the border . . .

(*2nd chorus*) Where I go, where'er I holler
I see them running
Along beaches, across valleys.

Where I go, where'er I holler
I see them running
I see them running
For a shot of light.

SCENE 24

The ferry yard. Minerva and Keck wait.

MINERVA. Clear across to Wales.

SOLDIER KECK. Is that where this goes?

MINERVA. One of these ferries got to go somewhere far.

SOLDIER KECK. Everywhere's the same.

MINERVA. It's not. Can't be. What? You don't wanna go now? After
all this . . .?

SOLDIER KECK. . . . A woman in a yellow dress met me. She was soaked in blood from her hem to her armpits. You could smell the burning plastic from a fire up ahead.

The burning plastic smell wouldn't stop. And this woman, she just wanted to see her daughter, right? She was looking for her daughter that I had killed.

MINERVA. You killed her daughter?

SOLDIER KECK. I didn't know it was her daughter. I didn't know anything. I saw movement in a house as we were coming upon it, my mates and I. There had been snipers in the area, and we were feeling up against it, y'know. Everything was messed up in our heads. I knew that. I knew were wrong inside somehow. We saw movement, we fired. They were just kids inside the house. That's all. Just kids. This woman's daughter . . . I didn't know what to say. I couldn't say anything. I just stared at her.

Go to hell, I said. Go to hell. Everything's been taken from me. Every bit of human-ness. . . . What's taking a ferry going to do? Is it going to change me?

MINERVA. We live inside ruin.

We become ruins.

We seek change?

Maybe it will happen.

BETTE AS A ROGUE FERRY-YARD GUARD (*appears*). You got the money?

MINERVA. Yes, ma'am.

BETTE AS FERRY GUARD. One, two . . . eight hundred, eh?

MINERVA. Yes, ma'am.

BETTE AS FERRY GUARD. Quit with that.

MINERVA. What?

BETTE AS FERRY GUARD. I'm not ma'am to you. I work here, that's all. I manage things, the ferries. I keep track. That's all I do. No niceties. No personal interaction. You pay me, I get you on a boat. There's one leaving in a minute.

SOLDIER KECK. Where's it going?

BETTE AS FERRY GUARD. Up to Skye.

SOLDIER KECK. Where?

BETTE AS FERRY GUARD. Some place called Skye. I don't got a map. You want to take it, you get on. Yeah?

MINERVA. Yes, ma'am.

BETTE AS FERRY GUARD. And quit with that. I'll have none of it. I'm nothing to you. The money's good. That's all I care about. Understand?

MINERVA. Yes.

BETTE AS FERRY GUARD. If you want to get on, you slip around the back. Where the tins are, and you get yourselves in there.

SOLDIER KECK. Tins?

BETTE AS FERRY GUARD. Sardine tins, oyster tins, mussel tins, canned fish, right? There's storage in the back. You slip in there among the tins, and you'll make it across. I've already got three dozen in there.

MINERVA. Three dozen people?

BETTE AS FERRY GUARD. Yeah. It's been a busy day. But don't worry, you'll fit in. They all do. Just squeeze tight, right? You'll be fine.

MINERVA. Thank you.

BETTE AS FERRY GUARD. I just take, y'know. I'm part of the grand exchange.

Bette walks away.

MINERVA. Fucking Skye.

SOLDIER KECK. I never heard of it.

MINERVA. Could be something.

SOLDIER KECK. Could be shit.

MINERVA. Don't say that.

SOLDIER KECK. Squeezed among tins?

MINERVA. We'll manage. I still got the chocolate bar you gave me.

SOLDIER KECK. Comet?

MINERVA. We could split it. Fight the pangs, Keck.

SOLDIER KECK. . . . You go on.

MINERVA. What are you talking about?

SOLDIER KECK. I don't want to go.

MINERVA. Look, I just handed somebody eight hundred dollars that I had to kill somebody to get. Right?

SOLDIER KECK. You can live like that?

MINERVA. I live how I can. . . . Come on. We'll miss it otherwise.

SOLDIER KECK. . . . We're not together.

MINERVA. Huh?

SOLDIER KECK. We're just . . .

MINERVA. Beside. Yeah. Right.

SOLDIER KECK. To Skye.

> *They head toward the ferry. They walk together, until they are out of sight.*

The End.

CHARACTERS

ILONA	20s, woman who's been through it all, forced now to work for Sondra.
ALAN+	30s, a pretender to civility, sex trafficking procurer/courier.
SONDRA**	30s, a brothel mama/madam to all the wild ones, wild herself, lives in a squat, speaks French argot occasionally (a language of her ancestry).
LILA (AICHA) BORGES	20s, 'outsider' artist, used to work for Sondra.
MAURICE	20s, Ilona's lover across the divide, underground political operative, revolutionary.
SONTILE**	Late 20s, professional soldier who served in the far desert, among other places, now does errands for Lila Borges and whomever else that can give him a gig (of French-Arab ancestry) (played by actor playing Maurice).
MAN IN TIRED HAT	30s, Low-level Spanish businessman, a john (played by actor playing Maurice).
TOURIST	20s, university post-graduate student from the US on holiday (played by actor playing Maurice).
CELINE	In her teens, tomboy hustler with a screwed-up aura, Fatima's street 'sister'.
BEATRICE+	20s, Alan's current partner, ambitious, driven (played by actor playing Celine, also plays Second Masked Figure).
FÁTIMA	In her teens, transgender street hustler (played by a male actor who also plays Second Glue Kid and Soldier Two).
ZULEM GRAZIA	Ageless, street *bruja*, trickster/seer (Creole, can be played by either male or female actor who also plays Third Glue Kid).
NICKY	30s, Sondra's client, will do anything to get by (also plays First Glue Kid, Soldier One and First Masked Figure).
L'ARGENT	20s, sex-trafficker, British (played by actor playing Fátima).
BEVY	Early 20s, Jack of all trades, locksmith.
ALETTE	In her teens, a girl on the road.
GLUE KIDS	In their teens, chorus of street kids, runaways, addicted to glue.

TIME	The continuous now.
SETTING	A city in an unnamed country, recently devastated by war.
PLACES	Fluid, multiple interior and exterior locations suggested with economy and elegance, with emphasis placed on a strong "map" of sound and light.

NOTE ON THE PLAY	This play should be performed with an interval after Part 1. Text in parantheses is not meant to be spoken. Melodies to original songs and song fragments written by the playwright may be obtained by contacting the author directly or the lyrics may be reset by another composer.
PRONUNCIATION	Names marked with ** should be spoken with a French accent. Names marked with + should be spoken with an English accent. Also, "Lila" is pronounced with long *i*, rather than a short *i*. "Borges" is pronounced with a Spanish accent, the same as the brilliant Argentine writer's surname. "Fátima" is pronounced with a Portuguese or Spanish accent.
SCRIPT HISTORY	This play was originally commissioned by Mark Wing-Davey, chair, and NYU's Graduate Acting Program. It received a production at NYU Tisch School of the Arts under the direction of Seret Scott in 2009. It subsequently received a production at the University of San Francisco's Theatre and Social Justice program under Roberto Gutierrez Varea's direction in 2010. It was further developed through the LoNYLa (London–New York City–Los Angeles) Spring Lab with directors Rachel Parish, Anna G. Jones and Sue Hamilton in 2011.

"Here we are crawling the cracks between walls of church state school and factory, all the paranoid monoliths. Cut off from the tribe by feral nostalgia we tunnel after lost words, imaginary bombs."

Hakim Bey, *Chaos: The Broadsheets of Ontological Anarchism*

PART 1

1. MERCY

Interior, in a makeshift squat. Daylight streams in.

MAURICE. Just go in, leave the bag . . . It'll be five minutes.

ILONA. I'm scared, Maurice.

MAURICE (*caresses her*). It's just a drop off. Stop by the factory, run, go.

ILONA. What if somebody—?

MAURICE. I'll take care of the guards. I told you, Ilona, it's all arranged. We bomb the factory, we strike at where they have their weapons stored. We have to do something for this country before it rips itself to pieces.

ILONA. It's already . . .

MAURICE. Before it's completely destroyed.

ILONA. . . .

MAURICE. What?

ILONA. I've never . . .

MAURICE. Hey. Hey. Come here . . . You'll do fine. We've talked through it. You'll be safe.

ILONA. You could . . . .

MAURICE. They've their eye on me. You know that. Have done for some time. They'd like nothing more than to . . .

ILONA. And if something (happens) . . .?

MAURICE. How many times are we gonna go over this? It's all been arranged. You're the drop off. That's what we agreed. You don't want to do this now? You don't want to help me? Help us?

ILONA. It's not that.

MAURICE. Love, love, you say. Oh, you love me so much.

IMAGE 5.1 **Ilona (Kathleen Wise) in despair.**

Rift, directed by Seret Scott at New York University Shubert Theatre, New York (2009)

Photograph by Ella Bromblin (Courtesy photographer and NYU Graduate Acting Program)

ILONA. I do.

MAURICE. Well then, do this, *cheri*. One drop off. One bomb. Strike the bastards where they hurt. And then we head to the border and try to make a new life for ourselves.

ILONA. Easy for you.

MAURICE. Huh?

ILONA. All these things . . .

MAURICE (*coughing, fighting strained health*). I do "these things" because I want to? I'd rather fight, than see my country eat itself from within. What should I do, Ilona? Leave it to those from the outside to save us, collect our dead, mourn our forgotten city? Easy, you say. Walk away, then. Walk the fuck away.

ILONA. Maurice . . .

MAURICE. I'll do it by myself.

ILONA. The guard . . .

MAURICE. Fuck the lousy guard. If he kills me, so be it. Let's all blow the fuck up. You stand there with your nice clothes on, staring at me. You've got options, right? You can get by in the world even when it's turned to shit.

ILONA. You don't know what you're saying.

MAURICE. I'm lying now?

ILONA. Look, my uncle . . . he always told me to . . .

MAURICE. Use your words to save the goddamn world? And when they kill your brother and your sister and your whole family, pieces of them stuffed in suitcases so you can't even tell whose leg belongs to . . .

(*He has a coughing fit. A moment.*)

. . . It's just one factory. That's all it is. A goddamn building.

ILONA. . . . Okay. I'll do it.

MAURICE. Yes?

She embraces him. A moment. They run off.

Sound of gunfire in distance escalates into . . . time shift . . .

ILONA. "Safe."

Dusk. Sounds of battle in the distance. Ilona and Maurice run in. It is clear they've been on the run for some time. Maurice is coughing. He is not well. Ilona leads him to a secluded area on the beach.

ILONA. They won't find us here.

MAURICE. Ilona.

ILONA. It's too far away.

MAURICE. I'm so cold.

ILONA. Give me your hands.

MAURICE. . . . So tired.

A moment.

ILONA. . . . I can hear the city burning.

MAURICE. Shh.

ILONA. Our beautiful city . . . When I was a child, I'd run along the water, pick up strange rocks along the beach.

MAURICE. Treasures?

ILONA. I'd call out to my uncle, "Look what I found. A blue shell. And over there, isn't that a line of red thread making a path through the sand and up to the fields?" "Silly child," he'd say. "Silly Ilona."

MAURICE. You're not.

ILONA. Listen to me. I know it's not much, but . . . I want you to have this.

She takes off amulet necklace.

My uncle gave it to me. For protection.

MAURICE. Little boat charm?

ILONA. He said if I carried this little boat with me, I'd always be safe.

MAURICE. Ilona . . .

ILONA. I love you.

(*She puts necklace on him. He kisses her, and then sings to her softly in French.*)

"chanson de l'exil" / "exile song (a lullaby)"

MAURICE. *Et quand on part* (And when we go)
le monde va savoir (the world will know)

She joins him in song.

ILONA and MAURICE. *tout-ce qui reste en bas* (all that lies below)
Une ville des anges (a city of angels)

un rêve de salut (a dream of salvation)
Une chanson rue d'exil. (a song of the exile's road.)

They repeat first part of the song together, trying to find comfort in each other, trying to stave off fear. Soldier One and Soldier Two burst in. (Lines in this following sequence overlap.)

SOLDIER ONE (*to Maurice*). Come. With us.

Soldier One pulls Maurice away from her.

MAURICE. What are you—?

SOLDIER ONE (*ordering the other soldier*). Hold her down.

ILONA. Maurice! Maurice!

SOLDIER ONE. Down.

Soldier Two puts gun to Ilona's throat and straddles her. Soldier One handcuffs Maurice.

MAURICE. I haven't done anything. I haven't done anything.

ILONA. Maurice . . .

SOLDIER ONE. Let's go.

ILONA. Where are you taking him? Where are you taking him?

MAURICE (*to Ilona*). Shh. It's okay. It's okay.

Soldier One puts a hood over Maurice's head.

ILONA. Maurice!

SOLDIER ONE. Shut the wog-lover up.

ILONA. Maurice. Maurice . . .

SOLDIER ONE. Shut her.

Soldier One exits with Maurice. Soldier Two starts to have his way with Ilona. The sound of a cluster bomb in the distance. Soldier Two exits.

Time has passed.

Day. In the city, in the background, Sondra crosses. She carries a large bag of useable, repurposed rubble: household objects, clothes, etc., flung over her shoulder. She calls out her work-song/sales pitch in French and English.

SONDRA *(freely). Venez! Décombres a vendre!*
Come. Rubble for sale.
Venez! Des roches a vendre!
Come. Rocks for sale.

Sondra continues to call out to whoever will buy. Time shift. On the road, she comes upon Ilona, left stranded, huddled, half-asleep. Sondra kicks her awake roughly. Ilona starts. A moment.

Sondra takes out a jacket and cap from her bag and tosses them onto Ilona. Ilona puts them on. She rises. Sondra turns her around, as if she were inspecting her. She grabs her and demands she open her mouth. She inspects. A moment.

Ilona tries to run off. Sondra grabs her roughly. There's no running here. She places locked anklet on Ilona, branding her as possession. She whispers in her ear, and sends Ilona back toward the city to earn her keep.

Sondra continues calling out her work-song and walks away, as Ilona now walks through the city. Time shift.

3. TEMPORARY ASYLUM

In the foreground, exterior of a bar in a train station on the outskirts of a metropolitan city.

TRAIN ANNOUNCEMENT (VOICEOVER). Track 2, track 2, extended delays on the southbound on Track 2 *(slight static, and then)* Executions at five o'clock; All plastic sheeting donations to the central square *(slight static).*

Alan is seen, standing at the bar. He has a row of drinks. He drinks, alternating, from all of them. After slight pause, Ilona approaches the bar. A moment. He slides a drink towards her. She takes it.

ALAN. Cheap liquor. The blessing of train-station bars.

ILONA. . . . There are other bars if you—

ALAN. I prefer the nearness of motion.

ILONA. Going somewhere?

ALAN. Traveling costs. There's not enough money to go around in this world.

TRAIN ANNOUNCEMENT (VOICEOVER). Track 1, Track 1, extended delays on the northbound, Track 1.

ILONA. Nice watch.

ALAN. A gift.

ILONA. A friend?

ALAN. Good friend. It's not a crime to have friends.

ILONA. It's useful.

ALAN. Sometimes . . . it's rather a nuisance.

ILONA. The burden of friends? You prefer to be alone, then? A man and his drink?

ALAN. I didn't say that.

ILONA. . . . Wonder when the next train . . .

ALAN. Headed far?

ILONA. Don't know yet.

ALAN. It's all wrecked. Shame . . . 'Cause this used to be a beautiful country.

ILONA. Still is.

ALAN. Where are you from?

ILONA. Nowhere.

ALAN. Nowhere . . . everywhere?

ILONA. I'm common. You?

ALAN. Oh, I'm quite common. Some would even say vulgar.

ILONA. That's very common.

ALAN. In these times.

ILONA. War's war.

ALAN. War's. Over.

ILONA. So they say.

ALAN. Don't believe it?

ILONA. I don't believe anything.

ALAN. You're here, though.

ILONA. How's that?

ALAN. Wouldn't be here if you didn't think . . .

ILONA (*ironic*). Life was worth carrying on?

ALAN. . . . Look, can I get you another (drink)?

ILONA. I'm fine.

ALAN. . . . Such pretty eyes.

ILONA. Don't.

ALAN. Don't like compliments?

ILONA. I told you: I don't believe anything.

ALAN. No sweetness, eh? No goodness? . . . Here.

ILONA. What?

ALAN. I want you to know there's good in the world. Actual good.
That is done. Every day.

He gives Ilona his watch.

TRAIN STATION ANNOUNCEMENT (VOICEOVER). Track 2, Track 2, all southbound routes cancelled on Track 2 (*static, and then*) Executions
rescheduled for four o'clock. Repeat: four o'clock (*slight static*).

ILONA (*looking at watch*). Beautiful inscription. Is she still . . .?

ALAN. No.

A moment.

ILONA (*tries to give watch back*). . . . I can't . . .

ALAN. I want you to have it.

ILONA (*pockets the watch*). . . . Not many like you.

ALAN. Too many like me.

ILONA. World's littered?

ALAN. World's a junk heap.

ILONA (*referring to his drink*). A drop.

ALAN. What?

ILONA. You spilled a—on your shirt.

ALAN (*referring to shirt*). It's cheap.

ILONA. You can get a new one?

ALAN. I can get anything.

ILONA. . . . What do you want, then?

ALAN. . . . We're just having drinks.

> *Ilona walks away. Alan restrains her.*

ILONA. . . . Let go.

ALAN. Gonna beg?

ILONA. Ain't too proud.

ALAN (*singing/referring to the 1966 Temptations pop song*). "Ain't too proud to beg, sweet darling, Please don't leave me, babe . . ."

> *A moment. He lets her go. Ilona slaps him. A moment.*

(*A turn-on.*) You wanna play games? Out here in the fucking open?

ILONA. I'll play any game you want, Alan.

ALAN. Is that who you think I am?

ILONA. Been told. Kilt babe on the street. Said you gave her plenty.

ALAN. I give all sorts of things.

ILONA. Give, then.

ALAN. You've the watch.

ILONA. Now.

> *Ilona pulls a knife on him. A moment.*
>
> *Alan reaches for his wallet, hands it to Ilona. She takes it and runs away. A moment.*

ALAN. Poor lost thing.

> *A moment. In the distance, a bomb blast.*

Shortly after. Day. Sondra, Celine, and Fátima are seen in the squat/shelter. Sondra tabulates numbers in her makeshift accounting book, trying to maintain her own sense of order. Celine blows soap bubbles (from a soap-bubble necklace). Fátima wears a snug top and her version of a kilt (fashioned from combination of fabrics).

SONDRA (*matter of fact*). Every day, another bomb.

CELINE. Pop pop. Like on the Wii.

FÁTIMA. Wii don't bang, girl.

CELINE. Wii got everything.

FÁTIMA. You need some kind of serious glasses to straighten out your sense of the world.

CELINE. I need your ass in my mouth is what I need.

FÁTIMA. It don't fit.

CELINE. I got more mouth than you can take, boy.

FÁTIMA. Hey. Call as you see me.

CELINE. All I see's a tit-crownin' pup who gives it hard in the back street when the sky blows hellfire and the rain comes down sticky, bloody cum.

FÁTIMA. Pushin' me, darlin'? You want a cruel taste of my hard lips on your soft crack?

SONDRA. Fátima.

FÁTIMA. I'm just tellin' it like it was, is, and ever will be.

CELINE. I push, you go down in a skinny-ass millisecond.

FÁTIMA. Is that right?

CELINE. Snip snip with a little knife, Fátima goes the way of Hades.

FÁTIMA (*as if quoting something heard once*). (If) You cut me, I'll carve out your tits and box with a butcher's knife and sell them to the junk-man on the street.

SONDRA. Shit talk.

FÁTIMA. My mouth is free, mama dear.

CELINE. Say that again, motherfucker. Say that nasty shit again and I'll—

FÁTIMA. What? What you gonna do, Celine? Celine of the pristine, Plasticine tits?

Celine tears into Fátima. A messy fight ensues. Sondra tries to intervene.

SONDRA. Celine! Fátima!

CELINE (*midst struggle*). Motherfucker.

FÁTIMA (*midst struggle*). Chilly cunt.

Fight continues.

SONDRA (*pulls them apart*). Enough! *Petits baiseurs* (Little bitches).

FÁTIMA. . . . Mama's got a temper.

SONDRA. Watch your tongue.

FÁTIMA. We're just playin', Sondra.

SONDRA. That kind of shit affection with its shit words—are you listenin' to me?—has no room in my house. In the street, say what you like. But here? There's no kind of bully-ass, nasty shit going down. Understand?

FÁTIMA (*routine*). 'Cause you won't put up with it.

SONDRA. Take that smile off your face, girl, or you'll see my animal. Or don't you think I have one? Mama Sondra got plenty animal inside her. And this no conjure talk. This ain't somethin' you can dismiss with a swivel of the hips and a wave of the hand. I got ancient animal inside me, kind that can rise up and cry havoc mighty enough to wake up the dead. You with your petty anger, your shit jealousies, what gods do you wake?

FÁTIMA. Whatever.

SONDRA. That how you answer me?

FÁTIMA. Answer how I like.

CELINE. Petty shit.

SONDRA. What?

CELINE. This all . . . petty shit. Like every day.

SONDRA. Every day you don't make somethin'. Numbers don't lie. What have you been doin'?

FÁTIMA. Same as you.

Sondra strikes Fátima.

SONDRA. You're in my house. We're ALL in this.

FÁTIMA. I can get me a place. Get a palace.

SONDRA. Wanna play with the gods? Think you can live in their world?

FÁTIMA. I'm a superstar, baby.

SONDRA. Dream and dream.

FÁTIMA. I don't mess up my head with dreams.

SONDRA. Fátima.

FÁTIMA. Honey bitch, this is real.

Fátima walks away.

SONDRA. Fátima!

Fátima is gone. Silence.

CELINE. She'll come back.

SONDRA. No need of her whimper here.

CELINE. . . . We were a good team.

SONDRA. You'll do fine on your own, Celine.

CELINE. . . . Nothin' but knots in my head.

SONDRA. Shh.

Sondra sings Celine to sleep.

Ghost Song (Surrender)

Surrender, sweet.
Sleep falls upon the mornin'.
Watch the ghost of your lover cry.

(*Celine is fast asleep from sheer exhaustion. Sondra continues. Ilona appears, observes.*)

Surrender me.
Dreams rise upon the evenin'.
Watch the back of your lover sigh,

As legend leaves your body hangin'
In the pale wash of a liquid sky.

ILONA. . . . Sondra's tragic and blue.

SONDRA. That's my veil, *cheri*.

ILONA (*handing money over*). Here.

SONDRA (*stashing money away*). Made good today. If it wasn't for you . . .

ILONA. . . . Where's Fátima?

SONDRA. Off somewhere.

Ilona takes off a layer of clothing, hot, tired . . .

SONDRA. . . . You get hit?

ILONA. No.

SONDRA. A bruise is blooming on your skin.

ILONA. It's nothing . . . Celine's fast asleep.

SONDRA. Makes nothin'. What right has she to sleep and sleep? *Vas-y* (Go on).

(*Ilona doesn't respond.*)

Vas-y.

ILONA. Let her—

SONDRA. *Je te posséde. Chienne.* (I own you. Bitch.)

ILONA. *Cette chienne pisse dans ton sang* (This bitch pisses in your bloodstream).

SONDRA. *Maudite garce* (damned bitch). Now, do (as I say). Like I taught you all how children are to be awakened.

Ilona walks over to where Celine sleeps. A breath.
And then pounds her with her fists, forcing her awake.
Sondra takes a sip of liquor from a flask,
and sings a reprise of her "Ghost Song (Surrender)."

Surrender, sweet.
Sleep falls upon the mornin'.
Watch the ghost of your lover cry . . .

Shortly after. In the foreground, in the present, outside the squat/shelter, Ilona cuts herself with a little knife—a ritual of cutting that is routine for her now.
She holds onto memory. She refuses tears.

ILONA. The sky burned. You held on to me.
    We held on to each other and ran and ran,
    Until we had no breath left,
    Until all we could do, Maurice, was . . .
    Zulem Grazia appears.

ZULEM. Dreamin' out in the open for the whole world to see?

ILONA. The world gives fuck-all we're here.

ZULEM. World gives fuck we keep the stink of dead bodies fresh in mind, but no(thin') more than that. Be wretched, stay wretched.

ILONA. I'm not.

ZULEM. Work the stations, streets . . . make your way . . . to where?

ILONA. Nowhere.

ZULEM. . . . . Sondra kick you out?

ILONA. I'm just resting.

ZULEM. Air's poison.

ILONA. Don't mind.

ZULEM. Because you dream about Maurice?

ILONA. Leave me alone, Zulem.

    Zulem sings with a mixture of irony and vulnerability.

Wild chil'

ZULEM. Hoodoo chil', runnin' wild,
    Let go the sorrow of your days.
    'Cause when you run from me,
    You'll be in the devil's disgrace.

ILONA. I don't believe in the devil.

ZULEM. You think the world just is?

ILONA. I think the world has no reason except itself.

ZULEM. But you cut all the same.

> (*Zulem grabs Ilona's arm.*)

> Little rivers of feeling.

> (*Ilona wrests herself from Zulem.*)

> Is this how you treat your lover?

ILONA. I treat as I'm treated.

ZULEM. You treat as you've been taught.

ILONA. As we've all been.

ZULEM. No room for tenderness?

ILONA. Stop.

ZULEM. Just a caress.

ILONA. To soothe your anguished soul?

ZULEM. I've no anguish.

ILONA. Zulem's free?

ZULEM. Zulem Grazia cries to no one about no one. I've no Maurice.

ILONA. Shut.

ZULEM. . . . I've seen him. Plain as day.

ILONA. He's dead.

ZULEM. All I know is what I see.

ILONA. Fuckin' lie to me.

ZULEM. Cool night by the quiet river, he was sinkin' down a long way. *Anba dlo.*[1]

ILONA. Drowned?

ZULEM. And then he come back up he did: Maurice come back up a whole new being.
Seek him out, *cheri.*

ILONA. Can't.

> *Ilona reveals locked anklet. (Sign of being owned by Sondra.)*

---

1 *Anba dlo*: Haitian voodoo phrase meaning "beneath the water, where lwa and ancestors reside."

ZULEM. Ah, Mama Sondra's leash.

ILONA. She's just doing what's done.

ZULEM. To those who . . .

ILONA. What? Go on, Zulem. You've all the answers. You've all the goddamn judgment in the world.

ZULEM. I didn't mean . . .

ILONA. No. No. You're a good soul. Right? You've all the pretty words and visions. When you look, you just see what you want.

ZULEM. . . . You know, I know someone who can (*refers to anklet*) trick the lock.

ILONA. Fuckin' gamin' me?

ZULEM. This is no game, chil'. Can be done. With expertise. I know this kid. Real clever. Goes by Bevy.

ILONA. Never heard . . .

ZULEM. Works the back end of the station sometimes. I'll ask Bevy, see what can be done.

ILONA. Why do this for me?

ZULEM. Why do we do anythin' for anyone in this world?
(*As she walks away, half-sung*) Hoodoo chil', runnin' wild . . .
Zulem is gone.

6. EVERYDAY EROS

Lights shiver-shift to the present uninterrupted by spectral dreams.

Twilight, in the city, in the background, Sondra is seen. She sells useable objects and rubble (from the latest ruins) and also uses her work-song to pitch her "girls"—Celine and Ilona—to potential clients. She calls out freely in French and English.

SONDRA. *Venez! Décombres a vendre!* Come. Rubble for sale.
Venez! Des roches a vendre! Come. Rocks for sale.
(*On the street, Ilona registers Sondra's presence and call. She heads to her prostitute work station. Pose. A snapshot of performed yearning.*)

Venez! Décombres a vendre!

(On the street, Celine registers Sondra's presence and call, and heads to her prostitute work station. Pose. Another snapshot of performed yearning.)

Venez! Des roches a vendre!

Alan appears. He's night-crawling, on a high.
In the background, music is heard from a dance club
(perhaps Karsh Kale's "Distance" from 2009 album Realize).
The music underscores a movement sequence
driven by a sequential portrait of Alan's carnal desires
(the movement sequence should not seem choreographed)
As captured in separate, intensely feverish erotic encounters
With Celine first, and then Ilona,
neither of which ultimately leaves him fully satiated.
He tosses money dismissively at both Celine and Ilona after each transaction.
They walk over to Sondra with it, and exit.
A moment.
Alan is alone: a portrait of the debauched self in inner sexual and addictive chaos.
The music takes a sharp turn, the movement sequence distills into a single encounter:
Fátima spills out from the dance club on a side street of a boulevard,
Dancing, lost to herself, strangely blissful.
Alan sees her. A moment of attraction and seduction.
And then Fátima is overtaken by Alan:
a strange, violent sensual transaction transpires between them.
Lights shiver-shift into . . .

7. BORGES RENDERS IN THE BLOOD QUIET / THE VALUE OF ART

A short time after. A gallery, which used to be a slaughterhouse. Lila Borges is seen. She speaks to herself as she scrolls through digital images she's taken, recording her thoughts into voice-recorder component, which is part of her digital camera / phone.

LILA BORGES. Look.

What do you see?

A stranger?

A lover?

An incendiary?

Sondra enters, unseen by Lila. She observes.

This is the face of sex.

This is the face of silence.

This is the face of . . .

SONDRA. Workin' on your art?

LILA. Fuck off.

SONDRA. Talk to everyone like that? Won't sell much.

LILA. What are you doing here, Sondra?

SONDRA. Used to work here. The hours I spent in this slaughterhouse . . .

LILA. Gallery.

SONDRA. Slaughterhouse to me.

LILA. Gut girl.

SONDRA. And I was proud of it. (*Approaching Lila's work area.*) You've got an eye for this art thing, Aicha.

LILA. Lila.

SONDRA. Aicha to me. Real good eye. Not my taste, mind. I don't go in for all this muck-of-life shit.

LILA. Really?

SONDRA. I like happy things. Nice pictures. World's got enough muck. . . . (*Looks at her for a moment.*) This your get-up now? (if) I put you back on the street, you'd make a fortune.

LILA. Not going back.

A moment. And then an embrace between them, full of history.

SONDRA. You may have clawed your way into another world, *cheri,* but you're still mine.

Lila takes Sondra's picture. A moment.

LILA. You want this picture, Sondra, I'll give it to you.

SONDRA. No. No. Sell it. Make a killing. (*Mimicking, in mockery, Lila when she was recording her thoughts earlier.*) Here stands the seller of ruins, selling those that have been ruined to get by.

Pity the poor under-sellers of the earth who have nothing, but their wits and muscles to stay alive.

LILA. *Va te faire foudre* (Go fuck yourself).

SONDRA. *Va niquer ta mere* (Go fuck your mother). You sell these images to the liquid rich, to the ones who say, "Oh, look at those poor people and their poor struggles, it's so comforting to contemplate over tea."

LILA. They're just pictures.

SONDRA. Is that what you tell the people who come to this slaughter-house?

LILA. Gallery. And I don't say anything.

SONDRA. Silent Aicha?

LILA. Lila.

SONDRA. That's not how I remember you, *cheri*.

LILA. How do you remember me? Trussed up? Slung from a god-damn harness?

The sound of a bomb in the distance. A moment.

SONDRA. The world goes.

LILA. . . . So should you.

A moment.

SONDRA. . . . The poor can't afford not to work.

LILA. I'm not rich.

SONDRA. I've this girl. (*Hands her photo.*)

LILA (*looks at photo, and turns it over, reads name scrawled on back of photo*). Ilona.

SONDRA. I want you to see her.

LILA. What for?

SONDRA. Lots of dreams in her head. You know what needs to be done.

LILA. I'm not an expert.

SONDRA. You're in another sphere.

LILA. Meaning what? Bring her 'round, make things nice, tell her all about the glory of being in Sondra's house, and then hand her over to get beaten down? Get someone else to do your shit work.

SONDRA. Lila. Lila Borges. It's a good name. Good name you've found for yourself. But you forget, *cheri*.

LILA. Sorry?

SONDRA. You want my silence, Aicha? You want to keep on living this little life of yours, making your little art?

LILA. What are you—?

SONDRA. Think hard. Think about everything you've done. In your "so-called" past.

LILA. . . . *Salope* (Bitch).

SONDRA. We've all a tongue, dear, until it's cut.

THE GAME OF LIFE / TO BE RID OF YOU

Alley. Evening. Nicky, client, and Ilona in midst of sexual transaction. Ilona pulls away.

NICKY. Hey. We're just getting started, honey.

ILONA. Time's up.

NICKY. Give me your mouth.

ILONA. Give me more, then.

NICKY. I'm not a bank, baby.

ILONA. Then this is all you get, Nicky.

NICKY. Sondra teach you that?

ILONA. I don't need anyone to teach me anything.

NICKY. Is that right?

Nicky moves toward her, a physical threat.

ILONA. What? What are you doing?

Nicky laughs and throws money at her.

NICKY. Good ol' Sondra. She taught you good . . . Come on.

ILONA. Not so fast.

NICKY. Hey. This ain't a game, girl. I'm paid up.

ILONA. Turn around, then.

NICKY. Wanna play? Be my daddy?

ILONA. Sure.

NICKY. Where are you from, Ilona? Where'd Sondra find you?

ILONA. Nowhere.

NICKY. Like everyone else, right? All from fucking nowhere until they're found out otherwise.

ILONA (*role-play*). Be a good son now.

NICKY. Do I get a treat?

ILONA. You get everything.

> *He laughs. She straddles him.*
> *Time suspension midst action. Interior. Close-up on Ilona.*
>
> Seek him out, she says.
> Seek his spirit re-born.
> You left me, Maurice.
> Fucking left me here.
>
> . . .
>
> Kill my dreams of you.
> Rid the trace of your ghost.
>
> *Time suspension ends.*

NICKY. Hey. Don't stop, honey. I ain't got all the time in the world.

ILONA. I'm here. I'm right here. . . . Come 'ere . . .

> *Shift to . . .*

8. IN THE PALACE OF SOME OTHER GODS

Early evening. In the silver loft, in the present, Alan and Beatrice walk in.

BEATRICE. Such a twat.

ALAN. That's graciously put.

BEATRICE. Like Lila Borges knows anything about anything.

ALAN. Well, you must admit: she has a point of view.

BEATRICE. . . . You want to screw her.

ALAN. Beatrice . . . .

He caresses her. It is a forceful, aggressive caress that leads into a messy kiss.

BEATRICE. You're salty.

ALAN. Dirty martinis.

BEATRICE. You're so old skool.

ALAN. I treasure history.

BEATRICE. The history of cocktails? I could use another.

ALAN. All right.

(*He goes to bar area to make drinks. She takes off jewelry.*)

Did you like her pictures?

BEATRICE. Screw her. And get it over with.

ALAN. Where are you . . .?

(*Beatrice goes to another area, unseen. Alan snorts heroin from a vial. A moment.*)

Love you.

BEATRICE (*from off, not in direct response to him*). What the fuck—?

ALAN. I love your mouth, Beatrice.

BEATRICE (*from off*). What?

ALAN. Your mouth. I love it.

He drinks.

BEATRICE (*from off*). When I have it on you, you mean.

ALAN. Must we go there?

BEATRICE (*emerges in a slip and robe or dressing gown*). Where else?

ALAN. I was thinking something a bit more . . . sanitized.

BEATRICE. Want me to wear a mask?

ALAN. . . . How 'bout a gag?

BEATRICE. Been through that war.

ALAN. I rescued you.

BEATRICE. A cool thousand, and the wog's yours.

ALAN. It wasn't like that.

BEATRICE. I remember it perfectly, Alan.

ALAN. Well . . . anyway . . . you're not a wog.

BEATRICE. I'm an interesting trophy. "Go on, Beatrice. Tell us your
sob story. Tell us how Alan is such a damned hero for saving
you."

ALAN (*an air of disappointment*). Nobody says that.

BEATRICE. People forget so easily.

ALAN. Come 'ere.

(*She doesn't oblige.*)

Beatrice . . .

BEATRICE. . . . How 'bout you, up there, as if you were on an auction
block?

ALAN. *L'enfant sauvage.*

BEATRICE. Ready for the bidding. Ready for the master's whip.

ALAN. That's what Fátima's for.

*Alan clicks remote control. A box in an area of the converted loft is
illuminated, revealing Fátima. Her wrists are shackled to a bar
that's attached to the box/cage's ceiling, her ankles are bound. She
is gagged with a silver sash (a decorative, rather absurd 'artistic'
touch). The box should appear, when unlit from within, to be a discreetly chic art object.*

BEATRICE. Such a creature.

Fátima tries to move.

ALAN. Steady now. We'll take a walk later; we'll play.

BEATRICE. . . . Such need you have for such shit.

ALAN. Such need have we all . . .

A moment.

BEATRICE. Turn her (light) off. I can't touch you with her . . .

ALAN. . . . You're still scared. . . .

Alan hits the remote control. Lights fade on Fátima in the box. Beatrice resumes foreplay.

BEATRICE. . . . You know . . . I'm as good as her.

ALAN. As whom?

BEATRICE. Lila Borges.

ALAN. You're still on about her?

BEATRICE. You're thinking about her. I can tell.

ALAN. Actually, I've invited her over.

BEATRICE (*breaks away, explosive, with vengeance*). To what? Put me en route with Fátima? Are you putting together a (*pushing him*) package deal, Alan? Trading us both out of here to (*slaps him*) goddamn Turkey or wherever?

ALAN (*slaps her*). It's not like that at all.

BEATRICE (*slaps him*). I fucking married you, Alan. I've played all your sick games, gone to all your parties, I've put up with a hella shit.

ALAN (*overlap*). Okay, okay.

BEATRICE (*throws lime or some other insignificant random object at him from the bar area*). For you to start making plans with goddamn Lila.

ALAN. You're escalating things—

BEATRICE. I'm not escalating anything. I see things exactly for what they are. I'm here, Alan. We're in this.

ALAN. The sanctity of marriage.

BEATRICE. You're not going to just let me go, put me out with the trash-like poor Fátima.

ALAN. Beatrice . . .

BEATRICE (*cocktail glass in hand—a viable threat*). I'll shatter your eyelids. Let's see who'll do business with you, then.

ALAN. Put the glass. In its place.

BEATRICE. Where would that be? On Fátima's tit?

ALAN (*he grabs her by the throat*). Okay, look . . .

BEATRICE. What?

> *Alan kisses her with force. A slight knock on the door. Neither of them registers it, they're so wrapped up in their rough sexual moment. Lila Borges walks in, witnesses the moment between Alan and Beatrice. Slight pause. She has a bouquet of white hyacinths in hand. She is followed by Sontile.*

LILA. Hope you don't mind. We're a bit early.

ALAN. No. No. It's fine. It's good to see you, Lila.

LILA. This is Sontile. He's my friend. . . . Remember? He was at the gallery.

BEATRICE. Of course. You were lingering about.

SONTILE. I don't linger.

LILA. He takes care of me. Don't you, hon(ey)?

SONTILE. Every bit.

ALAN. Right. Well. Sontile.

SONTILE (*looking around*). Fucking place this.

ALAN. Yes.

SONTILE. Fucking silver. Very retro.

ALAN. It's homage.

SONTILE. The past was shit but let's celebrate it?

ALAN. Not quite . . .

SONTILE. You're fucking pissin' in it.

ALAN. Sorry?

SONTILE. Pissin' in its mouth. Like everyone else behind these gates. Fucking privy-to-the-high house shit.

ALAN. Such *joie de vivre*.

LILA. Alan, don't I get a kiss? I brought hyacinths.

> *Alan kisses Lila. Slight pause. Alan holds out bouquet to Beatrice.*

ALAN. Beatrice, would you—?

> (*Beatrice doesn't respond.*)

I'll manage.

Alan takes hyacinths and goes to put them in a vase.

LILA. Beatrice?

BEATRICE. Drink?

LILA. If it's not too much trouble . . .

BEATRICE. Why would it be?

LILA. Some people, you know . . .

BEATRICE. Don't like serving? Our marriage is built on service. Isn't that right, Alan?

ALAN. It's a hot day.

LILA. The weather's turned crap. World over. You think anyone really cares?

SONTILE. You got beer?

BEATRICE. What?

SONTILE. Beer. I'm sweating my kit off.

ALAN. . . . I don't remember you.

SONTILE. What?

ALAN. At the gallery.

LILA. You must've missed him somehow. Sontile likes to move about.

ALAN (*mocking, referring to the Beatles song*). "Here, there, and everywhere?"

LILA. Actually, he's a genuine war hero.

SONTILE. Well, I wouldn't . . .

LILA. He was in the far desert fighting the good fight.

BEATRICE. Really?

SONTILE. Just doin' what had to be done. You know.

ALAN. Such a dutiful son.

SONTILE. Done piss more than you, mack.

ALAN. How do you know what I've done?

SONTILE. Can smell it.

ALAN. Like a damned ferret?

LILA (*to Sontile*). Lick me.

Sontile does so: a display of brazen affection.

BEATRICE. You know, I recycle.

LILA. What?

BEATRICE. You were talking about the crap world, the climate . . . I recycle.

LILA. You know how many landfills there are all over: toxic waste sites just sitting there, accumulating . . .

BEATRICE. Not 'round here.

LILA. No, they shove the trash outside this zone, don't they, Alan?

ALAN. Well, it's one way to—

SONTILE. Keep the shit out?

ALAN. I wouldn't put it like—

SONTILE. No. You got fuckin' words, right? All sorts of words up your tight ass. But when it comes to thinkin' about the country, our fuckin' house, you don't give fuck what.

ALAN. Such beauty of expression, Sontile.

SONTILE. Rim. Me.

LILA. Honey . . .

SONTILE. Honey, honey . . . Thousands of people dying of hunger, and you walk into a market around here, in the so-called Right district, and it's obscene.

ALAN. . . . Look. If it's any comfort, Sontile—

SONTILE. What?

ALAN. . . . I don't go to that market.

BEATRICE. We can't afford it.

ALAN. Shut up.

LILA. Sontile likes to go on.

SONTILE. Don't act all . . . we're the same. Sweet dirty . . .

Sontile and Lila are all over each other: another brazen display of affection.

ALAN (*a burst*). You are. So full. Of fucking. Shit.

Alan rises, remote in hand. Goes toward Fátima's box. He slips away behind it. Pause.

BEATRICE. Alan's a bit excitable. Must be the weather.

LILA. I brought hyacinths.

BEATRICE. Very sweet of you.

LILA. Had to go all the way out. Past the old district. Ruined my shoes.

BEATRICE. They're nice.

LILA. They were a gift.

BEATRICE. Lucky.

SONTILE. Lila can stick her tongue anywhere with her art.

LILA. Enough.

SONTILE. Enough, enough. What am I, your pup?

LILA. He's in a mood.

SONTILE. I'm not in anything. This is some place you got here, Beatrice. Can't get over it.

BEATRICE. The silver?

SONTILE. It's like I've been here before.

BEATRICE. Apparently it used to be a school once.

SONTILE. Fuckin' kindergarten?

BEATRICE. I don't know. Alan's the one who . . .

SONTILE. Can smell the old paint. Paint and piss . . .

LILA. What the fuck is Alan doing back there?

Alan composes himself a bit and emerges from the box, where he's been, unseen.

ALAN. How 'bout another drink?

LILA. What do you have back there?

ALAN. Look, let's just carry on, all right? We're here, we've having a time, let's have it.

LILA. Let me see.

ALAN. Drinks first.

SONTILE. I'm in.

ALAN (*to Sontile*). Little bitch. (*Shift to*) . . . Lila?

LILA. I'm waiting.

ALAN. Show and tell? Show and tell, tell and show . . .

A moment. Alan goes blank. A moment.

SONTILE. Hey. You're in the hatch there?

ALAN. What? . . . I'm fine. So. So, it's a light-box of sorts. Met up with this artist. Odd sort. But kind. Very kind.

LILA. You struck a bargain.

ALAN. Actually, it cost me quite a bit.

SONTILE. How's that?

BEATRICE. Business. It's always about business with Alan.

SONTILE. You got any chips or anything?

BEATRICE. Hungry, Sontile?

SONTILE. Fucking starving.

BEATRICE. Come with me.

Beatrice and Sontile head toward area, unseen, where Beatrice changed her clothes before. Lila and Alan go toward Fátima's box.

ALAN. It's pitch dark inside.

LILA. Like a cocoon.

ALAN. Yes. But when I click this (remote), I can blast it, dim it, whatever.

LILA. Show.

(*Click of remote. Lights fade up on the box. A moment.*)

Beautiful tortured thing.

ALAN. Fátima.

LILA. Can I have her?

ALAN. Not for sale.

LILA. Bastard. You've sold her already.

Fátima tries to move slightly. Sontile and Beatrice are heard from other area, unseen. They are laughing, engaged in their own dance of attraction.

BEATRICE (*from off, mid-conversation with Sontile*). Did what?

SONTILE (*from off, mid-conversation with Beatrice*). Rammed that shit down the wogs' throats.

BEATRICE (*from off*). Prick.

More laughter from Beatrice and Sontile, from off.

LILA. Keep the light on.

ALAN. What for?

LILA. I want to take her picture.

ALAN. I don't want—

LILA. It'll just be her face. I want her face. She's so beautiful. . . .

ALAN. Lila? (*At a loss, oddly vulnerable*) . . . What shall I—?

LILA. Make her cry. I want to get a shot with tears in her eyes.

Lila goes for the camera in her messenger bag.
Alan walks into the box and caresses Fátima's torso, nipples, and then throat; the caress leads to Alan erotically choking Fátima; Fátima cries.
Time shift.

9. A LOOK OUT OF / FOR ALL TIME (A CLOSE-UP / INTERIOR)

In suspended time, unshackled, ungagged,
Fátima describes what she feels as Lila photographs her.
It is as if she is watching herself—out of body, out of time.
This should be treated as a close-up. Direct, intimate address.

FÁTIMA. She held my tears.

She said she wanted to hold them for eternity.

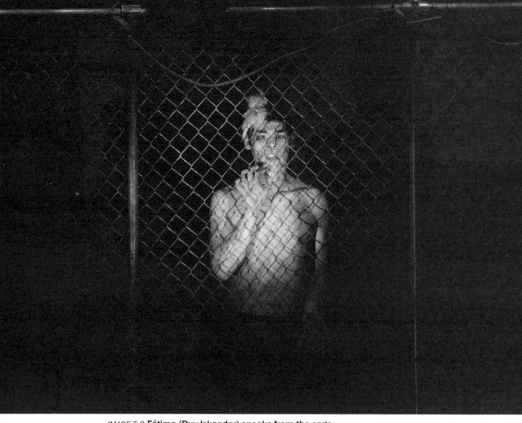

IMAGE 5.2 **Fátima (Ruy Iskandar) speaks from the cage.**

Rift, directed by Seret Scott at New York University Shubert Theatre (2009).

Photograph by Ella Bromblin (Courtesy photographer and NYU Graduate Acting Program)

I'll fix you, she said. I'll make you a star.

I thought, Sure. Okay. Why not? I've always wanted to be a star.

Anyway, it's not up to me. Is it?

He's refused my tongue, while he enters my body.

Lila smiles. She can't stop looking at me.

She closes in on my bruises.

Oh, I love this one, she says. It's got such terrible beauty.

I know her kind.

She wants a docile, wounded beast.

All right. I'll give.

I'll give you the best picture of suffering you're ever going to get.

10. WALKING WITH WATER

Morning. Celine and Ilona walk for hours. They each carry a large plastic container of water.

This is their mandatory morning task.

CELINE. I miss Fátima. We were a good team.

ILONA. You were, Celine.

CELINE. I liked talking to her. We talked all kinds of crap. You think she'll come back?

ILONA. Has to.

CELINE. Mama Sondra didn't give her an anklet. Not like us.

ILONA. No.

CELINE. Mama must've wanted her to get shot off somewhere.

ILONA. Just keep moving.

CELINE. You think Fátima's been shot?

ILONA. No.

CELINE. I dream about her being shot. I dream she's stuck in some hole with blood all over.

ILONA. Just keep moving.

CELINE. Why do I dream that?

ILONA. You're dreaming about something else.

CELINE. What do you mean?

ILONA. Look, my uncle would say, "Sometimes dreams deceive us; they make us think things are real when they're not." You can't go by what you dream.

CELINE. Your uncle sounds nice.

ILONA. He was a good man.

CELINE. You miss him? . . . I miss people. All the time. Sometimes I think I miss people I never even met.

ILONA. Celine.

CELINE. I got all this stuff in my head. Everything's . . . Your family get shot?

ILONA. Just keep moving.

CELINE. I only had my half-sister. They called her a wog. I don't know why they called her that. She was just in the kitchen making coffee. And they walked in and shot her. I wanted to stop them, but they held me down for a long time. All of them. Screwed me. I don't know who they were. Some boys up the road? They said they wanted to get rid of all the wogs. Do you think Fátima's a wog?

ILONA. We just have to get to the blue house, leave the water there, pick up the other container, and walk back.

CELINE. My arms hurt.

ILONA. When we stop, it gets worse.

CELINE. But I wanna stop. I wanna stop everything.

ILONA. Remember what Mama Sondra said.

CELINE. She got eyes on the road.

ILONA. Whole lotta eyes.

CELINE. And if they catch us restin' . . .

ILONA. . . . That's right.

CELINE. You think Mama Sondra does good by us?

ILONA. She does what she does.

CELINE. You'll leave her.

ILONA. No.

CELINE. You dream of leavin'. I hear you when you sleep.

ILONA. I don't dream of anything.

CELINE. You dream loud.

ILONA. Hush.

CELINE. Was Maurice your lover?

ILONA. Hush now.

CELINE. Was he a wog?

ILONA. Shut up.

CELINE. I wish I had a Maurice I could dream about leavin' with.

ILONA (*marking the path*). Half-way mark.

CELINE. What?

ILONA. Red stone on the road.

CELINE. Fátima used to dream.

ILONA. Fátima's not here.

CELINE. I hate mornings.

ILONA. Keep moving.

11. THE RULES OF FAIR TRADE

Exterior of bar area at train station. Alan and L'argent.

L'ARGENT. Fátima, is it? What kind of name's that?

ALAN. Just a name.

L'ARGENT. Sounds Catholic.

ALAN. You don't like her name, *l'argent*, change it. Deal's done, you put her in a van, ship her to Turkey . . .

L'ARGENT. Not so fast.

ALAN. Sorry?

L'ARGENT. Deal ain't done, friend.

ALAN. What?

L'ARGENT. Deal ain't fuckin' done. You owe us, remember? Last shipment. Was shite.

ALAN. Well, that was a . . .

L'ARGENT. Fuck-up? You talk and talk, Alan.

ALAN. I've given you . . .

L'ARGENT. Yeah. You've given us all sorts of girls. Especially that last one.

ALAN. You'll get everything you need with this one.

L'ARGENT. Is that right? What's this Fátima worth, then?

ALAN. Fair markup.

L'ARGENT. Said that last time.

ALAN (*memory blur*). Huh?

L'ARGENT. (You) Stood there, plain as day, and said, oh, yeah, she's a beaut, she'll do you plenty.

ALAN. All right, look . . .

Alan's face goes blank. A moment.

L'ARGENT. . . . You're in the fuckin moon, friend? Going out on a parade?

ALAN. No, I'm . . .

L'ARGENT. Thinking up a story for me, eh? Little bed-sit fable? If this Fátima don't work, mate, that's it. Game over. You owe us enough already.

ALAN. Look, I told you . . .

L'ARGENT. Good legs, ripe ass. Yeah. Struck gold with this one.

ALAN. *L'argent* . . . Fátima's perfect.

L'ARGENT. That's a big, juicy word, Alan. (You) do her?

ALAN. She gives. She takes.

L'ARGENT. Do her plenty, eh?

ALAN. I'm a reasonable man.

L'ARGENT. Flesh of fucking reason.

ALAN. We all go the way of flesh, L'Argent. You're abstaining?

L'ARGENT. Screw that. . . . So, perfect package . . . Well, as long as you're good for it . . .

ALAN. Such an ass.

L'ARGENT. Hey. We're friends, right? . . . (I'll) pickup 'round four, then.

ALAN. Make it three.

L'ARGENT. Fucking early.

ALAN. Set your alarm, friend.

L'ARGENT. Same place as always, then.

ALAN. Make it the gallery.

L'ARGENT. What?

ALAN. Slaughterhouse.

L'ARGENT. Won't go there.

ALAN. Sorry?

L'ARGENT. Don't go to that district. Got skinned there once.

ALAN. Wasting my time.

Alan walks away.

L'ARGENT. Alan . . . Alan!

(*Alan stops.*)

All right.

ALAN. Scared rabbit. . . . Remember: three. In the a.m.

L'ARGENT. Hey. What's in the gallery?

ALAN. Just art, friend. Fucking art. (*Exits.*)

12. THE COST OF WAITING

Twilight. The squat/shelter. Sondra waits. Nicky drinks. A short while after they've had sex.

NICKY. Sit with me.

She sits on his lap.

SONDRA. You're like a little boy, Nicky. Coddle me, coddle me.

NICKY. I'm not a boy.

SONDRA. I gave you drink, what more do you want?

NICKY. More time.

SONDRA. It'll cost you.

(*He hands her some money.*)

Need more than this.

(*He hands her some more.*)

NICKY. You're bleeding me dry.

SONDRA. With all your new government friends? You can afford it.

NICKY. We'll see how long this government lasts. All my so-called friends could be out on the street tomorrow. . . . I love your thighs.

SONDRA. What's this relish?

NICKY. Happy.

SONDRA. Happier still when Ilona and Celine get here.

NICKY. Three for one?

SONDRA. Not likely.

NICKY. I go out. I walk into any wog's house. I get my way.

SONDRA. That word is not allowed in my house.

NICKY. Come on. Uncle Nicky makes your day.

SONDRA. Uncle Nicky's full of shit. . . . They're late.

NICKY. They're on track.

SONDRA. Not all.

NICKY. You lose one?

SONDRA. Fátima.

NICKY. Oh, I liked her.

Celine walks in.

SONDRA. Where you been? It's dark already.

CELINE. Took a while.

SONDRA. Where's Ilona?

(Celine doesn't respond. She goes straight to her area of the squat to change her clothes.)

Celine.

CELINE. Don't know.

SONDRA. What'd you mean?

CELINE. We were talkin'. We were talkin'.

SONDRA. And what? She left you chatterin'?

NICKY. She's had a long day. Haven't you, sweet?

SONDRA. Answer me.

CELINE. We were just talkin'.

SONDRA. What'd you take? I see it in your eyes. What you doin' on the road? Losin' time on my time?

CELINE. She was right behind me. I swear. She was right behind me.

SONDRA. . . . Go on. Nicky's been waiting.

NICKY. I've time.

SONDRA. What do you think this is? Go. Take her out back with the stink of the rotten sheep.

Nicky and Celine head out to back of the squat/shelter.

13. AND A TRICK OF THE LOCK

Twilight. Disused area at back end of train station. Ilona and Bevy, the fixer.

BEVY (*undoes the lock on the anklet*). All set.

ILONA. This enough, Bevy?

Ilona hands Bevy Alan's watch. Bevy inspects it.

Zulem said you'd take it.

BEVY. Zulem says all sorts of things.

ILONA. Is it enough, Bevy?

BEVY. Don't talk much for a whore.

ILONA. I don't have time.

BEVY. Me? I got all the time in the world.

ILONA. Get off.

BEVY. Just a touch.

ILONA. Let go. (*Pulls out knife.*)

BEVY. Knife girl. Like at the circus? My cousin used to work the circus. He did all kinds of acts. Real good on the high wire. Real balancer. Everyone thought, oh yeah, he'll go far. But one day he slipped. Just like that. Fell off the wire. He was dreaming, you see. Dreaming of all the old cities of the world and the way they used to be. Broke his skull right open with dreaming.

ILONA. I don't dream.

BEVY. Is that right?

ILONA (*all business*). . . . Put your hand in.

BEVY. Girl, I just wanted to touch your face. A caress. Simple.

A moment.

ILONA. All right.

Bevy does so. A moment. Ilona starts to walk away.

BEVY. You know, Mama Sondra and me go way back. Before the war.

ILONA. You work for her?

BEVY. Once.

ILONA. She can't—

BEVY. Hey. Zulem sent you. I do what she says. I know who she loves.

Ilona walks away. Bevy watches her go.

14. IN THE PALACE DARK

After midnight. The silver loft. Beatrice sits in the dark. Alan enters. He doesn't see Beatrice.

ALAN. Dammit. Where's the—?

Beatrice lights a cigarette.

BEATRICE. Power's gone.

ALAN. What?

BEATRICE. Went out. About an hour ago.

ALAN. Did you call the—?

BEATRICE. They said it'd be a few hours.

ALAN. Fucking shit.

Slant of light through the window: perhaps from a battery-operated hurricane lantern in a neighbor's window across the way.

BEATRICE. How was the club?

ALAN. Dead. Fucking dead. . . . Smoking again?

BEATRICE. Yes.

ALAN. Nasty habit.

> *Alan snorts from his vial of heroin.*

BEATRICE. Keeping all the junk to yourself?

ALAN. I thought you didn't have a taste.

BEATRICE. Give.

> *He hands her vial. She snorts. A moment.*

ALAN. War zone out there.

BEATRICE. What?

ALAN. Sometimes it's as if nothing's changed.

> *Slight flicker of light (power surge). Alan looks at his new watch.*

BEATRICE. You've an appointment?

ALAN. Later.

BEATRICE. Transit day.

ALAN. Yes.

BEATRICE. I'll miss Fátima. Such a pliant creature.

ALAN. . . . I'm burning up.

BEATRICE. I'll get you a drink. Dark and Stormy.

ALAN (*sweetly*). How is it you always know what I want?

BEATRICE. That's why you married me.

ALAN. Dirty girl.

> (*They kiss.*)
>
> . . . I'm sorry if things have been a little . . .
>
> *Alan caresses her.*

BEATRICE. One dark and stormy coming up.

ALAN. Love you.

BEATRICE. Lemon, all right? We're out of lime.

ALAN. Lemon's fine.

> (*Light [power] returns.*)
>
> Light.

BEATRICE. Comes and goes.

ALAN. Fucking country.

BEATRICE. You know how it is. Takes forever to get anything back to anything.

Beatrice prepares drinks. Alan heads toward box. Clicks remote.

ALAN. Fucking hell.

BEATRICE. Sorry?

ALAN. Where's—? (*Goes within, toward unseen area of loft, from off*) Where's—?

BEATRICE. What?

ALAN. Fátima.

BEATRICE. I let her go.

ALAN (*walks in*). What?

BEATRICE. Freed her from captivity; she's back out in the wild again.

ALAN. . . . What do you think this is? Some game?

BEATRICE. You can get another wretched orphan somewhere.

ALAN. . . . how many times have I told you? . . . This is business, Beatrice. Fucking business.

(*He hits her. Beatrice falls.*)

What do you think happens now? What do you think happens to the courier when he doesn't produce the goddamn merchandise? Fucking wog. You're all alike.

(*Alan kicks her. Sontile emerges from the area, unseen. Sontile restrains Alan.*)

SONTILE. That's enough.

Alan struggles to wrest free from Sontile.
A messy, wild fight ensues between them.
As Alan and Sontile thrash about.

ALAN. Old-school ambush?

SONTILE. You hit her again, I'll kill you.

ALAN. You love her, Sontile? You love sweet, dirty Beatrice? She's a good fuck, but don't get your hopes up. She's nothing more than that.

SONTILE. Cocksucker.

ALAN. Monkey bitch.

After a while, Sontile finally manages to get Alan into a firm stranglehold.

SONTILE. Apologize, motherfucker.

ALAN. What for?

Alan struggles. Sontile holds him down, putting pressure on.

SONTILE. Apologize.

ALAN. . . . Sorry.

SONTILE. What?

ALAN. I'm sorry . . . Beatrice.

SONTILE. Good boy. Good monkey bitch talkin'. (*Calls out*) Beatrice.

BEATRICE. Right here.

Beatrice starts to tie Alan up.

ALAN. Fuck.

SONTILE. Easy now. This is just business. (*To Beatrice*) Tighter on the hands.

She does so.

ALAN. I'll have you arrested.

SONTILE. For what? I'm a patriot, motherfucker. I've shed blood for this country. What have you done?

ALAN. You've no right—

Beatrice gags him.

SONTILE. There now. Monkey bitch. We're going to do things proper, right? Just like you. No mess. No fuss. No trace.

Sontile grabs Alan and leads him to the door. Alan resists. Sontile hits Alan with enough force to knock him out. He exits with Alan. Beatrice follows them out, closing door behind her.

2:45 a.m. In the foreground, in the slaughterhouse/gallery, Lila sorts through photos from the Fátima (in tears) photo "session." She's trying to choose which one will become source image for the large-scale over-painting process. She hums to herself softly, perhaps a fado, as she works. Sontile walks in from within.

SONTILE. It's late. You should get some sleep.

LILA. I can't.

SONTILE (*refers to reworking of Fátima's image*). Fátima's too beautiful, eh?

LILA. I look at her and look at her and all I see is myself.

SONTILE. It's a good picture.

LILA. You think?

SONTILE. It's good. It works.

LILA. It has an effect.

SONTILE. Isn't that what you want?

LILA. I don't know.

SONTILE. You should get some sleep. Go on. I'll clean up.

Abrupt noise from outside.

LILA. What was that?

SONTILE. I'll go see.

(*Lila hums to herself softly, perhaps a fado, as she keeps working.
Sontile goes to back door of the gallery, L'Argent is seen.
Sontile pulls L'Argent away from view.
Muffled exchange of words [a transaction] is heard, and then the sound of a van driving off. Slight pause. Sontile reappears.*)

No worries.

LILA. What was that all about?

SONTILE. Nothin'. A friend.

LILA. What friend?

SONTILE. He's takin' his family up the road, near the border. I promised I'd get him some food. For the ride.

LILA. You're kind.

SONTILE. Just things he can't get there. That's all.

LILA. Figs and cherries?

SONTILE. Stop.

LILA. I wish I'd met you earlier.

SONTILE. Don't be sweet on me. We're fine like this. Friends.

LILA. More than that.

SONTILE. Lila . . .

LILA. I know. Get some sleep, girl. Stop being a sentimental mess . . . Do me a favor? (*Hands him snapshot of Ilona.*) Find her for me.

SONTILE. Who's this?

LILA. Just a girl.

SONTILE (*looks at writing on back of photo*). Ilona. . . . What's she?

LILA. Nothing. Portrait, you know. For a friend. Just like you.

16. TOWARD THE LIGHT

Ilona walks down the road, away from the city. She sings to keep herself going.

no mercy (bitter sea)

ILONA. Watch me burn
    Watch the river of me
    Go down.

    Send a soul
    Alight the ground

    'Cause when I go
    No mercy please.

    Here and now
    In the bitter sea.

    Here and now
    In the bitter sea.
    Ilona keeps walking down the road . . .

17. THE WILD DOGS OF NIGHT

Some time has passed. Night. In the country. Ilona is sleeping, curled up, on the ground. Her shoes and jacket have been stolen somewhere along the way. She trembles in her sleep. Occasionally she mumbles. Chorus of Glue Kids is heard in distance. First Glue Kid is the eldest of the pack, late teens.

FIRST GLUE KID. Fuckin' whacked that gyp.

SECOND GLUE KID. Fuckin' scolded that mutherfucka.

FIRST GLUE KID. Had it comin'.

THIRD GLUE KID. What you say?

FIRST GLUE KID. Had it fuckin' comin', huffin our sticky. Got no right to our shit.

> (*Chorus of Glue Kids is now seen on the path. On a glue high. First Glue Kid comes upon Ilona.*)

> What's this? City skank sleepin' in our yard?

THIRD GLUE KID (*catching up*). Looks a girl.

SECOND GLUE KID. Woggy shit. Eat her up.

FIRST GLUE KID. Take her. Fuckin' gyp.

> *The Glue Kids overtake Ilona, a strange, taunting, snarling attack that results in her being carried away by the pack. Light shift.*

18. WHAT USE IS A CUP?

In the country. In the small room of an old house.
Scant sunlight comes in through makeshift curtains.
Alan sits on the floor.
He is blindfolded. His hands are tied behind his back.
His legs are not bound.
He's been stripped of his clothes, and left with only a ragged pair of pants.
There's a small cup on the floor, at slight distance from him.
He shivers, makes intense kicking motions (from heroin withdrawal).
Common noises are heard from inside the house.

The kind of noises objects for everyday use make.
Alan shifts position. He can't stop shivering. He makes sounds.
Suddenly, a small slot in the door to the room opens.
A cupful of water is poured through.
A futile gesture, since the water will never make it into the small cup
that rests on the floor, away from the door. The slot shuts.
Alan moves, as best he can, trying to locate the trace of water on the floor.
Faint sustenance. Light shift.

19. A LITTLE PLEA (ABANDON SONG)

Morning. On the road, Celine talks to herself.

CELINE. Must've done somethin' wrong.
Must've done somethin' very wrong for Ilona to leave me just
like that.
Should've been more quiet.
Should've given her things.
That weird brooch that guy with the razor tattoo gave me.
I saw her looking at it.
Should've just given it. Wasn't worth shit.
Just a weird brooch. Sparkly.
Everyone leaves me.
Except for Mama.
She's always with me.
She says
Go with that one,
And that one . . .
And they all say,
You're so good, Celine;
You're a star, baby,
While they put their fires out on me.
I'm no star.
Everybody leaves me.

Time has passed. In the country. Night. Ruins of a house. Second Glue Kid stares out, dazed, replaying fragments of a video war-game in mind, his fingers cradle and maneuver an invisible joystick, occasionally he makes "war-game noises." Third Glue Kid sifts through a small pile of broken things, off to one side, pulls out anything that's shiny or glittery: pieces of fabric, etc. She hums to herself softly. First Glue Kid rests, down from his high. Ilona is collar-locked to an extended chain that's bolted to one of the stable fixtures of the ruined house. There's a feeling that they've settled in a routine here. Pause.

FIRST GLUE KID. Hella rain come down soon. I can feel it. If rain comes, we gotta find us another place.

SECOND GLUE KID. Rain rain go away . . .

ILONA. I need to piss. I need to piss.

FIRST GLUE KID. Keep her in line.

Third Glue Kid smacks Ilona very lightly like a dog that's misbehaved.

THIRD GLUE KID. Bad pretty.

FIRST GLUE KID. Gotta teach it manners. Manners have been lost in this world. Shame. 'Cause what's a world without manners? Fuckin' ruin.

ILONA. Please. I need . . .

First Glue Kid empties pants pockets, checking his personal stash/inventory.

FIRST GLUE KID. Let's see what we got ourselves today . . .

THIRD GLUE KID. Toys?

FIRST GLUE KID. Crazy girl. I ain't getting you any toys shit. Go on. Get out of my face.

(*First Glue Kid sorts through items.*)

Tie clip, pen, mobile crap . . .

Among the items is Maurice's boat charm amulet. Ilona sees it.

ILONA. Where'd you—?

FIRST GLUE KID. Huh?

ILONA. Where'd you—?

FIRST GLUE KID. What you on about?

ILONA. Where'd you get that?

FIRST GLUE KID (*holding up amulet*). This skank thing? Kept this. Off a wog. After I cut his tongue out. After he bled to death in this hole.

ILONA. Sonofabitch sonofabitch sonofabitch.

FIRST GLUE KID. Little boat, little tiny silly boat. Like this little piece of metal could do anythin' for his wog ass. (*Pockets amulet.*)

ILONA (*thrashes at him*). Fuck shit motherfucker.

FIRST GLUE KID. Steady now. Steady now, skank.

ILONA. What'd you do with him? Where's his body?

SECOND GLUE KID (*coming slightly out of dazed state*). What woggy . . .?

ILONA. Where's his body, motherfucker?

THIRD GLUE KID (*covering her ears*). Loud, pretty. Too loud.

FIRST GLUE KID. All I done . . . You listenin'? I was just doin' my duty. Understand? Like all us soldiers in the damn war.

ILONA. Where's his—?

FIRST GLUE KID. And no tears. They ruin things. I hate ruin.

ILONA (*toward First Glue Kid*). sonofabitch sonofabitch . . .

FIRST GLUE KID (*to Second Glue Kid*). Come on. Let's go.

First Glue Kid and Second Glue Kid exit. Ilona cries. Third Glue Kid tries to comfort her.

THIRD GLUE KID. Good pretty. Wanna play? Wanna kiss me?. . . I think it's hungry.

(*Third Glue Kid finds empty bag of potato chips and gives it to Ilona.*)

Eat, pretty. Eat.

Early evening. In the country. In the small room of the old house. Alan is still blindfolded, hands tied behind his back. He can't sleep. He has frequent muscle spasms.

Door opens. A Man in Tired Hat, wearing simple clothes appears. Door closes.

Man observes Alan for a moment.

MAN IN TIRED HAT. You're all right, son?

ALAN. Wha . . .

MAN IN TIRED HAT. There now. Come on.

Man takes heroin vial out of his pocket.

ALAN. Wha . . . wha . . . wha . . .

MAN IN TIRED HAT. Sniff.

ALAN. No . . . no . . .

MAN IN TIRED HAT. Easy now.

ALAN (*sniffs*). Fuckin' . . .

MAN IN TIRED HAT. Easy.

(Does his best to steady Alan. He sings to him in Spanish.)

Constante Soldado (Canción de Guerra) / Steady On (A War Lullaby)

Constante, hijo de la paz (Steady on, my good tin son)
Constante, buen soldado (Steady on, good soldier)
Constante, todos hacia el mar (Steady on, the sea wails on)
La orilla (nos) salvara (The shore will save us all one day)

ALAN. . . . Mother . . .

MAN IN TIRED HAT. Quiet. I need . . .

Man pulls down Alan's pants.

ALAN. . . . Wha . . .

MAN IN TIRED HAT. Like church.

Man penetrates Alan from behind. Lights shift.
In second frame of action, in the ruins of the house where the glue dogs live,

*Ilona is leashed, trying to sleep. She shivers. She calls out nondescript
words.
Third Dog approaches, and covers her gently with a thin blanket.
Third Dog kisses Ilona lightly and sings an ancient lullaby. A
moment.
Time shift.
Man in Tired Hat, having finished forced sexual encounter with
Alan, rests,
and sings quietly to himself (barely audible).
Alan shivers slightly, dazed, spent.*

DRUNK ON YOU

*Evening. In the city. In the makeshift squat/shelter. Sondra is drunk.
She's a steady, contained drunk, not a messy one. Nicky is with her.*

NICKY. Got the job.

SONDRA. Government man, eh?

NICKY. It's a start. With this job, I can make my way.

SONDRA. Come and save me, then? That your plan? I'm not setting
up house, *cheri*.

NICKY. Hey . . . What's wrong, baby?

SONDRA. Mind's all . . .

NICKY. . . . Thinkin 'bout Celine? Sondra, she'll be fine. You took her
to hospital, right?

SONDRA. . . . I don't know what I'm doin' anymore.

NICKY. What'd you mean?

SONDRA. She was tired all the time, Nicky, sick with those headaches
of hers . . . Had to . . .

NICKY. Had to what? . . . Sondra. Look at me. Had to what? . . . You
sell her off?

SONDRA. She wasn't makin' anything. Wasn't gonna make anything.

NICKY. So, you thought, make one last thing, while I still got the
chance?

SONDRA. Look, I'm dead sick just thinkin' about . . .

NICKY. Wasn't sick at the time, though. Who'd you sell her to? Where'd you put her?

SONDRA. They go cross the border . . .

NICKY. Put her with the dogs? In one of those killing houses? She'll be dead in a week.

SONDRA. She won't.

NICKY. Good Sondra with her good heart, eh?

SONDRA. Stop.

NICKY. What you done, baby? What the hell you done?

SONDRA. Nicky . . .

NICKY. Get off . . . off me!

SONDRA. There was nothing I could do, Nicky. She was sick, she was . . .

NICKY. You better get this house in order, Sondra. Y'hear me? Get Celine back.

SONDRA. Nicky . . .

NICKY. If you want a house . . .

Nicky exits. A moment. Sondra walks away.
Shift to the small room in the old house.
Man in Tired Hat unties Alan's hands.
Man in Tired Hat takes off Alan's blindfold,
And holds Alan's face in his hands for a brief moment, and slips away.
The door locks behind him.
Alan is left in the small room. Lights shift.

23. MOURNING NO ONE

Late evening. In the city. In the slaughterhouse/gallery.
Non-English-language expansive vocal music is heard (preferably Ana Moura's "Fado de pessoa" from her 2006 album Aconteceu*).*

Lila moves to the music. She is high. She has already selected which Fátima (in tears) photograph will become the source image for the final over-painting. She paints.
After short while, she becomes upset, as if she's in mourning, and not sure for whom or why.
She cuts off music (from CD player or other device).
Fátima appears in the doorway. Beaten, messed-up, lost: in a state.

FÁTIMA. Mom?. . . Mommy?

LILA. Fátima?

Lila goes to her.

FÁTIMA. Mommy.

Lila holds Fátima.

24. LESSONS TENDERED (IN SIMULTANEOUS FRAMES, OUT OF TIME)

In the country. In the small room of the old house.
Alan remains (untied, un-blindfolded).
A shaft of sunlight streams in.

ALAN. Mom . . . Mommy . . . Mom . . .
They were six today.
They smelled of liquor.
I drank them in.

In the country. In the ruins of the old house. Ilona remains, leashed.

ILONA. They were two today.
They smelled of liquor.
I drank them in.

ALAN. I count hands, fingers.

ILONA. I trace the night with my eyes.

ALAN. The sun.
Sometimes I think I see it through the cloth—a little speck.

ILONA. Holy god fuck.

ALAN. Creeping up my leg, like a little creature.

ILONA (*seeing him in mind*). . . . Maurice?

ALAN. Listen, it says.

ILONA. Don't listen to anything.

ALAN. Keep quiet. Like church.

> (*In the distance, Sondra is seen in low light, singing a hymn. She mourns Celine's absence.*)

> "Call to Heaven"

SONDRA. Where I go, Heavens above will follow.
Where I go, Heavens will allow.
As I go, the world in distant slumber.
Praise Heaven, won't be much longer now.

> *She keeps singing, repeating the refrain under* . . .

ILONA. And I pray.

ALAN. And for a while, everything fades
And it's just . . .

ILONA. A sky of rage.

ALAN. And I think
I could leave, I could leave this

ILONA. I could find what's left of you
If I just listen close

ALAN. The earth rumbles

ILONA. Tell me, Maurice.
Tell me where you are. Give me your body.

ALAN. My limbs shiver
And I remember how things used to be

ILONA. We're all innocent here

ALAN. Innocent as a drop of rain.

> *In the background, Sondra's singing subsides. Her image fades.*

ILONA. And I lift my eyes up to heaven again
And I think

ALAN. *And I think*

ILONA. *And I think*

IMAGE 5.3 **Alan (Michael Schantz) in abjected state.**

Rift, directed by Seret Scott at New York University Shubert Theatre (2009).

Photograph by Ella Bromblin (Courtesy photographer and NYU Graduate Acting Program).

ALAN. *And I think*

ILONA. *And I think*

ALAN. *And I think*

Tears fuck hold piss down tears can't stop . . .

And for a little while it's just the sound of Alan's weeping and Ilona's stifled sobs.

And then, footsteps are heard inside the house where Alan's kept.

And I do. What the creature tells me.

ILONA. Eat the floor.

ALAN. Teach me

what I should see.

Time shift.

25. ROUGH PASSAGE / AND THEY ESCAPE THROUGH
THE FLAMES (VISION)

Seconds later. In first frame of action, door to the room bursts open.
Two Masked Figures in everyday clothes come in.

FIRST MASKED FIGURE. Up. Up.

ALAN. Where—?

FIRST MASKED FIGURE. Move.

ALAN. Huh?

SECOND MASKED FIGURE. Useless bitch.

> *Second Masked Figure strikes Alan's leg, disabling him. Alan*
> *screams.*

FIRST MASKED FIGURE. Move it!

ALAN. Where—?

SECOND MASKED FIGURE. Trip. Going on a trip.

> *Alan is dragged out by the Masked Figures. A moment.*
> *In second frame of action, in the country. Ruins of the old house.*
> *Ilona at very edge of leash.*
> *Maurice appears (a vision).*

ILONA. Maurice?

MAURICE. Shh. Don't let them see.

> *Maurice undoes Ilona's collar and leash.*

ILONA. Maurice . . .

> *Ilona goes to embrace Maurice. He stops her gently.*

MAURICE. We don't have time.

> *Ilona and Maurice walk away.*

PART 3

26. AGAINST THE COMMON GOOD

Train Announcement (voiceover) is heard: "Northbound trains back on
schedule. Stand-by." Mid-day. Exterior. Bar area of train station. Nicky

is on his break from his government job. He's checking his mobile phone.
Sondra approaches.

SONDRA. Looks like rain.

NICKY. You shouldn't be here.

SONDRA. Can't be seen with Mama Sondra out here?

NICKY. I'm on a break, baby.

SONDRA. Scared what your lil' government friends might say?

NICKY. You know what I mean.

SONDRA. Missed you, *cheri*.

NICKY. Been busy.

SONDRA. Too busy for Sondra's thighs?

NICKY. Not here.

SONDRA. Nobody can see.

NICKY. . . . Enough.

A moment. He hands her some money.

SONDRA. You think all I want . . .? . . . Nicky . . . It's been a long time.

NICKY. A lot needs to be done in this country.

SONDRA. My place, Nicky . . . it's a wreck.

NICKY. It's been like that . . .

SONDRA. Gettin' worse.

NICKY. Bad for business, baby?

SONDRA. Could use a new place. Yes.

NICKY. I can't do that.

SONDRA. You've friends.

NICKY. Look, I told you . . .

SONDRA. I don't want to work for you. I just want a decent place.
Like anyone else.

NICKY. . . . I'll see what I can do.

SONDRA. You're kind, *cheri*.

NICKY. . . . I'm late.

He walks away.

Day. Ilona at edge of road, faint . . .

ILONA. Road turns.
An invisible line of red thread escapes . . .
You whisper, Maurice.
Can't make out . . .
Can't hear what you . . .

Zulem comes upon Ilona on the dirt road.

ZULEM. You're shivering, chil'.

ILONA. Huh?

ZULEM. Put this on. Come on.

Zulem hands Ilona dress and boots.

ILONA. Leave me alone, Zulem. I don't need your fucking hands.

ZULEM. Tired, chil'. So tired. You need rest.

ILONA. I don't need anything.

ZULEM. Given up on the world?

ILONA. I lost him. I lost Maurice.

ZULEM. You saw him, then? In dream?

ILONA. Came to me as real as day. Could feel his hands, fingers, didn't
want to let go, but I couldn't . . . couldn't . . .

ZULEM. There now. Rest your head.

ILONA. Is he with me, Zulem? Seek him out, you said. And what? . . .
I don't even know where his body . . .

ZULEM. In time . . .

ILONA. I want to bury him. I just want to . . .

ZULEM. He could be scattered all over the earth. Stomach in the
mountains. Tongue in a little stream.

ILONA. You lie to me.

ZULEM. What I see is not my possession. I give.

ILONA. Saint Zulem, eh?

ZULEM. I'm foolish to you. With foolish ways. My family—full of
seers, healers. *Mémère—*

She'd come upon a man with blisters from head to toe with disease and heal him with nothing more than a simple water glass and a cheap cigar. With no more than her mere breath and a bit of smoke. You think the gods choose only the so-called "good"? The gods recognize we're ALL in this world.

ILONA. Gods don't know shit.

ZULEM. I put my hands on you. I give you peace.

ILONA. Lay off.

ZULEM (*spell begins*). Breath, breath . . . like a good chil' again.

ILONA. I am not a good child. There's nothing good in me.

ZULEM. Breath, breath . . . like an innocent child again.

ILONA. I'm not.

ZULEM. Breath, breath . . . all will be forgiven.

ILONA. I don't want forgiveness. Blast me to hell. Send me ruin. It's what I deserve.

ZULEM. . . . This not your heart.

ILONA. What do you know of my heart?

ZULEM (*vision*). A church. In sky.
A boat. On water.
A girl walking. Uncle.
Sand under feet. Ocean and memory.
Girl full of promise. Girl looks up. Uncle.
Girl reaches. Hands. Mercy.
Girl looks. Maurice.

ILONA. Maurice.

ZULEM. Girl waits. Bag. Factory.
Girl leaves. Bag. Sound.
Girl cries. Red.

ILONA. Yes.

ZULEM. Girl cries. Maurice.

ILONA. Maurice.

ZULEM. Girl runs. Dreams.
Uncle's eyes.

Kind. Mercy.

Hands. Prayer.

Forgiveness.

Ocean crests.

(*In the near distance, Maurice is seen* [*a conjured image*].)

Weight of bones. Weight of death.

Zulem reveals the boat-charm necklace.

ILONA. How did you—?

ZULEM (*puts necklace on her*). Rest now. You have days and days to go, days and days like this.

ILONA. . . . Everything's burning.

ZULEM. World goes, mind goes. Spirit has its day.

Time shift. The sound of gunfire in the distance . . .

MAURICE (*through memory*). Ilona, Ilona.

28. MERCY (IN TIME BEFORE / MEMORY STREAM)

In real time, in time before, as they're on the run, in a field.

MAURICE. Ilona.

Ilona walks into her memory.

ILONA. I'm right here, Maurice.

MAURICE. Won't be long, right? Say it. Say we'll be okay.

ILONA. I think there were people in there.

MAURICE. What?

ILONA. In the factory.

MAURICE. What are you—?

ILONA. I heard voices, rustling . . .

MAURICE. There was no one. I told you. Just weapons. Nothing else.

ILONA. I could've sworn . . .

MAURICE. Don't worry your mind now. It's over. We just go a bit farther, and we'll meet my friend on the other side, and we'll start again. (*Coughs.*)

ILONA. You should see a doctor.

MAURICE. Just need to rest. That's all.

ILONA. Could hear them screaming.

MAURICE. Hey. Hey. (*Caresses her.*)

ILONA. What'd I do, Maurice? How many people did I—?

MAURICE. Shh. Shh.

ILONA. Don't.

MAURICE. You did what had to be done.

ILONA. If I killed a hundred, two hundred . . . my conscience should be fucking clear?

MAURICE. Ilona.

ILONA. Don't.

MAURICE. Leave, then. Go back. I'll go cross the border alone.

ILONA. They'll kill you.

MAURICE. I'm dead anyway. We're all dead.

Sound of gunfire in distance escalates into . . . time shift . . .

29. STRANGE PIETY

In present time, day, exterior, Ilona stands before the remains of the bombed-out factory. She reads the names (of the dead) written on what's left of one of the walls.

ILONA. Jairo, Adela, Hassan, Yasmin . . .

Lila is revealed near one of the ruins, camera in hand.

LILA. Were they your family?

ILONA. What?

LILA. The dead.

ILONA. No.

LILA. This used to be a factory. They used to make uniforms here for soldiers, nurses; during the war, it became a kind of storage site for weapons and the like. Then it got bombed. There were people inside. They were hiding. I don't think the bombers knew that. Those names on the wall . . . those are the names of the people that were in there.

Ilona is suddenly overcome with emotion.

LILA. They were family, then?

ILONA. No . . . it's . . .

LILA. I knew one of them. We were close. I suppose that's why I still come by here. Record what's left of the fucking wall before it all gets torn down. Fewer and fewer people want to remember what things were like. (*Takes another photo.*)

ILONA. My uncle, he loved taking pictures. He was a lousy photographer. He always made mistakes. But he said it didn't matter, as long as you remembered why you were taking the picture in the first place.

LILA. Sounds a good man.

ILONA. He was.

LILA. This area's going to be a hotel now. That's the rumor anyway. In a few years time we won't recognize this city. Won't recognize it at all. . . . You're trembling.

ILONA. I'm okay. I'm okay. I just . . . I don't know what I . . . I should go.

Ilona turns. She is confused, lost, not sure where to go.

LILA. Low valley. You should try there first to find who you're looking for.

ILONA. I'm not—

LILA. I'm sorry. I thought . . . Sometimes people ask, y'know, look for their . . . Sometimes I come here and think about everyone that's gone. I think if I could just have their pictures, I can prove they were here. And then sometimes I just write down names on the wall, the names of those I remember, the names of those I met once that are no longer . . . You want to write a name?

ILONA. . . . Yes.

(*Lila hands her marker or the like. Ilona writes discreetly, in small letters, on the wall. A moment.*)

Low valley, you said?

LILA. Try there first. Yes.

(*Ilona walks away.*)

Ilona?

ILONA. How'd you—?

LILA. Take care. Take good care.

(*Ilona walks away. Lila looks at wall, reads the name Ilona's inscribed.*)

Maurice.

A moment.

30. LOOKING FOR THE MOON

Late afternoon. Slaughterhouse/gallery. Lila sits, looking through her things. Sontile tends to Fátima.

SONTILE. Come on. Drink up.

FÁTIMA. Hot.

SONTILE. (It's) good for you.

LILA. I thought you said you'd take her to hospital.

SONTILE. . . . You look a little spooked.

LILA. I'm fine. Is there any chocolate, Sontile?

SONTILE. There's been nothing decent in the market for weeks. You're craving?

LILA. I just want something sweet.

SONTILE. Kiss me.

LILA. You're foul.

SONTILE. I thought you liked it . . .

FÁTIMA. Sticky moon. Happy there.

LILA. . . . We should get her some proper care.

SONTILE. I got friends in the country. They can look after her.

LILA. . . . Making plans with Fátima?

SONTILE. What are you talking about?

LILA. I asked you to find Ilona, right? A simple favor. And what'd you say? "Friends in the country." Every day . . . (I'm) trying to do something, trying to make some sense of . . . and you're here . . . looking to put Fátima in a van, take her God knows where . . .

SONTILE. What is this? Another one of your tantrums?

LILA. Get out of here.

SONTILE. Lila . . . You're beautiful.

LILA. Let go. Of me.

SONTILE. . . . Over a fucking bitch? . . . Screw your art. Fucking screw it.

He exits. Pause.

FÁTIMA. Moon.

LILA. You like the moon? My camera's like a little moon. You know, when I was a girl, I'd make these circles with wire . . . The circles needed to be just big enough so that a bird could come through and catch itself inside it. I'd tie it to a branch low on the ground and wait. Sometimes I'd wait for hours. But by end of day, a bird would always come through, its gorgeous feathers fixed in the slim wire.

Lila continues speaking, but we only see her mouth move as: close-up on Fátima. Interior. Intimate address. It is as if Fátima is watching herself, as Lila takes her photo.

FÁTIMA. I watch her mouth move.
A story about her childhood,
as if I'd know what it was like.
Smiles.
Full of her story.
I think about
the boys that came up behind me,
the boys with hard fists and steel toes,
that cut my flesh open
in the dead of night.
And I dream about

some swell party I'll be at some day
where no one
will recognize me

A moment. Time shift.

LILA. Come. We should go to hospital.

Lila helps Fátima up. They walk away.

31. BURY THEM TO BE SILENT

Night. In the silver loft, Beatrice and Sontile have just made love.

BEATRICE. Wonder if it's a villa.

SONTILE. What?

BEATRICE. Where Alan's been put.

SONTILE. Standard issue, I suppose. Grey walls. Bucket to piss in. Remorseful all a sudden?

BEATRICE. Just wondering.

SONTILE (*reveling in her*). Sweet Beatrice.

BEATRICE. . . . Want a drink?

SONTILE. No. I should get a move-on. It's late.

BEATRICE. I don't think we should see each other anymore, Sontile.

SONTILE. What?

BEATRICE. I've been thinking about it a lot, actually, and I think we should just stop.

SONTILE. But we've . . .

BEATRICE. I don't want to talk about it.

SONTILE. You don't wanna—? You think I can just be your puppy for a while and move on? All the shit work I've done for you. All the fucking shit.

BEATRICE. I'm grateful.

SONTILE. You owe me.

BEATRICE (*hands him an envelope with money*). Will this do?

SONTILE. . . . This your game?

BEATRICE. Sontile, I'm trying to be—

SONTILE. Whatever.

BEATRICE. Look, maybe we should . . .

SONTILE. Put Sontile in another war, another bunker, another window shooting some kid?

BEATRICE. That's not what I . . .

SONTILE. You're all the same.

BEATRICE. Sontile . . .

SONTILE (*Judas*). Fucking silver.

> *He exits, money in hand. A moment. She heads to bar area. She drinks.*
> *Then goes to door, as if she's remembered something she wanted to say to Sontile, when Alan staggers through the door.*

BEATRICE. What the—?

ALAN. Left me . . .

BEATRICE. Get out.

ALAN. Didn't know where else to . . .

BEATRICE. Get the fuck out of here, Alan.

ALAN. Beatrice . . .

BEATRICE. Out!

ALAN. Please.

> *He tries to hold onto her. She pushes him out, closes the door. Pause.*

BEATRICE. . . . Hell.

32. CARNIVOROUS VULTURES / BORGES'S CONFESSION

In the slaughterhouse/gallery, Lila is clearing the space. As she does so, Sondra walks in, observes for a moment.

SONDRA. Going somewhere?

LILA. Looking for scraps, Sondra?

SONDRA. I don't look, *cheri*.

LILA. No, you just find them and fuck them up, don't you?

SONDRA. Aicha . . .

LILA. Leave me be.

SONDRA. I told you . . .

LILA. What? . . . Find one of your girls? Is that why you've come all the way down here? And what if I did find her? What if I found her and told her to just walk away?

SONDRA. With everything you've done. You know, I still got a tongue, *cheri*.

LILA. Use it.

SONDRA. (You're) Above it all with your fuckin' art?

LILA. I'm rather below, as a matter of fact. See this place? Your beloved slaughterhouse? It's getting the crawler in the morning. It'll be all torn down. They're putting up another fuckin' hotel. So, all your little games, Sondra, all your stupid games . . . Do what you have to do. I don't care anymore.

A moment, as Sondra watches her put things away.

SONDRA. Where will you go?

LILA. I'll figure it out.

SONDRA. You know, I could . . .

LILA. Friends, Sondra? No.

A moment.

SONDRA (*refers to a small photo that Lila took of her that's in a stack about to be cleared way*). Can I have that?

LILA. Your face?

SONDRA. Memento, *cheri*.

LILA (*a moment of odd tenderness/recognition, as she hands her photo*). You look beat.

SONDRA. I'm fine, Lila. I'll be . . .

A moment. Sondra walks away.
Lila takes in the space, which is clear, save for one painting.
She turns it over. It is the completed over-painting of Fátima in Tears.
She looks at it. She takes out her recording device, turns it on.
Slight ambient sound. And then, the recording kicks in.
We hear Lila's voice, recorded earlier.

LILA (VOICEOVER). Look.
>What do you see?
>A girl?
>A construct?
>A transient being.
>This is the face of silence
>This is the face of last things.

She turns the painting, away from view, gathers her things, and leaves the painting in the space, as the recording continues . . .

>There's a story that'll go round.
>About a girl named Aicha.
>They'll say she killed a soldier one night after he raped her.
>They'll say she bombed a crumbling palace in the old city.
>They'll say all those people were flattened
>under her bomb
>and they'll say . . .
>This is the face of . . .

She exits. Static on the recording. Time shift.

33. BITTER PRESENCE (PASSAGE)

Ilona's journey to the low valley. As she journeys, Maurice is seen in background (a vision). He sings to her.

Low Valley

MAURICE. You walk along the yellow moon.
>You walk in paths of red.
>You walk as if the world is still.
>There is no place to rest.

>Oh bitter earth, surrender me.
>Find me in lower ground.
>Oh quiet song of lucid blood
>down in low valley.

>(*At the edge of the valley.*)

And when I wait,
I wait for you
down in low valley.

She holds out her hand. A gesture of prayer.
The sound of the world envelopes her. Time shift.

34. AND WHEN WE GO

The road. Alette carries water container on her head. She sings to herself
freely, joyfully.

down-bound train

ALETTE. Oh say don't you know can you see him
  he's comin on the down-bound train
  he's got shells on his eyes—

ILONA (*appears on the road*). Need a hand?

ALETTE. Don't got far. Just few more miles up the . . . (*Teeters.*)

ILONA. Let me. (*Helps her.*)

ALETTE. Just to the yellow house and back, 'cept—

ILONA. Arms get tired.

ALETTE. Yeah. Arms real tired. (*Ilona carries the container.*) You sure
  you don't—?

ILONA. No.

ALETTE. Thanks. . . . You from the city?

ILONA. Yes.

ALETTE. You look like from the city.

ILONA. How's someone from the city look?

ALETTE. I don't know. Like you.

ILONA. My uncle would say, "People are people; shouldn't matter
  where they're from."

ALETTE. That's weird.

ILONA. How's that?

ALETTE. Sounds weird . . . I hear it's pretty. Hear they're gonna make the city all new, put up all sorts of buildings and things.

ILONA. Maybe.

ALETTE. I seen pictures once. Of the city. From way back. Years and years ago. Black, white, and silver pictures. Looked so beautiful. I wish I was from the city. One day I'll go . . . What? You tired already? Give me, then. I'm used to it. I can walk for miles. My mama says, "Alette, you're stronger than any of the girls I've ever had. You're gonna be stronger than all of them."

(*A moment.*)

I say something wrong? Got a face.

ILONA. What?

ALETTE. Like them that been to the low valley.
Like all them when they come back down this road.
Some crying. Some like stone. Some just tired and not a word to them.
Lookin' for their people, lookin' for things gone.
I tell 'em, Nothin' in low valley. All there's burnt. Ash.
Bones just floatin' now. All along the water. All along and under.
I seen 'em. In pieces. Comin' up from the liquid blue . . .

ILONA. Yeah?

ALETTE. I call out. "Hey." Like they can hear me.
Mama said, "Hush. Quiet now."
I call out anyway. When I'm out here on the road . . .
I call out loud.
I don't care what Mama . . . I don't care what anybody . . .
Mine's floatin' in some water, I've a right to call out.

ILONA. Hey. Hey.

ALETTE. Yeah.

Ilona shouts to the world, releasing pain, rage . . .

ILONA (*extended, free, beyond herself*). Hey. Hey. Hey.

ALETTE. . . . That's right. . . .

ILONA. Hey . . .

ALETTE (*refers to water container*). Give me. . . . I gotta go to the yellow house. I gotta get back before sundown.

ILONA. You'll be all right?

ALETTE. Go on. Go.

> (*Alette walks down road with container on her head; she sings*
> *"down-bound train."*)

> He got shells on his eyes
> And a pocket full of rye
> and he's comin' to take you away . . .

> *Alette disappears down the road.*
> *In the distance, in the train station, Train Announcement*
> *(voiceover) is heard: "Southbound, coastline trains on stand-by."*
> *Ilona turns toward the city . . .*

35. FRAGILE

Day. Exterior bar area of the train station.

TRAIN ANNOUNCEMENT (VOICEOVER). Track 2, Track 2, all southbound
trains back on schedule now on Track 2. Coastline trains, Track
2. Standby . . . standby.

Ilona at the bar. Alan wanders in, mumbling to himself. He wears thin
layer of clothes that have been lived in for many days. His walking is
impaired. He's a wreck.

ALAN. It's just that, well, things are . . . uh . . . fragile, you know.

ILONA. It's war.

ALAN. War's over. We can all go home. Wherever that . . .

ILONA. Lost yours?

ALAN. In a manner . . .

ILONA. I'm sorry.

ALAN. Fucking stranglehold. If you know what I mean.

ILONA. You'd rather the freedom of the open field?

ALAN. Out in the . . . open. Yeah. Like uh . . .

> *Alan goes blank. Longer than has been usual for him in the past.*

ILONA. You're all right?

ALAN (*sings from "Steady on the War Lullaby"*). "Steady on, my good
tin son.
Steady on, my soldier.
Steady on, the sea . . ."

ILONA. I miss it.

ALAN. Ocean? Is that where you're . . .? . . . Know all about that.
Oceans and the like. Yeah. We're all fucking the same in the
end. Same god.

ILONA. Not really.

ALAN. No. Gotta have the goods, right? Don't have the uh . . . can't
walk into church. Trains (are) like church. Stations. You walk
in . . . feel the light.

ILONA. I don't like trains, actually. Stations.

ALAN. Sometimes you just have to find the Elsewhere.

Alan pulls a knife on her. A feeble attempt to get by.

ILONA. What are you—?

ALAN. Give.

ILONA. Don't have—

ALAN. Give.

ILONA. Don't . . .

ALAN. Ticket. Got a ticket, don't you?

She laughs.

ILONA (*laughing*). Ticket? You think I've . . .? Day's end, night's end,
I'm the same as you, man. Looking for a way out of this fucking mess.

ALAN (*overlap*). Shut.

ILONA (*continuing*). How's that for a laugh? How's that for a good
goddamn?

She wrests knife away from him.

ALAN (*overlap*). Easy.

She succeeds in doing so. A moment.

He looks down, as if seeking a connection to something . . .

ALAN. Nothing. Nothing. I'm nothing. Nothing. Nothing.

Pause.

ILONA (*a kind of blessing*). . . . Go.

Alan walks away, as best he can on his cane, lost to himself.
Ilona keeps her eyes on him until he's out of sight, and then allows
herself to openly cry—
Something she hasn't allowed herself to do for a very long time.
In the station, Train Announcement (Voiceover): "Northbound
trains, Track 1: Shut all doors. Repeat: Shut all doors."
The sound of waves; time shifts, and we're at . . .

36. ELECTRIC DREAMS

The beach. Day. Ilona faces the water. She calls out softly.

ILONA. Hey. Hey. Hey . . .

A moment.

Tourist approaches. He wears simple clothes and a shell necklace. He
carries a digital camera.

TOURIST. I'm sorry. Would you mind—?

ILONA. What?

TOURIST. I know it's a tourist-y thing to do, but . . . the beach is so
amazing.

ILONA. . . . Sure.

(*He hands her digital camera.*)

How do you . . .?

TOURIST. It's simple. Like this.

ILONA. Oh I see. Very simple.

TOURIST. Yes.

ILONA. . . . For your girlfriend?

TOURIST. What?

ILONA. Back home?

TOURIST. No, just friends. On the Net.

ILONA. Facebook.

TOURIST. I can't believe how amazing it is here. Not at all what I expected.

ILONA. What'd you mean?

TOURIST. Well, you see pictures, the news, you know, you think–

(*An indecipherable sound in the distance. Ilona reacts to it [flash of memory].*)

You okay?

ILONA. Fine. . . . Would you—? Too much sun on this side.

(*Tourist stands where she indicates.*)

That's better.

TOURIST. Yeah?

ILONA. That's nice.

TOURIST. You can see the water? I wanna make sure you can see the water (in the picture).

ILONA. I can see the whole beach.

TOURIST. That's good.

ILONA. Ready?

TOURIST. Yeah.

ILONA. And smile.

He poses. She takes picture.

TOURIST. Thanks.

ILONA. . . . One more? For luck?

TOURIST. Well, I don't really . . . Why not?

ILONA. Ready? And . . .

(*She takes picture.*)

There. Looks nice.

She returns camera to him.

TOURIST. Doesn't matter, really.

ILONA. What?

TOURIST. If it's a nice picture, as long as you know why it got taken in the first place, right?

ILONA. My uncle would . . .

TOURIST. Huh?

ILONA. Nothing.

TOURIST. . . . Hey.

ILONA. What?

TOURIST. There's this cafe down the road. Looks kinda interesting. Would you—?

ILONA (*simply*). No. Thanks.

TOURIST. Sorry.

ILONA. It's all right.

> *He takes her picture. A sweetly impulsive gesture. He laughs awkwardly, perhaps embarrassed at his own impulsiveness. She smiles. A moment.*

TOURIST. . . . You've a beautiful country.

ILONA. Yes. It is.

> (*A moment. Tourist walks away. As he does so, Ilona sings English version of "Exile Song," which she sang to Maurice in French earlier in the play.*)

And when we go
the world will know
all that lies below
a city of angels
a dream of salvation
a song of the exile's road.

> *She continues humming the song.*
> *As she does so, she takes off the boat charm amulet necklace,*
> *and hangs it on a fence between land and sea,*
> *and walks away on the road, disappearing from view.*

The End.

STEAL BACK LIGHT FROM THE VIRTUAL

CHARACTERS

TIMOTHY	A man who is unsure in his skin, of where he is or where's been, impulsive, and a bit trusting.
NADJA	A woman who eats words and steals images through a camera's lens, slightly feral and mindful of her own tenderness.
LAME	A young man who wants to be somewhere he's not, a hustler, immediate in his needs and desires.
ANGE	A young woman who eats ice cream and watches movies, exclusively, a runaway, practical and a bit uncentered.
MESMER	A journalist with a lighter in his hand, opaque and intelligent.
ARIADNE	His wife, who drinks and guards her intimacy, elegant and vengeful.
PLACE	The present. A labyrinth.

NOTE ON THE PLAY

This play may be performed with an interval.

This play was developed at the 2009 HotINK International Festival in New York City under Jose Zayas' direction (curator: Catherine Coray), and in earlier versions of the script at Evidence Room and Theater of Note in Los Angeles, and also at New Dramatists in New York City under Anne Kauffman's direction.

It was also presented as a reading (in translation by Jasen Boko) at Zagreb Youth Theatre as part of the 2010 US–Croatia Exchange hosted by Wax Factory, New York, and was a finalist for the 2010 XYZ Festival at About Face Theatre, Chicago.

". . . I fall down as if I'm dead I am on the milky
way floating into this turbulent sky some space."

Gus Gus, "Acid Milk," *This is Normal* (1999)

STEAL BACK LIGHT FROM
THE VIRTUAL

ACT 1

SCENE 1

A mobile phone rings. The sound of a crash, and car wheels screeching.
Silence.
4 a.m. Cramped square of a space. Graffiti on the walls. Light falls
through a slat high up. Timothy and Nadja are seated. He is smoking
incessantly. She gnaws on an edible bracelet.

NADJA. I eat words.

TIMOTHY. I smoke shit.

NADJA. My mouth is full. My belly pops. I need more.

TIMOTHY. Have a lie-down.

NADJA. I need to taste them.

TIMOTHY. It's four in the . . . It's late. My lungs are shot.

NADJA. If you have another smoke . . .

TIMOTHY. It's this, it's this . . . I can't even . . . Everything's shit.
Clothes, the newspaper, the tube, value meals the size of a
quarter, breakfast that doesn't sit in your stomach for more
than an hour and you have to vomit 'cause the bacon and
cheese turns into cardboard, speed-dial buttons that don't
advance you even a tenth of a second while you hang on the
line waiting, investing minutes in nothing, blankets made of
some synthetic what's-it that doesn't even warm you, not like
when you were a kid and you could curl up into anything for
hours and read . . . who reads? I can't even keep my eyes
straight for . . . fucking virtual orgasms. That's what we have
now.

NADJA. Have a word.

TIMOTHY. What?

NADJA (*offers bracelet*). Come on.

TIMOTHY. What's that?

NADJA. "Bubble."

TIMOTHY. Bubble?

NADJA. It's a good word.

TIMOTHY. It's round.

NADJA. Go on.

TIMOTHY. Don't you want it?

NADJA. I give freely.

TIMOTHY. You spoil me.

NADJA. I'm still capable of love.

> *Timothy mouths the word "bubble" silently, then eats what's left of her bracelet. Dark.*

SCENE 2

Night. Light barely falls through the slat high up. Nadja watches Timothy sleep. She takes off his red sneakers. She sings to him softly.

In the Stolen Part

NADJA. Would you give a toss
     if all was lost?
     Would you hide away with me?
     In the stolen part
     of my battered heart
     You could be . . .

     Would you let me go
     if the world was blown?
     Would you still look out for me?
     In the stolen part
     of my screwed-up heart
     You could be . . .
     You could be . . .

     Dark.

SCENE 3

Light. Time has passed. The cramped square of space is filled with cigarette butts. We can now see that Timothy's trousers are stained with blood. He is smoking. Nadja is buttoning her blouse.

TIMOTHY. Give me more.

NADJA. I'm out.

TIMOTHY. You're rotten.

NADJA. I give freely. Just tired now. Need rest.

TIMOTHY. Where the hell . . . ? I can't even move in this place. We're in some . . . what? A global what's-it?

NADJA. Flat.

TIMOTHY. Fucking two-by . . . I feel your stink.

NADJA. It's late.

TIMOTHY. Yes. And we've been . . . fucking.

NADJA. All this time.

TIMOTHY. . . . I got to get on the autobahn.

NADJA. We're not in Germany.

TIMOTHY. But I thought . . .

NADJA. Give a think.

(*Pause.*)

Do you remember now?

TIMOTHY. I was smoking.

NADJA. You still are.

TIMOTHY. I was looking at you. I was standing outside a building that used to be a TV station.

NADJA. A Teletubby on your back.

TIMOTHY. My life's possessions inside the belly of a plastic-headed plush creep.

NADJA. Your eyes were tearing.

TIMOTHY. My girl had left me. All the girls leave me.

NADJA. We went inside a club.

TIMOTHY. Inside a church. Your skin was glowing.

NADJA. Under the ultraviolet.

TIMOTHY. We were dancing.

NADJA. Holding hands.

TIMOTHY. Like a couple of kids.

NADJA. Your kisses on me . . .

TIMOTHY. We were in a car.

NADJA. Do you remember now?

TIMOTHY. After dancing, after everything.

NADJA. We crashed.

TIMOTHY. The windshield fell out.

NADJA. We crawled . . .

TIMOTHY. Feet and arms . . .

My mobile is ringing.

(*The sound of a mobile phone ringing outside.*)

I can hear it.

. . .

You must've carried me. You must've dragged me from the car and carried me on your slim back to this flat, this squat-sit . . .

NADJA. You're imagining things.

TIMOTHY. That's a hell of a lot, isn't it? A hell of a . . .

NADJA. Nadja.

TIMOTHY. What?

NADJA. That's my name.

TIMOTHY. It's a Samaritan thing, isn't it? Like in the Bible. A good turn.

Nobody does that anymore. I don't know of anyone . . .

NADJA. Thank you.

TIMOTHY. What?

NADJA. You could say "thank you." You could lean on me, rest your head.

TIMOTHY. Yes? Thank you, Nadja.

He leans upon her, rests his head. From outside, the mobile phone rings. Dark.

SCENE 4

Day. Outside the window. The mobile phone is on the ground. It is ringing. Lame and Ange look at it.

LAME. You answer it.

ANGE. Ain't mine.

LAME. Can't listen to it . . . driving me . . .

(*Ange smashes the phone against the sidewalk.*)

You didn't have to do that.

ANGE. You said you—

LAME. Won't know who it is now.

ANGE. Wasn't yours anyway.

LAME. It's the principle, isn't it? The principle of the thing.

ANGE. What are you—?

LAME. The phone rings, you pick it up.

ANGE. Where'd you hear that?

LAME. It's a rule.

ANGE. You need to get yourself sorted.

LAME. I'm all right, Ange.

ANGE. You've got everything backwards.

LAME. What do you mean?

ANGE. There are no rules. No principles. Where've you been?

LAME. Blowing cock.

ANGE. You don't know a thing.

LAME. Good money it is.

ANGE. You like it.

LAME. Yeah, but it's still good money.

ANGE. They pay you in euros.

LAME. Same as dollars.

ANGE. Not the same.

LAME. It is.

ANGE. Where's your math?

LAME. In my head.

ANGE. Lame. That's what you are.

LAME. That's who I am, not what I am. Look, it's just my name.

ANGE. It suits you.

LAME. Fuck off.

ANGE. It does.

LAME. You smashed the fucking mobile. We could've made some money off it.

ANGE. If it was up to you . . .

LAME. What?

ANGE. Money all the time . . .

LAME. It's good, isn't it?

ANGE (*on top of him*). Like cock?

LAME. Don't.

ANGE. Why? Can't I touch it?

LAME. Not here.

ANGE. What's wrong with here?

LAME. It's the street. There are rules, Ange.

ANGE. Yeah?

LAME. The street's one of them.

ANGE. I'll sort you out.

LAME. Don't.

ANGE. You want a mobile? I'll get one for you.

LAME. I don't like the new ones. They've got too many options. There's too much to remember . . .

ANGE. I'll get you anything you want.

She stays on him.

LAME. You're a cow.

ANGE. Yes.

She goes down on him. Dark.

SCENE 5

High-rise. Lounge—lush, pristine. A wide window that looks onto the city. Mesmer is writing. Ariadne is drinking.

MESMER. "In this world, in this world there is a proclivity for behavior that doesn't preclude . . ."
Fuck it.

ARIADNE. You were doing fine, Mesmer.

MESMER. I can't write this. I can't write when I don't even believe in what . . .
Look at the street. It's all gray.

ARIADNE. It'll be spring soon.

MESMER. I'm a fraud, Ariadne. A damn two-bit journalist.

ARIADNE. You've won prizes.

MESMER. A complete fraud.

ARIADNE. That's why I'm with you.

Pause.

MESMER. They catch a crime scene on a home camera.
It makes the news, and everybody wants their hands on it, don't they? Because it's what?

ARIADNE. Hot.

MESMER. A property. Yes.
A car crashes on the road. Two people fly out of a window: a man and a woman.
A few seconds later seven young men are killed by a man who is said to have the head of a bull.

ARIADNE. A Minotaur?

MESMER. Yes. And the bodies of the man and woman have disappeared. A camera captures everything.

ARIADNE. Including the Minotaur?

MESMER. His face is unseen, just out of the camera's eye.

ARIADNE. Shame.

MESMER. You'd like to see one?

ARIADNE. It's not every day, is it, that you get to see a man with the head of a bull?

MESMER. True.

ARIADNE. Where did the bodies go?

MESMER. The two people from the car? Perhaps the Minotaur ate them.

ARIADNE. It doesn't work like that.

MESMER. What doesn't?

ARIADNE. Nature.

MESMER. How does it work then?

ARIADNE. The Minotaur sees the woman standing before him
and decides to spare her.
He decides she is too beautiful to waste in this world, in this world of men,
so he gives her wings, and sends her into the sky so that he can watch her at all times,
from wherever he is: the cinema, the phone booth, the hole at the peep show . . .
He can watch her and keep his watch safe over her. He guards her strange beauty.

MESMER. What about the man?

ARIADNE. Which man?

MESMER. There was a man in the car.

ARIADNE. He hid inside the woman's wings.

MESMER. He escaped the Minotaur?

ARIADNE. Yes.

MESMER. He is kind, this beast.

ARIADNE. He understands the meaning of mercy.

MESMER. What about the boys?

ARIADNE. The seven slain?

MESMER. Yes.

ARIADNE. For someone to be saved, there must be a sacrifice.

He kisses her. Dark.

SCENE 6

The cramped square is wider now. Light fills it in streaks. Time has passed. Timothy is bent. Nadja is putting on lipstick.

TIMOTHY. It must be morning.

NADJA. It's midday. You slept through the night, and another day.

TIMOTHY. The room has changed. This is not the same . . . you've moved me.

NADJA. This is the same flat. See the graffiti?

TIMOTHY. Blackbirds are singing. There are no blackbirds in Germany.

NADJA. We're not in Germany. I told you before.

TIMOTHY. My mobile has stopped ringing. There are bruises on my legs. What have you done to me?

NADJA. Have a lie-down.

TIMOTHY. You've tricked me.

NADJA. I saved you.

TIMOTHY. I dreamt there was a beast, a strange animal, half-bull . . . his teeth dug into my flesh. He wouldn't leave me.

NADJA (*walking away*). Go to sleep.

TIMOTHY. Where are you going? Are you going to leave me like all the other girls?

NADJA. I'll come back.

TIMOTHY. I don't want that beast to . . .

NADJA. He's only in your dreams.

TIMOTHY. I can't sleep if you're not with me.

NADJA. Timothy. Please.

TIMOTHY. Nadja? Where are we?

NADJA. See the ravens through the window? We're home, love.

TIMOTHY. Do you love me?

NADJA. Be still now.

TIMOTHY. Where are my sneakers?

NADJA. You haven't any.

TIMOTHY. I can't go out without my sneakers. Nadja?
Tell me you won't leave me.

NADJA. I won't leave you.

TIMOTHY. Tell me again.

NADJA. I don't have time.

> *She exits. Dark.*

SCENE 7

Lame and Ange stand outside the ice cream shop. Ange is eating ice cream in a sugar cone. Lame watches her.

LAME. We could make a killing.

ANGE. Another one of your schemes. I ain't saving you, Lame.

LAME. They're giving out a fucking reward for those dead boys.

ANGE. Who are you going to blame?

LAME. The suit who had me last week.

ANGE. Which one?

LAME. I'll get me a fucking PlayStation, an MP3, one of those nylon mesh jackets with the non-woven fibers, a frock of the week. I could be rich.

ANGE. I don't get a frock?

LAME. Only if you're with me.

ANGE. I want an Alexander McQueen.

LAME. I want a leather number slit up the front with a tight bodice.

ANGE. You're dreaming.

LAME. You don't think I look it?

ANGE. You'd need black kohl eyeliner, glitter varnish, get yourself fixed up.

LAME. I could do it. I could be a damn rock 'n' roller.

ANGE. Yeah?

LAME. Like Bowie.

(*Sings from chorus of Bowie's "Young Americans"*)

"All night

You want the young American

Young American, young American, you want the young American . . ."

ANGE. Who'd fuck you then?

LAME. Upper-class twits.

ANGE. In your dreams.

LAME. . . . That suit burned me, all right?

ANGE. So you'll blame him for the killings?

LAME. He burned a hole on my tit. See?

ANGE. Cigarette?

LAME. Fucking bastard.

ANGE. Poor Lame.

LAME. Shut up.

He had me cuffed. Fetish queen, but married. He had his ring on. I could see.

He runs his forefinger on it to prove to himself what he's doing with me is nothing.

I don't mind except he starts flicking his Zippo too close, with his damn filtered cigarette, in his hand, and I think, "What's he . . .?"

He burns me. Right on my tit. Takes the lit cig straight into my skin. And he's smiling.

I can't even rub salve on it. It hurts too much. Hole in my fucking chest.

Who the hell does he think he is? Leaves me cuffed to the damn bed and he walks out with his Paul Smith trousers and Gucci cufflinks. Click, click.

I'm lying there with damn smoke cresting my skin. I can't even scream.

He comes back in an hour and uncuffs me.

He had ink on his fingers.

ANGE. Ink?

LAME. Like from a pen.

ANGE. A goddamn writer?

LAME. I don't know. I blew him for a hundred.

ANGE. Whore.

LAME. I was scared.

ANGE. Liar.

LAME. It's the truth, Ange. I swear.

ANGE. What was his name?

LAME. Mesmer.

ANGE. You're making it up.

LAME. He wants to see me again.

ANGE. What kind of name is that?

LAME. God of sleep.

ANGE. What?

LAME. That's what he said. Comes from the God of sleep. From the Greek.

ANGE. That's Hypnos.

LAME. Yeah?

ANGE. Hypnos is the God of Sleep.

LAME. What's Mesmer then?

ANGE. Fucking twit.

LAME. . . . Gave me his number. Said I should call him again. He's got nerve, right?

ANGE. So, you're thinking you go to the cops and say this Mesmer, this twit who burned a hole in your tit, killed seven boys off the highway?

LAME. That's right. Seek my reward.

ANGE. Rotten scheme.

LAME. He's fucking scared of his wife. He'd do anything for her not
to know about me.

ANGE (*offers ice cream*). I'm full. You want?

LAME. Give here.

(*He licks.*)

Got nuts in it.

ANGE. It's pistachio. You don't want it?

LAME. It's all right.

ANGE. The way you eat . . .

LAME. What?

ANGE. Like a damn girl.

LAME. Quit.

ANGE. You're worse than me.

LAME. Fuck it.

He tosses ice cream.

ANGE. Didn't have to do that.

LAME. I don't like pistachio. It's warped.

ANGE. There's nothing warped about pistachio.

LAME. So, what'd you think?

ANGE. Your scheme? I think it's shit.

LAME. Yeah?

ANGE. I like it.

Lights fade.

SCENE 8

*High-rise. Mesmer is standing. A Zippo lighter in hand. Ariadne is
seated, half-seen.*

MESMER. I don't always burn them. It's not something I do. I'm a
quiet man.

My wife Ariadne knows this. I abhor violence.

But certain boys? I want to burn them.

This boy on whom I was particularly keen . . . he called me last night.

He's looking for me. Will let me do it again, he said. On his other tit.

In his armpits. On the backs of his knees.

He is offering himself to me on the phone.

Who does he think he is?

I'll see him tonight. Same hotel. Off a side street.

He says he wants a frock: leather with a slit up the front and a tight bodice.

Off the shoulder. Exposed. He mentions a shop. Designer boutique.

"It's in the window," he says. "It's a girl's frock, but it will fit me."

My wife looks at me. She asks me again about the boys who were killed.

Have I written the complete story yet?

They have tracked down the person who shot the crime scene, the person who saw everything. It's a woman.

I tell my wife that she is lying.

Who would put a camera on her lover going through a window,

on seven boys cut open with a knife?

What kind of woman would be spared by a minotaur?

My wife smiles.

I want to meet this woman. I want to burn her skin.

The flick of the Zippo. Dark.

SCENE 9

The cramped square of space. The window is now even higher. Timothy reaches for it. He jumps. Higher and higher. Silence.

A mobile phone crashes through the window. Timothy picks it up. He goes to dial. The mobile starts ringing. It won't stop. Timothy looks at it. Timothy smashes the mobile phone. Dark.

SCENE 10

Hotel lobby. Stale quiet, potted plants, wet drinks. Ariadne is seated, an unlit cigarette in hand. Lame enters.

ARIADNE. Light?

LAME. What?

ARIADNE. Have you a light?

LAME. Yeah.

ARIADNE. You look like you smoke. I wouldn't ask otherwise.

LAME. I smoke. Yeah.

ARIADNE. Not filters, though.

LAME. Screw that. I like it strong.

ARIADNE. American cigarettes.

LAME. Yeah. Camels, Marlboros . . . If I'm going to smoke, I might as well do it right.

He lights her cigarette.

ARIADNE. Thanks.

LAME. You're waiting for someone?

ARIADNE. Hmm?

LAME. A guest?

ARIADNE. I like hotels. I like sitting in lobbies. I'm not waiting for anyone. You?

LAME. Might be.

ARIADNE. You don't know?

LAME. I can come back another time.

ARIADNE. Stay.

LAME. Yeah?

ARIADNE. I like you.

LAME. That's a line, isn't it?

ARIADNE. Everything's a line. My husband specializes in them. He's a journalist.

He stages crime scenes so he can write about them as if they were real.

That way he gets the exclusive, right? On his own damn story.

LAME. He does that?

ARIADNE. All the time. Wins prizes, the lot. He's a regular star.

LAME. You're proud of him?

ARIADNE. Wouldn't you be?

LAME. He's a liar.

ARIADNE. We're all liars. Just a bit. You're going to tell me you're through and through?

LAME. Well, I . . .

ARIADNE. You see? We're all the same. Drink?

LAME. What?

ARIADNE. Want a drink?

LAME. I shouldn't.

ARIADNE. Why not?

LAME. I'm waiting for someone. It wouldn't be right if I was all . . .

ARIADNE. You don't look the type.

LAME. What'd you mean?

ARIADNE. Like you'd have any sort of morality.

LAME. I believe in things.

ARIADNE. I've stopped believing.

When I was a girl, I believed in the Trinity, in faith, in the vespers, and the lighting of candles. I believed that if you prayed, good things would happen in the world, that there would be answers. Simple. Yes. But I believed it.

But then one girl in my class got killed, and then another,
and I couldn't do anything, no matter how much I prayed.
The Trinity couldn't save me. Couldn't save those girls.
I stopped praying. I stopped lighting candles and bowing my
head.
I stopped waiting for a man to be good to me.
And I met my husband. A man with infinite qualities, none of
them particularly good,
except that he does take care of me. He pays for my upkeep.
You see?
The nails must be manicured, the hair must be done, the
clothes must be . . .
I look good, don't I?

LAME. Yeah.

ARIADNE. You don't mean it.

LAME. I do.

ARIADNE. Don't lie to me. I don't need lies.

LAME. You look a mess.

ARIADNE. That's better. A mess . . .

LAME. I could fix that.

ARIADNE. With your cock?

LAME. I didn't mean . . .

ARIADNE. Yes, you did. It's all right. I don't want you. You see?
I don't want anybody. I only want my husband. And he
despises me.

LAME. You're waiting for him?

ARIADNE. I found a matchbook in his pocket with the name of this
hotel. Classic. I know. I'm a cliché. The wronged wife sitting
in a hotel lobby with an empty matchbook in her purse, hoping
to find her husband, hoping to see the woman he's screwing
tonight. I don't wish to confront him. I just want to see what
she's like. I want to study her.

LAME. Tips?

ARIADNE. What?

LAME. You want to get tips from her?

ARIADNE. I don't need tips. I know what to wear. I know what looks good on me.
I know my worth. No. I just want to see. I want to see how he behaves with her.
Does he caress her neck?
Does he slip his hand inside her pants, down her crack, like he does to me?
Does he wear the same cologne, the one I got him in Spain for his birthday?
Or does he wear something cheap so as to be disguised?
Does he want her the same way he wants me?

LAME. I should leave.

ARIADNE. Are you tired of waiting?

LAME. I think I got the wrong night.

ARIADNE. Stay with me.

LAME. I can't. It's not right.

ARIADNE. Such a principled man. I bet you wouldn't resort to killing.

LAME. What?

ARIADNE. Cutting boys open with a knife, sweet adolescent boys with eager faces . . .
You're not the kind to do such a thing.

LAME. I don't know what you're talking about.

ARIADNE. The news. The boys who were killed. The seven slain.

LAME. Right.

ARIADNE. They show their faces every day at six and eleven.
I see them in my sleep. My husband says I am willing them into me, into my dreams.
Do you think that's possible? Do you think you can will someone into your sleep?

LAME. I wouldn't know.

ARIADNE. You have such a kind face.

LAME. I should leave.

ARIADNE. Have a drink. Stay with me. I'll caress your skin. I'll give you whatever you need.

She offers him money.

LAME. Don't.

ARIADNE. Am I doing this wrong? Teach me.

LAME. Not here. We'll go up. Yeah?

ARIADNE. Of course. A room.

LAME. Yeah.

ARIADNE. You like hotel rooms, love?

LAME. They're quiet.

ARIADNE. We could all do with a bit of that, eh?

LAME. Finish your drink.

ARIADNE. Will you hurt me?

LAME. I need to think.

She downs the glass. Lights fade.

SCENE 11

The cramped square of space, which is wider now. Timothy is seated. Nadja walks in with a bag.

TIMOTHY. You came back.

NADJA. I keep my word.

TIMOTHY. I didn't think you would.

NADJA. Eat your fritters.

TIMOTHY. Did you miss me? Did you think about me waiting for you? Did you dream about me?

NADJA. I got us money.

TIMOTHY. Where?

NADJA. Man with a coat.

TIMOTHY. He gave it?

NADJA. We bargained.

TIMOTHY. How much?

NADJA. The price of flesh.

Pause.

TIMOTHY. The fritters are cold. Where'd you get them?

NADJA. Day trip.

TIMOTHY. What? The man in the coat gave you a ticket? An excursion pass?

NADJA. He wanted a ride.

TIMOTHY. I hope he paid you plenty.

NADJA. We rode all the way up to Aberdeen.

TIMOTHY. Aberdeen?

NADJA. Up north a bit.
The train was empty, except for some kids on their mobiles calling home.
They were sweet. They were calling their parents, tugging at their sneakers and sipping from concealed bottles of Becks. They were talking about football and their favorite teams, ticking away minutes on their mobiles for a bit of home. We sat in the back facing the wrong way.

TIMOTHY. The wrong way?

NADJA. We sat in the opposite direction of where the train was heading.

TIMOTHY. How could you stand it? I always get a headache when I do that.

NADJA. It's what he wanted. He was paying. The kids talked and he ran his hand for a while. Just rubbing. I wanted him to open me but he wouldn't. He said "Not until we are further north and it's all gray."

TIMOTHY. You shouldn't have had to do it.

NADJA. I got us money, didn't I?

TIMOTHY. Cold fritters in my mouth.

NADJA. You need something in you. You can't go out like that.

TIMOTHY. I can't go out at all. You lock the door.

NADJA. I saved you.

TIMOTHY. You picked me up from the street, but I looked out for you, didn't I?

NADJA. I don't need it.

TIMOTHY. I don't even remember what air feels like on my skin. You shut everything out.

NADJA. It's safe here.

TIMOTHY. Damn squat-sit. Everything's ash. Did he screw you?

NADJA. He pushed me down onto the seat of the train as we closed in on Aberdeen
and I could see the gray buildings come into view.
Then he pulled the cigarette from his mouth and started burning me.
I think he expected me to give him a good cry, but I wouldn't.
So he burned me more. All down my belly. See?
It was a day trip. He wanted a look at me. A good look. That's what I gave him.

TIMOTHY. He didn't screw you?

NADJA. He left me lying on the seat until the train stopped. Then he said, "Let's go for some fritters." I said, "Sure, I love fritters. My father used to make them on Saturdays before he'd go drinking."

TIMOTHY. Did he?

NADJA. I lied. I was hungry.
He walked me over to a stand and ordered a couple of bags.
Then we sat on the edge of a row of concrete blocks, and ate silently.
Like old people do.
Old married couples who sit in parks watching the birds shit as they eat with salty hands.

TIMOTHY. What was he like?

NADJA. Polite. Nice cufflinks.

TIMOTHY. You met him before?

NADJA. No.

TIMOTHY (*at end of bag*). What's this?

NADJA. A treat.

TIMOTHY. Tastes sweet.

NADJA. Mars bar. Thought you'd like it.

TIMOTHY. It's warm.

NADJA. I got it on the way back. It's fried. Do you like it?

TIMOTHY. I can't think about you with that man . . . with your stomach all . . .

NADJA. Shh. Be still.

TIMOTHY. I'm falling asleep.

I can't remember anything, Nadja.

Something about dancing and a car and going through glass . . .

NADJA. You'll be fine, love.

TIMOTHY. Do you love me?

NADJA. Be still now.

TIMOTHY. Your voice sounds strange, like it's far away, somewhere else.

Where are you from, Nadja?

NADJA. I'm from right here.

TIMOTHY. I can't make you out. I can't find my sneakers. I don't think these clothes are mine. They've been put on me by someone else. I can't find anything, not even my backpack . . .

NADJA. You tossed it.

TIMOTHY. Why would I do that, Nadja? Why would I toss my Teletubby?

NADJA. He was a creep.

TIMOTHY. Did I say that?

NADJA. I'll buy you another.

TIMOTHY. No. It's just I . . . I need a cigarette. My brain's mush.

I think I must've killed someone.

I keep seeing these boys' faces. Their bodies lie off the side of a road.

They stare at me.

They've got blood in their hair. I don't know where they're from.

They look like me when I was seventeen.

NADJA. Have a word.

TIMOTHY. I'm full. My stomach's turning.

NADJA (*offering the word*). Aberdeen.

TIMOTHY. Aberdeen?

NADJA. Slow doon.

TIMOTHY. What kind of language is that?

NADJA. Just take the words, love.

TIMOTHY. Do you love me?

NADJA. Slow doon.

TIMOTHY. . . . Slow doon.

NADJA. Ah go tae bed.

> *He closes his eyes. Nadja touches her stomach, weeps. Light disappears from the window.*

SCENE 12

Hotel room. Mesmer is on the mobile phone. This is a close-up.

MESMER. She had the camera tight on me. She wanted to X-ray my eyes, she said.

"It's the flicker effect." I looked straight ahead on the train.

She had the kind of voice I imagined: a trace of everywhere.

She said she'd been to Mexico

and that's where she learned to shoot crime scenes.

They happen all the time down there, she said. Somebody has to record them.

So, she got into the habit of carrying her camera everywhere.
"I have seven hundred stacks of film. Murders, kidnappings,
virtual suicides,
sexual coercion, dead boys, girls . . . I have everything.
I'll sell them to you for the right price. I'll sell anything."
She has warm eyes. I could lose myself in her.
But I keep my gaze. Straight ahead.
She places her hand in between my thighs. She starts rubbing.
I will not be aroused. I will not let her . . .
She keeps rubbing. Her fingers are insistent. She has practice.
I think of her in flames.
I think of the man with the head of a bull who haunts me. I
will not give in.
The train pulls to a stop.
We are in a town whose name I cannot pronounce.
She says, "Mesmer, Mesmer . . ." How is it she knows my
name?
I squeeze her hand. I break her fingers. I feel the snap. She will
not win.

*Lights reveal Lame at Mesmer's knees finished with a blowjob. He
wears the leather dress with the tight bodice, and black kohl eyeliner.
Lights fade.*

SCENE 13

Nadja watches Timothy in the near distance. She dreams in real time.

NADJA. I wake up in London. I go to bed in New York.
Glasgow is at the other end of the train, at the other end of
Aberdeen,
and the northern country: Caledonia.
Los Angeles is the layover of a layover that never ends. Mexico
finds me in sleep.
Berlin . . . Berlin steals my dreams.
Voices call out on invisible speakers in languages I cannot
understand:

"Aspekten der Hypnose, Aspekten der Hypnose . . ."

This is the suitcase of never-ending cities that merge in my brain.

Everything is the same.

We are on a piece of cardboard. Points equidistant from each other.

The infant universe is flat. Draw a line from one city to the other.

Aberdeen lies near Seattle.

The seven slain boys haunt me.

"Aspekten der . . . *slow doon . . .*"

Words from one country fall into the other.

I see Timothy leaving.

Walk on, boy. Lose me.

There is a glitter on my eyelash from where you kissed me last, from when you were leaning on my cheek.

I am an atlas that questions itself daily.

(*sings*) "Would you give a toss

if all was lost?

Would you still look out for me?"

In the near distance, Timothy is seen crawling out of the window high up of the square space. Dark.

SCENE 14

Morning. Outside the window. Timothy is standing. Ange is thrown onto the street.

ANGE. Damn restaurant prick. All I wanted was an ice cream.

TIMOTHY. Is that all you eat?

ANGE. What?

TIMOTHY. I've seen you through the window. You're always with a cone in hand.

ANGE. Who are you?

TIMOTHY. Timothy.

ANGE. You look a wreck.

TIMOTHY. I feel all right, actually. Just my legs sometimes . . . hurt . . . did he hit you?

ANGE. What?

TIMOTHY. The man in the restaurant.

ANGE. Damn prick threw me out.
Didn't want a fucking what's-it in his establishment. Socialist pig.

TIMOTHY. What are you to him?

ANGE. Eh?

TIMOTHY. What kind of what's-it?

ANGE. I muck about. I steal things.

TIMOTHY. You're a . . .

ANGE. A pisser, rotter, spoiler, a spoil on the earth.

TIMOTHY. A junkie.

ANGE. I don't use. Haven't in years. Where are you from?

TIMOTHY. I don't know.

ANGE. Eh?

TIMOTHY. Cities keep changing on me. I thought I was in Berlin for a moment.

ANGE. That's far, isn't it?

TIMOTHY. But then I woke up and I could've sworn I was in London, right?
There were ravens outside the window, blackbirds singing, foxes all around.
But then I had these fritters, these ice-cold banana fritters that tasted like nothing,
and I thought I was in Aberdeen, that a part of my body was walking the concrete,
and then I looked at my lover, this woman who found me, and I thought, I'm in New York, right? I'm in goddamn Manhattan in a walk-up on 10th Street or somewhere on a hundred and eleventh, but she looks at me and I see in her eyes that we're

in Mexico or maybe it's Los Angeles. I've never been to Los Angeles but her eyes look like LA must look, and she says she doesn't know what I'm talking about.

She's half-Russian and her father is from goddamn Paris, and she doesn't remember speaking French as a child, but she does have a vague memory of Berlin, and I think,

"Right. That's where we are, that's the city I'm in." But she shakes her head and says, "No." She says, "Look out the window. You'll see where we are."

But all I see out the window are feet, a boy with Cherry Docs and jeans, and you holding an ice cream. Pistachio, I believe. And I think, "This is a damn labyrinth.

There's not even a map for me to figure this out."

And this woman who's become my lover who saved me from a car crash I don't even remember, except all I do remember is glass breaking, she says "Look again."

And I think "Okay. We're in Toronto. That's where we are. We're in a northern place where everyplace you've been burns into the pavement and tricks your eyes." But she smiles again, and shakes her head, and says

"Go to sleep, Timothy. You need a good long rest before you can see where you are."

And my head falls and my dreams turn, and I watch myself crawl out of the window that I couldn't reach . . .

The window that seemed heavy is light as feathers, and I crawl out with ease.

I see that my eyes have been shattered by a windshield, which is why I can't make things out. I have been through a crash, you see?

If I hadn't been pulled out by this woman whose eyes look like LA or some other place I've never been, I'd still be in a car stranded on a road with a wad of money in my backpack. I wouldn't be here looking at you with your bruised eyes, hurt by a man you don't even know, who wears a suit and tie and works in a restaurant to make ends meet.

I'd be lost and more than a little confused. But as I'm here, looking at you, I'm fine.

I know everything is a labyrinth, and that's all right.

ANGE. . . . You buy me an ice cream?

TIMOTHY. What?

ANGE. There's a place on the corner. Double-dip . . .

TIMOTHY. I could do anything.

ANGE. The name's Ange.

TIMOTHY. What?

ANGE. That's my name.

TIMOTHY. Ange? That short for something?

ANGE. Let's get an ice cream.

Lights fade.

SCENE 15

High-rise. Evening. Ariadne is sitting. Mesmer walks in.

ARIADNE. You're late.

MESMER. The city is a bitch.

ARIADNE. That's a strange way of putting it.

MESMER. What do you mean?

ARIADNE. Doesn't sound like you, Mesmer.

MESMER. What? You've never heard me use the word bitch?

ARIADNE. You sounded so young for a second.

MESMER. I am young.

ARIADNE. You're not twenty.

MESMER. Neither are you. Are you, dear?

ARIADNE. . . . How much work was there?

MESMER. What?

ARIADNE. You're late.

MESMER. I'm always working. Curse of the writer.

ARIADNE. You didn't call.

MESMER. Stop.

ARIADNE. What?

MESMER. You're playing "the wife." Stop it.

ARIADNE. I am your wife.

    (*Pause.*)

    I go to hotels. I sit in a different lobby every night surrounded by plants, soft chairs, cold drinks. It's amazing what you see in a lobby, if you look.

MESMER. I'm glad you're entertained.

ARIADNE. Do you think I'm completely stupid? I could shoot you. I could slay you, let you fall into a ditch like the murderer did with those boys.

    I'm capable of anything.

MESMER. Have they caught him yet?

ARIADNE. You screwed him, didn't you?

MESMER. Who?

ARIADNE. That boy. The one with the smile, with the distracted smile.

MESMER. I don't screw boys.

ARIADNE. He's a tart. He'll do anyone for money.

MESMER. Have you met someone? Is this what this is about?

ARIADNE. He showed me his tit.

MESMER. He only has one?

ARIADNE. I could shoot you.

    Reveals gun.

MESMER. What are you doing?

ARIADNE. Lame. That's his name, right? Your wretched tart.

MESMER. He's not wretched.

ARIADNE. I married you. I trusted you.

MESMER. Put that gun away.

ARIADNE. I let you humiliate me every night. And you still . . . with a fucking boy . . . Pig.

MESMER. Listen to me.

ARIADNE. Pig, pig, pig . . .

MESMER. Nothing means anything, you see? It's sport, a game, a test of living.

I'm not even there.

I don't even screw them. I try, but I can't. I won't let myself. Because I love you, you see? I love you too much.

ARIADNE. Pig.

MESMER. I walk down one street. I walk down another. I memorize directions. Nothing means anything. We're a transglobal accident passing each other,

going through each other,

through vaginas and cocks . . . furious, rapid, not knowing what . . .

Seven boys are killed, thrown into a ditch, sacrificed for the well-being of this city,

so that people can become concerned, feel connected for a second,

so that they are distracted momentarily from their petty lives, but it doesn't mean anything. The boys are dead. A minotaur walks the streets. Someone else will be sacrificed. Our accident, this accident we live in, is a dream.

We go from city to city pretending we're the same, pretending everything is all right,

but we're substituting real feeling for something else: virtual pleasure, virtual pain.

I can't even walk into the office without thinking about your eyes, your body waiting for me at night. My dear Ariadne . . .

And on the other side of the city,

the boy with the distracted smile and the slender waist,

and the delicate earring waits . . . You see? I can't think of anything.

So I walk the streets until it is too late, and you are angry from waiting, and you want to kill me with a gun that has sat in a drawer for too long. And I'm even willing to accept killing, to accept death, because it would be something, wouldn't it? It'd be real feeling. Not some . . . You see? I'm nothing.

I can't even walk into our apartment without shaking.
The minotaur enters my sleep and I let him devour me, because
I know whatever I do, however much I try, I won't love you
enough. I'll never save you. And that's what you want, isn't it?
You want to be saved. You want the promise of religion. You
want ecstasy and beauty and some kind of transcendence. And
what do you get instead?
You get a butcher boy, a freak, a man with eyes that spin in a
trance who cannot, who . . .
Mesmer falls in a fit.

ARIADNE. Mesmer?

The fit continues. Ariadne sets the gun down. Lights fade.

ACT 2

SCENE 16

Outside the ice cream shop, Lame and Ange stand. It is cold.

LAME. A fucking brain scan.

ANGE. What?

LAME. He's in the damn hospital.

ANGE. Some scheme . . .

LAME. It's got nothing to do with that. He's ill or something.

ANGE. Sick?

LAME. Yeah.

ANGE. Did he pay you?

LAME. What's it to you? You've got a new outfit.

ANGE. I met a guy. Fucking loon.

LAME. You screw him?

ANGE. We eat ice cream. He takes me out.

LAME. Day trips?

ANGE. We go to the movies.

LAME. . . . I've got to see him.

ANGE. Who?

LAME. Mesmer.

ANGE. You're stuck, aren't you?

LAME. Am not.

ANGE. He bought you the frock and everything.

LAME. Looks good on me.

ANGE. Yeah. It does.

LAME. Shiny black lipstick.

ANGE. Is that what you wore it with?

LAME. Yeah.

ANGE. Goddamn coven.

LAME. Nothing like that.

ANGE. You're turning into a fetish queen.

LAME. I like the way it looks. That's all.

ANGE. What? Rock 'n' roller?

LAME. Yeah.

> (*Sings from Bowie's "Heroes."*)
> "I, I will be king
> And you, you will be queen . . .
> We can be heroes, just for one day . . ."

ANGE. . . . You've got to see him.

LAME. I hate hospitals.

ANGE. You've got to sit by his bed. Watch him.

LAME. His wife will be there. She won't like it.

ANGE. You screw her?

LAME. She wanted to try me. I let her.

ANGE. You're a moo, you are.

LAME. She had a sad look.

ANGE. If you don't go to that hospital, he'll die.

LAME. Ain't that serious.

ANGE. Brain scan? That's mortal.

LAME. He's got some kind of disease.

ANGE. You should be ashamed of yourself.

LAME. I didn't know.

ANGE. He rub your tit?

LAME. It's better.

ANGE. Healed, has it?

LAME. Still hurts a bit, but . . .

ANGE. Your poor sorry heart has decided it's better to have a flaming tit than lose Mesmer's love, is that it?

LAME. Oink.

ANGE. At least I admit it.

LAME. Going to the movies, eating ice cream . . . going out with a schoolboy.

ANGE. He's all right.

LAME. He's probably a fucking murderer.

ANGE. Hey.

LAME. That's what they're like, the worst ones. They come on all nice and then they stab you fifteen times.

ANGE. Fuck off.

LAME. I'm only trying to warn you.

ANGE. You're a fucking cow. A goddamn moo. Go on. Go to your sick boyfriend. Bring him wildflowers.

LAME. He's not my boyfriend.

ANGE. What is he then?

LAME. . . . He's Mesmer.

ANGE. Cow.

She walks away.

LAME. Where are you going?

ANGE. To the movies.

Lights fade.

Nadja turns her gaze onto the street. In the background, the flicker of a film.

NADJA. Under the duvet, I dream of Caledonia way up north,
    I dream of Catalan boys and street singers,
    scabs on twins in the middle of a square,
    a black sleeveless T on a body, and an ambient muse.
    That's what I see, what I listen to, as I turn on my camera and dream.
    Timothy's left me. He's stolen away.
    He's looking for another dream.
    He's looking out for me. Even though I don't need it. I don't need anything.
    I've got money, cold fritters, and a bag of chips.
    I've got chocolate, too. Kit-Kat bars in my pocket in case he comes back to me.
    I know he likes sweets. Not all the time. But to have . . . to stick between his teeth.
    It's raining smoke. The shops are closed and I turn the other way.
    Past another street. There's another boy with a bottle of Becks in his hand
    and a bouquet of wildflowers. He doesn't know where he is. He doesn't see me.
    He's got a distracted smile and a hint of contempt on his lips.
    I'd like to have him under a little tartan blanket,
    put mirrors on his nipples, so he can reflect everything.
    I want to make everything private in my life public, including my love,
    even though it's misplaced, displaced, gone from view.
    I don't care. Love is a labyrinth. It doesn't know silence.
    It questions everything.
    There is a voice on the loudspeaker. All flights have been cancelled.
    Barcelona will have to wait for another day, so will Caledonia,
    and everywhere else on this cardboard map.

I'm on the lip: a place of landing where all facades are dropped.
My suitcase holds the future as I stand across from a midnight car park.
"Get out and don't come back" are the words I hear.
as I weep alone under the glow of the TV aerials in the dark.
Lights fade.

SCENE 18

Hospital. Mesmer is in bed. Lame stands before him with a bouquet of wildflowers in hand.

LAME. I brought you these. I thought you'd like them. Wildflowers . . .

I didn't know what else to get. You look so pale lying there. So fragile.
I don't think I'd recognize you.
You've got such blond eyebrows. I never noticed that. What do you do, eh?
Do you dye them? I'd dye mine but they're so thin, there's no point.
My hair would fall out.
I got you wildflowers for luck. They say they're lucky.
That's what the woman in the shop said. Cost me a fiver.
You think she stiffed me? I didn't know what to get.
I hate hospitals. Last time I was in one . . . was when my uncle got cut up. They cut off his leg. It was rotted from the inside. Cancer . . . I couldn't look at him. I couldn't stay in the room. I can't even walk by hospitals without getting the shivers.
Always feel like taking a piss, a real piss, you know what I mean?
You've got a soft mouth. I don't think I noticed that. I always think of you in the dark.
But it's so light here. You can see everything. Can't you? Why do they make hospitals so light? It's not like anyone wants to see how sick they are. Fucking cruel it is. What? You're laughing? It looks like you're smiling. Like you're going to laugh.

I didn't want to see you. I didn't want to come near you. Ange told me to come. She made me. You'd like her. She's not afraid of anything. She picked out my frock, the one you got me. She teased me about it, but she picked it out. I was going to wear it, but I didn't think they'd let me in. It's enough I'm some pug off the street, right?

They said they're testing your brain. Something to do with your fit . . . I don't know what any of it . . . I don't even know how they can get into your brain. What are they going to find? I'm having that dream, the one you told me about, the one about the man with the head of an animal. I dream he's eating me, biting off my toes,

then my fingers, nipples, earlobes . . . the delicate parts first, then everything else.

Like those boys on the news, they had their fingers bitten off, did you know that?

They said it in one of the papers, one of the ones you're not supposed to believe.

But I believe it, because it's in my dream,

in the dream you gave me by telling it to me.

Some man with the face of an animal bit the fingers off of those boys after they were killed. In my dream, I see your eyes in the face of that animal, and I have to hide under the duvet or else I will scream. I don't even know why I'm here. You've fucking poisoned me. I feel you in my flesh, and every part of me hurts. I was going to seek a reward, some kind of scheme, but fuck that, fuck everything.

They say you're ill, the nurses . . . They say your brain doesn't work right.

Something happened during your seizure. Oxygen left and some part of you stopped.

I brought you wildflowers. I thought you'd like them.

They'll make you think of the country, eh? Foxes and trees . . . But there's no water for them. There's no vase. They're starting to stink.

Lights fade.

SCENE 19

Outside the cinema, Timothy and Ange look away from each other.

ANGE. That was a crappy movie.

TIMOTHY. Sorry.

ANGE. Why'd you take me to it?

TIMOTHY. I didn't know what was playing.

ANGE. You could've told me it wasn't a slasher. Would've saved your dime.

I only see slashers.

They're the only kind of movies I like.

TIMOTHY. Why?

ANGE. Everything else is boring. You feel all right?

TIMOTHY. I think so.

ANGE. You're getting your eyes back?

TIMOTHY. Yes. I'm starting to focus better.

ANGE. What was it like?

TIMOTHY. What?

ANGE. Going through glass?

TIMOTHY. I don't know.

ANGE. Was there blood everywhere? Were any of your bones sticking out?

They say you can go up to 10,000 feet if you've got enough oxygen in you. Like you're flying, right? Only without wings.

TIMOTHY. I don't want to talk about it.

ANGE. It helps to forget?

TIMOTHY. Yes.

ANGE. It's all a lie.

TIMOTHY. Sorry?

ANGE. Forgetting. It's a lie. Nobody forgets anything. We just pretend we do.

TIMOTHY. I don't mind.

ANGE. You're a coward.

TIMOTHY. Is this what you're going to be like?

ANGE. What?

TIMOTHY. I took you to a movie. I bought you ice cream.

ANGE. I'm not a schoolgirl, am I?

TIMOTHY. I'm trying to be nice.

ANGE. Why?

TIMOTHY. I don't think I was before.

ANGE. . . . Got amnesia, is that it?

TIMOTHY. Of a kind.

ANGE. Like a sci-fi?

TIMOTHY. Yeah.

ANGE. You're my real live sci-fi.
I like slasher sci-fis. You ever seen those? People get killed with strange objects.

TIMOTHY. . . . Kiss me.

ANGE. What for?

TIMOTHY. I want you to.

ANGE. Buy me a gelato.

TIMOTHY. That's Italian, isn't it?

ANGE. So?

TIMOTHY. There's not an Italian place around here.

ANGE. Look for one.

TIMOTHY. Kiss . . .

ANGE. No.

TIMOTHY. What's wrong?

ANGE. I don't want to.

TIMOTHY. Look, I'm sorry about the movie.

ANGE. You're a fucking cow . . .

She starts crying.

TIMOTHY. I'll buy you a gelato, all right? I'll find a place.

ANGE. Goddamn moo . . .

TIMOTHY. What did I—?

ANGE. He's going to die.

TIMOTHY. What?

ANGE. Lame. I dreamed it last night.

TIMOTHY. I thought you didn't . . .

ANGE. I love him, all right?

TIMOTHY. Lame?

ANGE. Yeah. What? I can love him.

TIMOTHY. Does he know?

ANGE. Are you crazy? He'd fucking kill me.

TIMOTHY. What do you mean?

ANGE. He's a cow. A moo minder.

TIMOTHY. I don't understand . . .

ANGE. He goes into any hole, drinks up.

TIMOTHY. I see.

ANGE. Do you?

TIMOTHY. But you still love him?

ANGE. I'm crazy as well.

TIMOTHY. . . . In this dream . . .

ANGE. It was horrible. He was all bit up. Like an animal. Flesh in
     pieces.
     It's that suit he's seeing: Mesmer. He's no good for him.
     He's a bad egg. You know him?

TIMOTHY. No.

ANGE. You made like you did.

TIMOTHY. I don't think so.

ANGE. You made a face.

TIMOTHY. The name, that's all.

ANGE. Some kind of god, isn't it?

TIMOTHY. . . . It helps to forget.

ANGE. Convenient amnesia you've got. Mesmer burn your tit, too?

TIMOTHY. There are lives one has. There are lives that exist in ruins, in circular ruins that enclose the heart. They move inside of you, slipping in and out of your memory, in and out of feeling. You watch them. You tuck them away. You excavate them. You see, sometimes you want to bring them back, try them out again.

See how that life used to feel inside your skin. But mostly you leave them in ruins.

'Cause there's no other place for them anymore. Not in any way you can make sense of.

ANGE. Which life is this?

TIMOTHY. Hmm?

ANGE. Which life are you living now?

TIMOTHY. The one of forgetting.

Lights fade.

SCENE 20

Hospital. Day. Ariadne sits to one side. Mesmer is awake in bed. Lame is resting on Mesmer.

MESMER. I'm fine.

ARIADNE. He's fine.

MESMER. Just my head sometimes . . . hurts.

ARIADNE. Lame?

MESMER. It'll go away.

ARIADNE. Lame?

MESMER. He's crying.

LAME. I'm not.

MESMER. The boy awakes.

LAME. Don't call me that.

ARIADNE. What else is he going to call you?

LAME. I'm not a boy. I haven't been a boy for years.

MESMER. Don't cry now.

ARIADNE. Such a shame . . .

LAME. Stop laughing at me.

ARIADNE. He's imagining things.

MESMER. He doesn't look it, but he's got a lively mind. Don't you, Lame?

LAME. Leave off.

MESMER. What did you do with the flowers, eh?

LAME. I tore them up.

ARIADNE. Why did you do that?

LAME. How can you sit there? How can you sit there and look at me?

ARIADNE. I like looking at you. You remind me of things.

LAME. Cock?

ARIADNE. Don't.

MESMER. I'm devoted to Ariadne.

LAME. Yeah? What about me?

MESMER. You tore up my flowers.

LAME. They were no good. They were cheap.

MESMER. I would've liked to have seen them.

LAME. I don't know anything.

ARIADNE. Such a boy . . .

LAME. You used me.

ARIADNE. We used each other.

LAME. I believed you.

MESMER. The world is full of mystery. Just the other day, I was fine. I was working on my story, meeting deadlines, not thinking of anything.

ARIADNE. Except your dreams.

MESMER. And then my brain snaps, blood runs, oxygen leaves, and I'm here.

ARIADNE. At everyone's mercy.

MESMER. Flowers are left, and I don't even see them. A boy weeps.

LAME. I didn't.

MESMER. I hear things. In my sleep. I even heard Ariadne, even though she didn't show up until . . .

ARIADNE. I can't stand hospitals.

LAME. I fucking hate them.

MESMER. Nothing can be explained. Not even the fact that I am perfectly fine now.

ARIADNE. You could have another fit.

LAME. Another?

MESMER. There's always the possibility.

LAME. Hell . . .

MESMER. It's what I live with.

LAME. Will you still see me?

MESMER. I'm seeing you now.

LAME. I mean . . .

MESMER. Money?

LAME. I don't want anything.

MESMER. Then why don't you leave?

LAME. Everybody around me . . . they're always screaming, asking for things:
girls on the street selling frozen steaks out of plastic bags, knackered boys looking for a bit of a cuddle, old tarts handing me dodgy drinks . . . I'm nothing. You see? Even Ange. She doesn't believe in me. And I've known her longer than I've known myself.

ARIADNE. What are you saying?

LAME. I feel at peace here.

MESMER. With me?

LAME. You could burn every part of me.

MESMER. What's happened to you, Lame?

LAME. I don't want to lose you.

ARIADNE. You don't know what you're saying.

LAME. Burn me.

ARIADNE. Such a boy . . . such a shame . . .

MESMER. Tell me your dreams.

Lame folds into Mesmer's arms. Lights fade.

SCENE 21

The cramped square of space. Nadja is smoking. Timothy walks in.

NADJA. You've come back?

TIMOTHY. I left my sneaks.

NADJA. I'm smoking. See?

TIMOTHY. There will be nothing left of you.

NADJA. Words don't work anymore. What use are words? They do
    not educate, they do not change . . .

TIMOTHY. Where have you put my—?

NADJA. I sat on the train and let him screw me with his inky fingers.
    I stood on the street and let a car run over a child.
    I walked into a room and told a boy to undress me so that three
    men could watch.
    What are you doing?

TIMOTHY. I'll wear these.

NADJA. Shoes?

TIMOTHY. Why not?

NADJA. They won't fit.

TIMOTHY. They suit me.

NADJA. You'll get lost.

TIMOTHY. I'm already lost.

NADJA. I should have never saved you.

TIMOTHY. You did the right thing.

NADJA. So you could leave?

TIMOTHY. I go to the movies, Nadja. Every day. I see slasher movies. First show is at eleven in the morning, last one at midnight. I watch them all.

At the multiplex, at the corner cinema where the vinyl seats stick to your ass, wherever I can . . . Slasher movies are my favorite.

I've seen three hundred deaths this week.

And next week, I'll see more. I can't stop.

NADJA. You're killing yourself.

TIMOTHY. I've stopped smoking.

NADJA. Have you?

TIMOTHY. Nothing but amyl nitrate and ice cream now.

NADJA. Together?

TIMOTHY. Sometimes it's the only way I can come.

NADJA. You're crazy.

TIMOTHY. I feel alive, Nadja.

NADJA. Lace your shoes. You'll fall like that.

TIMOTHY. They are laced.

NADJA. Missed a hole.

TIMOTHY. Where?

NADJA. Your eyes don't work right yet.

TIMOTHY. I'll be all right.

NADJA. You'll fall all over yourself.

TIMOTHY. I'll use some of this tape, fix the laces in place.

NADJA. You shouldn't be out walking.

TIMOTHY. I saw a movie the other day. I looked at the screen and saw myself.

NADJA. What'd you mean?

TIMOTHY. It wasn't advertised, this movie . . . It didn't have a name. The reel must've slipped in somehow. There was the sound of a crash, wheels screeching,

the screen went black for a second, then it's me.

NADJA. You?

TIMOTHY. Up on the screen. Like a fucking star. Walking out of a car on a bare road with blood all over my trousers. I think it's Berlin because I hear a voice.

Someone is speaking in German. The voice belongs to a woman. The woman is laughing.

I turn around. The screen goes black again. There is the sound of a car door opening.

Light fills the screen. Radiant colors. I am standing by the guard rail on the road.

I'm looking down.

There's the sound of speeding cars and the voice of the woman. I can't see my eyes. It is as if they have been eaten by the sun. The blood on my trousers is dry. The woman's voice calls to me "Timothy?"

There are legs and hands below me. There are fingers missing. I look closer, keeping my foot on the rail.

They are the legs of boys, age twelve, thirteen . . . dead boys . . . The woman calls to me again "Timothy?" I turn to her. I cannot see her face.

The camera moves. My foot slams against the rail. I feel as if I am falling.

The screen goes black, and when light returns, only the car can be seen.

Neither the woman nor the man, which is me, can be found. Are you listening to me?

NADJA. You saw a movie.

TIMOTHY. The man on the screen was me. It was your voice, Nadja.

NADJA. I don't speak German.

TIMOTHY. Who did we crash into?

NADJA. We didn't crash into anything.

TIMOTHY. Why do you lie to me?

NADJA. I misuse affection. But I don't lie.

TIMOTHY. From the day you met me.

Aiming that camera at me, calling to me, sinking your tongue
into my mouth,
 messing up my hair.

NADJA. I didn't mean anything. I just wanted to—

TIMOTHY. Locking me up in this room, bringing me cold food to eat.
 Stealing all my things: my sneakers, my backpack.
 What did you think you were going to do with me?

NADJA. I wanted to protect you. I wanted to . . . hold you.

TIMOTHY. Fucking . . . make me sick.
 Give me your mouth.

NADJA. . . .

TIMOTHY. No more lies.

Timothy tapes Nadja's mouth shut. Dark.

SCENE 22

*The cramped square of space, which feels narrower now. Half-light.
Mesmer cradles Nadja. Her wrists and ankles have also been bound with
tape. She remains gagged, from previous.*

MESMER. Are you crying? Is that what you do when your lover
 leaves?
 Dry your eyes. Stop now. The tape is wet. You'll ruin
 everything.
 Come. Let's set you down over here. The light will not come
 into your eyes.

(He sets her down in another part of the room.)

It's safer here. Away from the window.
 You don't know what could come through that window.
 Does your body hurt, dear? Are your joints tired of being
 locked?
 You shouldn't cry. It only makes things worse. You know that
 better than anyone.
 Don't you, Nadja?
 I've seen you. You stood by the road as the boys went down.

You recorded everything.

What makes anyone keep their eyes fixed on atrocity? Do you take pleasure in it?

I take pleasure everyday. In bits. You see this boy?

(*Light reveals Lame in a corner. There are cigarette burns all over his naked body.*)

He came to me. One day. Unknowing. A transaction. That's all he was.

A little hell-child off the street. He let me touch him. He let me do my will.

Look at him. He can't even look at me without drowning his eyes . . .

I can't touch him anymore. There is no part of him that is unknown to me.

I found every bit of pleasure I could.

Stop shaking, Lame. Stop looking at me.

I give him to you, Nadja. I offer him to you. Do with him what you will.

He's my sacrifice.

I'll take the camera now, and the slice of film where the minotaur's face can be seen.

You've been good to keep it here. To keep it for me.

It will help me write my story, the story of seven boys killed . . .

Thank you for everything.

Mesmer picks up camera and exits. Lame slowly makes his way toward Nadja. Lights fade.

SCENE 23

The square space. Time has passed. Light falls from the window and onto Nadja and Lame's bodies. Nadja is unbound. Lame rests, near her. He remains naked. Silence.

NADJA. Bubble.

LAME. Bubble.

NADJA. Do you like it?

LAME. It's a good word.

NADJA. Try another.

LAME. Don't know . . .

NADJA. Try another.

LAME. Can't think . . .

Pause.

NADJA. Plenty.

LAME. Plenty?

NADJA. Yes.

LAME. I don't like it.

NADJA. Try another.

LAME. Sorrow.

NADJA. Sorrow?

LAME. Yes.

NADJA. There's no room for it.

LAME. Leave it on your tongue.

NADJA. Sorrow.

Pause.

LAME. It's a word my Mom used. I remember.

NADJA. I can't remember my mother.

LAME. She made custard pies, and creamy strawberries.

NADJA. I can't remember anything before Timothy.

LAME. Who's that?

NADJA. Someone I knew.

LAME. I'm hungry.

NADJA. Sorrow . . .

Pause.

LAME. Kiss me.

NADJA. Can't.

LAME. Lips hurt?

NADJA. Everything does.

LAME. Same as me.

NADJA. I'm not . . .

LAME. The same.

NADJA. You fall in love. Not me.

LAME. What about Timothy?

NADJA. I try not to think.

LAME. Loved him, didn't you?

NADJA. Out in the open.

LAME. He left you here, in this squat.

NADJA. So did Mesmer.

LAME. I wanted him to.

NADJA. You could barely breathe.

LAME. I asked him to destroy me.

NADJA. Sick with love.

LAME. I didn't want to feel anything anymore.

NADJA. Through with feeling?

LAME. Yes.

NADJA. Everyone lies.

> *Pause.*

LAME. I wonder where Ange . . . Give me a word.

NADJA. Empty.

LAME. Empty.

> *Lights fade.*

SCENE 24

Nadja watches Lame sleep. She sings to him "In the Stolen Part."

NADJA. Would you give a toss
> If all was lost?
> Would you still look out for me?

In the stolen part of my . . .

(*Lame stirs. He is crying. She stops singing.*)

Shh.

(*She continues singing.*)

You could be . . .

Dark.

SCENE 25

High-rise. Wide view of the city. Mesmer is writing. Ariadne stands, looking out onto the expanse of city below.

ARIADNE. I'll miss Lame.

MESMER. You were jealous of him.

ARIADNE. At first. Yes. I wanted to kill you. But after the hospital . . . There was nothing to say, was there? He was just a boy. I could see that. He only wanted a bit of pain, a bit of meaning in his life.

MESMER. Like the boys on the news.

ARIADNE. They found him, you know.

MESMER. Who?

ARIADNE. The killer, the butcher . . . The Minotaur.
A man out of uniform shot him through the eye, punctured his spine. The beast fell.

MESMER. No more dreams . . .

ARIADNE. You've posted your story?

MESMER. Everything's sorted now.

ARIADNE. . . . I would've liked to have seen him.

MESMER. The Minotaur?

ARIADNE. His face.

MESMER. What for?

ARIADNE. So I could put him in my dreams. Along with the boys.
I like everything to have its place.
You taught me that.

MESMER. Have I?

ARIADNE. And Lame.

MESMER. Still jealous.

ARIADNE. I'd like someone to hide me in their wings.

Pause.

MESMER. Sky's turning.

ARIADNE. Looks like Barcelona.

MESMER. We should go. How long has it been . . . ?

ARIADNE. Honeymoon.

MESMER. Did we . . . ?

ARIADNE. Don't you remember?

MESMER. The Twin Hotels.

ARIADNE. On the sand.

MESMER. We baked.

ARIADNE. Fried our skin.

MESMER. We offered ourselves up.

ARIADNE. To the gods?

MESMER. To everything.

Lights fade as the city gleams.

SCENE 26

A side street. Timothy and Ange are bruised.

TIMOTHY. Sucked my fingers. Licked your crack.

ANGE. Paid up, didn't he?

TIMOTHY. If he hadn't cuffed me, I would've beat him. I'm getting
old.
Too old for this.

ANGE. What'd you mean?

TIMOTHY. What am I doing with you?

ANGE. We have a laugh.

TIMOTHY. I want something more.

ANGE. Go back to Nadja.

TIMOTHY. You don't know her.

ANGE. Is she a good egg?

TIMOTHY. Found me on the street, gave me sweets.
Gave me words. "Bubble." A round word. It filled me up.
She said "Slow doon." We'd fuck all night, and she'd just hold onto me.
We were on the road, my foot was on the guard rail, there was a man coming up to me.
It was as if he knew every part of me.
But I couldn't place where I had met him.

ANGE. Another life?

TIMOTHY. Nadja pulled at me, tugged at my Teletubby, tucked me under her arm.
We flew over a million cities—Berlin, Glasgow, New York . . .
I could see everything—intersections and tollbooths and boys pissing on the street;
there was blood on my trousers, and glass in my eyes.
"Hold on," Nadja said. "Hang on, love."
And we kept flying over nameless cities,
as the man's face turned away from me.
Nadja set me down in a room.
I wanted to hold her all the time. Even if I didn't know where I was.
What does it matter where one is anyway
if you have to spend all your time watching people die?

ANGE. . . . I'll buy you a frock. From the boutique. Alexander McQueen.

TIMOTHY. I don't want one.

ANGE. How about a helmet?

TIMOTHY. Why would I want that?

ANGE. They're expensive.

Pause.

TIMOTHY. They found the man. The one who killed the boys.

ANGE. You knew him?

TIMOTHY. Why do you say that?

ANGE. Sounded like you did, the way you said it.

TIMOTHY. He was a stranger. Let out from some institution.
They say he had a knot under his tongue.

ANGE. You believe that?

TIMOTHY. It was online.

ANGE. Rubbish.

TIMOTHY. It will be safe now.

ANGE. You're dreaming.

TIMOTHY. Safe from him.

ANGE. . . . What am I going to do with all this money?

TIMOTHY. Get an ice cream.

Lights fade as Timothy walks away.

SCENE 27

The cramped square of space. Graffiti on the walls has faded. Lame and Nadja face out. He is wearing Nadja's blouse. She is wearing one of Timothy's shirts, and a skirt.

NADJA. I filmed children. I watched them through the lens.
Different schools, different cities.

LAME. Why'd you stop?

NADJA. Went in one day, all the children in the school had been shot.

LAME. You film it?

NADJA. I started to turn my camera on everything after that.
I struck a bargain with God.
I looked Him in the eye and said, "I will conquer death by looking at it over and over again." I went from one city to the other until I found this room,
where I thought I would not have to conquer anything.

LAME. Quiet.

NADJA. I don't know now what it is I see.

If I stop the images in my brain, what's left to me?

LAME. There's a game I used to play.

NADJA. No games. Please.

LAME. Hand over eyes. Go on. Don't be afraid.

NADJA. I can't . . .

LAME. I'll do it with you. (*He places his hand over his eyes.*) One, two . . .

NADJA. Where'd you learn this game?

LAME. When I was a boy and all the pretty-ugly lads would take turns screwing me.

Go on. Count.

NADJA. One . . . two . . .

LAME. Keep your hands over your eyes. Take your time.

Nadja continues counting silently, then . . .

NADJA. I think I could walk out of this room with my bones aching, and I wouldn't care what would find me.

LAME. I'm not afraid. I'm not afraid of anything.

NADJA. It's like when I was ten years old.

LAME. On the beach. No sand. Just pebbles. Wind beats. And the change machine at the arcade spits out euros by the hundreds, and everyone is playing. Bowie blasting through the speakers with his mad-idle face looking at me, bare and gleaming. And I want him in my mouth, between my legs. I want the euros in my hand to buy me everything.

NADJA. Ten years old and I can't even see the beach. There is only land here.

Tall hills. And leaves I collect with my bare hands.

I try to pretend I am somewhere else. Sometimes I forget the words to things.

The leaves are full of dirt. I carry them with me.

LAME. I got mirrors on my nipples, and black galaxy varnish on my toes.

Everything glitters: my eyes, hair, tits . . . It's time to nick a little, steal a little . . . light.

NADJA (*counting*). Fifteen . . .

LAME. I see a poster for Barcelona on the walkway. I can't feel the holes that have been burned into me. I am unmarked, unbroken.

NADJA. I see a poster for Barcelona on the walkway, outside the door, on the other side of the street. This is somewhere I have never been.

LAME. Barcelona.

NADJA. Barcelona.

LAME. A mobile rings in the distance.

NADJA. Don't answer anything.

The world doesn't need any more stories of slain children.

LAME. And slain beasts. I walk slowly.

NADJA. Out of the labyrinth . . .

The room falls away, no walls, no windows. Warm Catalan sun beats down. Mesmer appears.

MESMER. I dreamed I was in a city that was a dream.

NADJA. What did you see?

MESMER. I saw you looking at me when I was dead to feeling.

You came to me holding a camera to my heart, and said

NADJA. Enter me in your dream.

MESMER. And the atlas turned, and the skies shivered, and we remembered pieces of ourselves

NADJA. Bits we had left behind

MESMER. Lives we had abandoned because we wanted to destroy everything.

Pause.

NADJA. Out of this,

MESMER. Out of this,

NADJA. Out of this world . . .

MESMER. Everything is within our compass.

NADJA (*simultaneous*). . . . Let's make . . .

MESMER (*simultaneous*). . . . Let's make . . .

MESMER. A senseless act

NADJA. Of beauty . . .

> *Mesmer and Nadja begin to devour Lame. Light bathes them, then fades.*

The End.

CHARACTERS

LEE	Low-key and slightly contemplative, at a crossroads (preferably US Latino).
FLACO	Practical with something of a slacker-philosopher air, at ease with himself (preferably US Latino).
CORY	Spirited. And a bit dramatic, genuinely so, not camp (preferably US Latino).
KAYLA	Intelligent, warm, dynamic yet tentative at one and the same (preferably Anglo).
MONICA	Impulsive, a bit high-strung, slightly confused, but well meaning (US Latino or Asian).
LESLIE	Naturally flirtatious, confident with buried insecurity (preferably Anglo).
DANIEL	Has been through a lot in life, has a Romantic streak, Brazilian.

PLACES	Luna Park: the sky, the cliffs, the ocean, the band-shell, the Victorian pool, the rides, the grove, the runner's path, the lemonade and ice cream stand, the other path.
	And several interior locations, suggested simply.
TIME	Act 1: Summer. The recent past (before), and the present (after).
	Act 2: Later the same summer. In the moment (between time), and the present (after).

NOTE ON THE PLAY

This play may be performed with six actors, if need be. If so, then the actor playing Cory also plays Daniel. Melody to the original song featured in the text can be obtained by contacting the playwright, or lyrics may be reset by another composer.

Luna Park is the name of one of the first amusement parks in the US; it became a prototype for others around the country and abroad (Melbourne, Australia, and other cities). It is also the name of a concert venue in Buenos Aires, Argentina, and of restaurants in various metropolitan cities. The central site for this play is imagined, and not based precisely on these existing and pre-existing locations. However, this play is inspired, in part, by the US Latino/a youth scene in Los Angeles that is devoted to The Smiths and Morrissey.

SCRIPT HISTORY

This play was commissioned and presented (in an earlier version) by the French American International School (Lycée Français) in San Francisco in November 2005 in a workshop staging directed by Martha Stookey with musical arrangements and sound design by David Williamson, and videography by Matthew Perifano. Ben Yalom of foolsFURY Theater Company served as movement consultant. It was subsequently developed at Center Stage-Baltimore's First Look Series under the direction of Stephanie Gilman. The earlier version of this script was published by Playscripts. This version has not been produced or published.

This play is dedicated to the memory of Jonathan Zablotny.

PRELUDE

Luna park.

In ones, twos and threes, three young women and three young men[1] appear.

Expansive, classical music plays—perhaps Vaughn Williams's "Fantasia on a Theme by Thomas Tallis."

A dance of gestures and little moves begins: a dance of flirting.

Singles become pairs and become singles again.

Some pairs are together longer than others.

The dancing is alternately stop and start, joyous and fluid, and slow and slightly private in nature.

There are occasional solo break-outs, where someone is overcome perhaps by the music or simply the freedom of the moment.

The dance as a whole is a dance of a disparate community nevertheless finding commonality on a very hot, summer day.

As the dance draws to a natural close, and pairs go off to unseen areas of the park, the figure of Lee emerges.

---

1 If played with a cast of seven, then four young men appear instead of three.

1. THE SADNESS OF RICKY MARTIN

Images of the amusement park and the sea in the background: digital projections of memory. In the present (after).

LEE. So, we went for a swim.

It was hot.

Sun just bakes here in the summer. You have to swim. Otherwise it's hell.

The sky was . . . azure-deep. Everything was shimmering.

It was a perfect day. We didn't want to see the end of it.

So, off we went, me and Flaco and Cory, to the park right by the beach.

Luna Park. You've heard of it. It's named after some place in Argentina or Italy.

It's a destination. People dream of it.

Well, maybe not dream . . . I mean, who dreams of parks?

But you get what I mean . . . it's a place to be . . .

And we were joyous, me and Flaco and Cory.

We had our Morrissey T-shirts on, and we were going to let it rip . . .

We were every word there is for what's ultimate.

We weren't into miserableness. Despite Morrissey.

'Cause we didn't think of him that way.

Maybe he was some angsty rock 'n' roll god for some other boys way back when,

but for us, for Flaco and Cory and me, he was . . .

the perfect embodiment of something pure,

even if he is a racist prick.

I mean, I'd still take Morrissey any day

over Ricky Martin living *la vida loca*.

'Cause you knew even though he's smiling all the time

he has sadness in him,

and not an eloquent sadness like Johnny Cash and those ol' country dudes,

But a cheap sadness, which is the worst.
I know, 'cause it's what I feel sometimes . . . .
Cory and Flaco wanted to head to the cliffs
Right at the park's edge, after the Victorian pool and the kiddie train ride.
There's great diving there. And the best view.
You can see everything: the whole world.
I was trailing. I just wanted it to be night
So we could all cool down, have drinks, and get lost.
Kayla was staring at me from down the way.
I gave her a smile. She waved.
My T-shirt was sticking to me. Morrissey's face clung to my torso.
But I wouldn't take it off. 'Cause . . . well, I liked his face . . .
Cory and Flaco went ahead. They were full of light.
I loved looking at them. There was nothing sad about them ever.
"How do they do that," I'd think.
"How can make themselves be so joyous when everything's a mess really?
How have they figured it all out?"
And then I'd think, "Maybe they haven't.
Maybe they're just pretending like Ricky Martin with his sad smile."
"Hey," Flaco called out, "Come on, Lee, what are you waiting for?"
I was distracted. My mind was . . .
Everything was too beautiful: the sky, the trees, beach . . .
By the time I looked up
There was nothing
except a great big noise this side of sleep.

Projected images in the background fade.

In the recent past (before). Interior: Lee, Cory, and Flaco getting dressed for the park and beach.

CORY. Ok. Which song?

LEE. What'd you mean?

CORY. Which one's your favorite?

LEE. I don't do that.

FLACO. What?

LEE. Pick favorites.

CORY. You like all songs equally?

LEE. That's not what I said. Songs fit a mood. It depends what mood I'm in . . . Why? You got a favorite?

CORY. Sure.

LEE. What is it?

CORY. What do you care?

FLACO. . . . . Cory doesn't want to say. Do you, Cory?

LEE. Are you afraid?

CORY. Never. I'm not afraid of anything. It's just . . . Why should we reveal anything intimate about ourselves? It's better to live in a bubble.

FLACO (*as if quoting*). 'Cause Risk is our greatest fear.

CORY. You take the words right out of my mouth, Flaco.

FLACO. I steal from the best.

CORY. Don't steal too much from me, sweet.

FLACO. I won't.

CORY. Promise?

---

2 This is the title of a Smiths song. While there are overt references to the 1980s UK band throughout the entire text, the figures in this play are not seeking to recreate time past but rather to re-invent themselves through the appropriation and celebration of another time, culture, and music. (That is, the phenomenon of US Latino youth—especially in Los Angeles—and their devotion to Morrissey and the Smiths).

FLACO. Cross my heart.

CORY. You're so full of shit.

FLACO. You love it.

CORY. I know.

LEE. So, what's with the philosophy crap?

CORY. What?

LEE. "The bubble, risk, fear . . ."

CORY. It's not philosophy. It's reality. We're shaped and formed by deep fears that we apply to every part of our lives.

LEE. Says who?

CORY. Says me. And I know 'cause I've been living in a bubble for years.

FLACO. That's not true.

CORY. I use myself to make a point, but you get what I mean.

FLACO. We get your drift, yeah.

Messes up Cory's hair.

CORY. Hey. Don't mess. It's taken me two hours to get my hair to do anything.

FLACO. It looks better that way.

CORY. I hate you.

FLACO. You don't mean that.

CORY. I want to look good, Flaco. Can I look good, please?

FLACO (*sings*). "Please please please let me get what I want."

CORY. You got it.

LEE. What's that from: "please, please, please . . ."?

FLACO. Don't you recognize it?

LEE. No.

CORY. It's my favorite song. The Smiths. *Hatful of Hollow.* (*Sings*) "So for once in my life / Let me get what I want."

LEE. Oh.

CORY. Is that all you're going to say?

LEE. What?

CORY. Oh?

LEE. It's just a song. What do you want me to say?

CORY. Something extraordinary. Don't you want to be extraordinary in all things?

LEE. Not right now.

CORY. Rise up, Lee. Abhor mediocrity. Be noticed. Be like Icarus. Dare to risk it all, including your life, so you can touch the sun.

LEE. Icarus didn't want that.

CORY. Huh?

LEE. He wanted to fly. He didn't want to touch the sun.

CORY. Do you really want to be like everybody else, Lee? Walking round on autopilot not even risking anything 'cause it's not safe? Why don't you risk something? Why don't you speak your mind and do something?

LEE. About what?

CORY. You don't know what your favorite song is; you don't have a firm opinion about anything; you don't even know who it is you love, let alone what you believe in.

LEE. What does it matter?

CORY. 'Cause it matters. 'Cause you and me and Flaco matter. 'Cause it's not good enough to just miss out on life, while your friends are standing right next to you.

LEE. Look, I thought we were going out. Isn't that what we're doing? Aren't we getting ready to go out?

CORY. Would you listen to him?

FLACO. He's hopeless. I know.

LEE. You two are shutting me out now? Is that what this is? 'Cause of some damn Morrissey song?

CORY. Not 'cause of some song.

LEE. You are shutting me out.

FLACO. Nobody's doing anything, Lee. Come on. We're friends. We always have been.

LEE. But not anymore. Is that what you're saying? I said or didn't say something, I did or didn't do something, I recognized a song or didn't recognize it and suddenly Lee is out of the game, is that right? Listen, if you're messed up, don't take it out it on me.

CORY. In what way am I messed up? Tell me.

LEE. I'm not getting into this.

CORY. Afraid to get angry? At least with anger comes passion.

LEE. Just quit, all right?

CORY. Why?

LEE. I don't want to fight. Not now.

CORY. Later maybe?

LEE. . . . What the hell's gotten into you today?

CORY. I've always been like this. Haven't you noticed?

LEE. I guess not.

CORY. Stay sharp. Don't sleep through life.

LEE. . . . Is this T-shirt all right, Flaco, or should I wear the other?

FLACO. The one you got looks all right.

CORY. What about mine?

FLACO. It's fine.

CORY. Not too loud?

FLACO. Not a bit.

CORY. I like you, Flaco.

FLACO. And I like you. We're one big happy . . . right?

CORY. Yeah.

FLACO. Lee?

LEE. Yeah, yeah . . .

FLACO. Come on, then. Or we'll get there too late.

LEE. What'd you mean?

FLACO. You don't want to go now?

LEE. It's too hot.

FLACO. It'll be good. Come on. It's Luna Park, for Chrissakes.

CORY (*chanting*). Luna. Luna. Luna!

LEE. I'll go. I'll go, all right?! . . . One thing, though.

FLACO. What's that?

LEE. I'm not doing the kiddie rides.

CORY. Why not? They're fun.

FLACO. . . . He's got a crush.

CORY. Really? On who? Don't tell me. Monica? Leslie? Kayla? It's Kayla, isn't it?

LEE. It's not Kayla.

CORY. Then why are you blushing?

LEE. I'm not.

FLACO. Kayla's got good moves.

CORY. Yeah, but I can't see her with Lee . . .

LEE. Why not?

CORY. I don't think they'd mesh.

FLACO. They already have.

CORY. He hasn't even talked to her for real. Have you had a real conversation?

LEE. Real enough.

CORY. So, what'd she say?

LEE. Look, maybe we shouldn't wear the Moz T-shirts.

CORY. Morrissey is god. He is It.

LEE. In what century?

CORY. Moz transcends centuries and you know it. Anyway, you like Kayla, so it doesn't matter.

LEE. Is she going to be there?

CORY. Everybody's going be there.

LEE. . . . To Luna, then.

CORY & FLACO & LEE. Luna! Luna! Luna!

Images of the cliffs and the beach near the amusement park, and Lee's face in the background. In time (after).

KAYLA. It was so hot. We had to go out. The whole city was out.
Monica and Leslie wanted to go to the desert,
But I said "Let's go to Luna."
We always had fun there even if some of the rides were lame.
And you could spend the entire day and not feel it, you know . . .
In other places, time doesn't move. It just stands. And you wait and wait
And you do all sorts of stuff and it's still, like, two o'clock or something.
But at Luna, time passes. And there's so much space.
It's not my favorite place, though. Well, I don't believe in playing favorites.
'Cause that's discrimination, right?
I don't go for that. The world's full of that already.
I don't want to contribute to the greater advancement of discrimination.
But if I had to pick, sure, Luna would be up there in my top whatever . . .
Monica and Leslie and I, we went pretty early in the day.
It wasn't noon yet.
You could walk around and not bump into people you didn't want to bump into.
There was a band playing songs by dead pop stars in the old bandshell.
They did all the suicide rockers: Joplin, Hendrix, Joy Division, Parsons, Cobain, Hutchence . . .[3]
They didn't cover the dead plane crash rockers 'cause they said they belonged to a different category altogether. To them, it was all drugs and rock 'n' roll.

---

3 Janis Joplin, Jimi Hendrix, Gram Parsons, Kurt Cobain, Mitchell Hutchence.

Sad songs, sad stories, and great beautiful faces to go with them.

Wasn't Kurt Cobain beautiful?

Is that too weird to say? Does that make me a necrophiliac or something?

It's true, though.

I think he would've remained beautiful even if he hadn't died young.

Monica and I listened. Leslie looked at the boys running around.

They weren't like men at all, but like little kids all over again.

And they were wearing those *cholo* Morrissey shirts

like they were born in London or something when they've never even been . . .

Yeah, they were funny. I recognized them from school, from when we used to hang out in large groups and do things. Not like now. Now we float . . .

A soccer game started on one end of the field; the Moz boys joined in,

While the band slipped in a Ricky Martin song just for kicks 'cause we know he's not dead—

but in the dustbin of history, sure, that's where he is.

"Livin' la vida loca." What a sad song.

Phenomenally sad in that pop kind of way. But we sang along anyway.

It was hot, and time was passing.

Monica wanted to go on the Shock Drop. Leslie was being a *guapa* with the boys.

The band took a break from their suicide songs, and I headed toward the cliffs.

People were diving and making great big splashes in the ocean blue.

Lee, Cory, and Flaco were already on their way.

Cory's shirt was too loud, but so what? Cory was Cory. He'll never change.

I felt a breeze skimming in.

It felt good. You need a breeze on a hot day.
 . . . And then there was nothing,
The last thing I remember was Lee's face.
Images in the background fade.

4. THERE IS A LIGHT THAT NEVER GOES OUT

Before. Lee, Kayla, and Flaco at the lemonade and ice cream stand in view of the Shock Drop ride.

LEE. I should've gotten a beer. You want a beer?

FLACO. I'm fine.

LEE. A beer is better than a lemonade or ice tea on a hot day.

KAYLA. I'm not a beer person.

LEE. Why not?

KAYLA. No reason.

LEE. That's weird.

KAYLA. Why?

LEE. You gotta have a reason to flat out object to something.

KAYLA. I didn't say I objected to beer.

LEE. You didn't?

KAYLA. You're not listening to me.

LEE. Of course I am. I always listen to you, Kayla. Don't I, Flaco?

FLACO. What?

LEE. Kayla. I listen to her, right?

FLACO. Yeah. Sure.

KAYLA. But you like Morrissey.

LEE. It's just a shirt.

FLACO. Every Thursday. Moz night at the club. All the gloom and romance you can stand. You should go.

KAYLA. It's boys only.

LEE. There's everything. Girls too.

FLACO. Yeah, it's not exclusive. If you like the sound, you celebrate it. That's what we do. We just take one night and celebrate. For us, it's Moz, for others it's the Ramones—the rockers, the punks—we go against things. It's dress up, not dress down, you know. Others got their hip-hop crews and reggaeton to validate themselves with. We got Moz. What matters is being part of something, to have a sense of ownership even if it's just about someone else's music or a certain time in history . . . Everybody's so isolated, you know. In their own little islands doing their own little things. It's hard to . . .

KAYLA. Get through the bubble.

FLACO. Exactly. I mean, what is it? What are we afraid of, right? Losing ourselves?

LEE. Are you quoting Cory again?

FLACO. This is pure me.

LEE. Really?

FLACO. Absolutely. You don't think I think things? I think plenty. I do nothing but think. There's so much fear, you know . . . just to look at someone straight in the eye, and make a little contact is like . . .

KAYLA. Impossible. I know. What we don't say . . .

LEE. Huh?

KAYLA. What we don't say to each other, and yet we want to so bad.

FLACO. It's fear.

KAYLA. All around us. Inside of us.

FLACO. I think maybe all of my life I've been afraid.

LEE. What are you talking about?

FLACO. Not in an obvious way, but little things, you know . . . can really spook me . . . I don't let on, but it's there . . . it's natural; after all, it's part of the human condition. What's that saying? "Fear is what keeps us alive, and what gives us our stories?"

LEE. I've never heard that.

FLACO. Well, maybe it's not quite like that, but that's the gist of it.

LEE. "Fear keeps us alive?"

FLACO. Yeah, like, as opposed to sleepwalking through life . . .

LEE. That's one weird saying.

KAYLA. There's truth in it, though.

LEE. I think of fear differently. Less of a survivalist thing, more of a deep-seated thing.

KAYLA. Unknown?

LEE. Yeah. Something like that.
       Hey, is that Monica on the Shock Drop?

KAYLA. She loves getting her adrenaline pumped.

LEE. I never would have figured her to be a Shock Drop type.

KAYLA. Why not?

LEE. Don't know. She seems kind of . . . I don't know . . . muted.

KAYLA. Monica's not muted. Are you sure you're thinking about the right Monica?

LEE. Yeah . . . Monica . . . with the braids.

KAYLA. She's relentless.

FLACO. Look at her.

KAYLA. I know. She's like a kid when she comes here. She hits all the rides.

LEE. Hey! Monica!

KAYLA. She can't hear you.

LEE. So what? (*Toward Monica*) Hey!
       Good to shout. Let the air out . . . See? She's waving.

KAYLA. She is not.

LEE. She's moving her arm.

FLACO. I think she's waving a mosquito away.

LEE. What mosquito?

FLACO. It's summer, Lee. Mosquitoes thrive in summer.

LEE. I don't attract them.

KAYLA. Really?

LEE. No. Mosquitoes don't come near me.

KAYLA. That's a godsend.

LEE. Well, I wouldn't put it that way. But yeah, it's . . .
. . . She looks a little like Ricky Martin.

KAYLA. Ricky Martin's a boy.

LEE. So? Don't you think she looks . . .?

FLACO. Sure. I can see it.

LEE. See? Even Flaco thinks so.

KAYLA. You're both completely crazy, drunk from the sun.

LEE. I'm just observing . . .

KAYLA. Out of your minds.

LEE. You don't have to get worked up about it.

KAYLA. I'm not.

LEE. You don't look like you're not.

KAYLA. What are you: twelve?
The way you say things . . .

LEE. I just say what I say.

FLACO. . . . . I don't like the Shock Drop. It's too abrupt. I like being on an even keel.

KAYLA. Really?

FLACO. Yeah. I like flow. You know, going with it, riding it. Flow is good. Leave shock to somebody else.

KAYLA. Sometimes, it's good. It wakes you up to yourself and the world. As long as nobody's getting hurt, a little shock can be a good thing.

FLACO. Yeah, but then you're all awake and what? You realize how crappy your life is, what you planned to do and still haven't done, what dreams you've let fall by the wayside . . . it's awful.

KAYLA. You can always change what you dream.

FLACO. What'd you mean?

KAYLA. Change your goals . . . it's asking for defeat to think you can achieve what you set out to do when you were fourteen or fifteen.

FLACO. Why?

KAYLA. 'Cause it's impossible. I mean, what did you want from life when you were fourteen?. . . The best of everything, right? Nobody can achieve that.

FLACO. Maybe you're right.

KAYLA. Of course I'm right. Don't beat yourself up about it. It's not worth it. You get all depressed and then what? You don't even enjoy the day, and it's perfect.

LEE. That's what I was going to say.

The day. It's perfect. And you know it's not so bad . . .

KAYLA. You're funny.

LEE. Why?

KAYLA. Nothing. You just are.

FLACO. . . . Look at that kid.

KAYLA. Where?

FLACO. With the earrings.

KAYLA. How sweet. What is it about little kids, huh?

LEE. They're full of hope.

KAYLA. Some, yeah. This one definitely.

LEE. Heartbreaker. That's what she's gonna be.

KAYLA. I'm not so sure about that.

LEE. You don't think so?

KAYLA. She's too self-possessed.

LEE. That's what I mean: heartbreaker.

FLACO. She reminds me of my cousin. Two years old and she already walks around with gold hoop earrings and bare feet like a princess.

KAYLA. A Latina goddess.

FLACO. Yeah.

LEE. . . . How 'bout a beer, Flaco?

FLACO. I like lemonade. Organic, right?

KAYLA. Is it?

FLACO. That's what the sign says.

KAYLA. They lie.

FLACO. It tastes good, whatever it is. You want a sip?

LEE. I could use a beer.

FLACO. So, get one.

LEE. It's better if you go. I'm a little . . . From the match. You know.

FLACO. You get hurt?

LEE. No. I'm just . . . would you?

FLACO. . . . Here you go, Kayla. Finish my drink for me.

KAYLA. Are you sure you don't want anymore?

FLACO. Nah. It's super-jumbo size. I've had enough. Beer, right?

LEE. Uh-huh.

FLACO. What kind?

LEE. Whatever they've got.

FLACO. Rock 'n' roll, then.

Flaco walks away.

KAYLA. He's a good friend.

LEE. Yeah. We've known each other since . . . Funny how you don't think about things and then . . .

KAYLA. What things?

LEE. You meet someone, and then for one reason or another this person ends up being your friend for, like, life. Like you and Monica . . .

KAYLA. I think Leslie and I are closer. We've gone through more stuff together. Lots of late nights, you know, up all hours, talking about things, crying . . .

LEE. Oh.

KAYLA. It's good. What? You don't cry with your friends? Don't give me that "men don't cry" crap. I used to pick up my little brother at baseball practice all the time. When they lost a game, believe me . . . there were tears and plenty of them.

LEE. I'm just saying I don't make a habit of it, that's all.

KAYLA. I don't either.

LEE. I didn't mean . . .

KAYLA. I know. I'm just letting you know.

LEE. . . . Monica's having fun.

KAYLA. Yeah. She goes up and waits two turns and then goes up again. Shock. Rest-rest. Shock. She's got the routine down.

LEE. She's going to get sick.

KAYLA. She'll stop soon. Then she'll come running over here and order a large soda, down it in one gulp, wait five minutes, and go right back over there again. . . . You hurt yourself in the match?

LEE. Nah, just . . . out of practice. I haven't played soccer in a while.

KAYLA. You were good at it, too.

LEE. In junior high . . .

KAYLA. . . . I wonder where Cory is.

LEE. Why? You'd rather he be here than me?

KAYLA. . . . I think the heat is getting to you.

LEE. What'd you mean?

KAYLA. Nothing.
    Did you get to hear the band? They were pretty good.

LEE. You gotta be kidding me. Give me the surfing safari sounds, the Tex-Mex pastiche, the bad pop songs. It's Luna Park, for God's sake. It's ninety-some degrees. Who wants to listen to Nirvana?

KAYLA. I do.

LEE. Listen, if Kurt Cobain hadn't died, if he wasn't a gorgeous kid, would you be all swooning to his music?

KAYLA. It's the same with you and the Smiths.

LEE. It's a completely different thing entirely. Morrissey's not dead.

KAYLA. He might as well be.

LEE. I can't believe you just said that.

KAYLA. The band broke up ages ago.

LEE. Nineteen eighty-seven.

KAYLA. Right. And you're still pining away every Thursday night at the club like a little teenager. Smiths wasn't even your generation.

LEE. Look, first of all, I don't pine. Second of all, I go to the club 'cause it's fun. Like Flaco said. We feel connected to something, and it's our own little mini-rebellion against whatever trend we're supposed to be a part of. We're anti-trend, anti-market, anti-cultural segregation, if you want to get political about it; I mean, we don't get political about it, but it is political in its own way. And third . . . in the grand scheme of things, appreciating some old pop music, having a little bit of devotion to something that went before you, and is not even part of you and who you are necessarily, but that somehow still speaks through time, is not the end of the world. It's a minor pastime in the millions of pastimes there are out there. Life is screwed up enough as it is. Might as well get whatever little pleasures you can.

KAYLA. And that's all?

LEE. Yes. Why? . . . What is it with you?

KAYLA. With me?

LEE. I don't get you at all. One minute you're perfectly laid-back and cool, easy to get on with, and the next . . . Do you want me to go? Is that it? 'Cause I can. It's a big ol' park. I can go anywhere.

KAYLA. I didn't say anything.

LEE. Sorry. I'm sorry. I'm having a weird day. I don't know what's wrong with me.

KAYLA. . . . Premonition. I woke up this morning, looked out the window and everything was so perfect. Not extraordinary. Just perfect. The sky, the angle of the sun reflected in the water . . . everything was in harmony. It made me scared somehow. . . I know. It's strange, but . . .

LEE. No, I felt the same thing. Too perfect.

KAYLA. Exactly. So, I thought, "I don't want to think about it. Let me just go out, distract myself." But I can't stop feeling it's all a bit . . .

LEE. Screwed up.

KAYLA. Yeah. Definitely screwed up. Is it weird to feel that?

LEE. It's how things are.

KAYLA. So, what? We resign ourselves to screwed-up-ness?

LEE. What can we do? Protest, march, put a flag up, put a ribbon on a car . . . Put a sign in a window . . . Graffiti . . . slash billboards . . . throw bricks . . . fast . . . keep fasting . . . and what? . . . a centimeter of change, of real difference . . . that's all you get.

KAYLA. Sometimes more than that. Look at MLK . . .

LEE. My little cousin knows who 50 Cent is and doesn't even really register MLK . . .

KAYLA. That's sad.

LEE. It's what it is. Where the hell is Flaco? I'm starting to get beer pangs.

KAYLA. You wanna text him?

LEE. He doesn't text.

KAYLA. Get out.

LEE. He doesn't believe in it or something. And he thinks I'm messed up . . .

KAYLA. Maybe we should go, then . . .

LEE. No, it's nice here. Look. They're turning the lights on.

KAYLA. Where?

LEE. By the Grand Prix.

KAYLA. I hate that ride. Lots of lights and noise, but it's still an old-fashioned bumper car ride.

LEE (*sings*). "There is a Light and it never goes out / There is a Light and it never goes out . . ."
"And if a double-decker bus / Crashes into us . . ."

KAYLA. What are you singing?

LEE. I think that's my favorite song.

KAYLA. What is?

LEE. "There Is a Light That Never Goes Out."

5. RICKY MARTIN SLEEPING

Images of Monica in the Shock Drop at the amusement park in the background.
In time (after).

MONICA. I was going for the record that day.
　　Nobody'd done the Shock Drop more than ten times.
　　Certainly not in Luna Park, anyway.
　　At first it was just routine. I just wanted the thrill of testing myself
　　The way I always did. But then I got fierce about it. Like Lance Armstrong or something.
　　I didn't even care if I got sick. I would wear my sickness with pride.
　　I took over the ride.
　　The guy running it knew I was on a quest.
　　Like when my cousin Marcy took over karaoke night at the Vinyl Lounge
　　And belted out every song in the song bible until she got through every one.
　　Or like when that artist said she wanted to film Ricky Martin sleeping
　　Every night for twelve nights,
　　and then exhibit the video on a huge plasma screen across from city hall
　　like a shared ritualized something or other . . .
　　Can you imagine twelve nights of staring at Ricky Martin in deep REM?
　　I mean, I'm not into him, but if I was . . .
　　Anyway, I was on the Shock Drop on my little quest,
　　And I didn't even know why.
　　It was like "Today I will kick some Shock Drop ass."

It wasn't logical. I didn't plan it out. I just went on impulse.
I do things like that. You can ask Leslie or Kayla. They know.
I just go.
And the guy running the ride was really cool.
He respected my quest.
'Cause he understood on some spiritual, earth-baby level
That some things are meant to be done.
At first I got sick. And I don't usually get sick
'Cause I've got major stamina,
and then it was like I was on some supernatural high.
My body was in this ride,
Being plunged from zero to fifty, and I couldn't even feel it.
I didn't get dizzy or freaked out.
I was above things somehow. Everybody in the park was this
gigantic blur,
And I was pure adrenaline like those drinks at the nutritional
store:
Ripped Fuel. That was me.
And then everything stopped. Just like that.
The blur crystallized,
And all I could think about was what Ricky Martin would look
like sleeping.

6. HOW SOON IS NOW?

*Before. Lee, Monica and Flaco near the bandshell, just as the band has
stopped playing.*

MONICA. Why'd they stop?

FLACO. Maybe they forgot which song they wanted to play.

LEE. They've probably gone through their set-list and are trying to
figure out what to dredge up now.

MONICA. They're not so bad.

LEE. If you like suicide rock.

MONICA. Don't call it that.

FLACO. Why not? That's what it is.

MONICA. Creeps me out.

LEE. . . . Remember Erika?

FLACO. Oh. Right. Sorry.

MONICA. It's all right. I don't think about her anymore. I don't mean that as cold as it sounds but you know . . . you can't obsess about stuff. She wanted to kill herself, she did. She followed through in her own way. There's nothing I could've done or any of us could've . . . And even if we could've . . . what would we have done? If somebody has their mind made up . . . no point going back . . . no sense staying in the past.

LEE. Only now.

MONICA. Now. Now. Now. That's right.

FLACO. Good to remember, though.

MONICA. No, it isn't.

FLACO. So people aren't forgotten.

MONICA. I don't forget. I didn't say I forgot about her. Erika was my best friend.

FLACO. I still can't believe she threw herself off some ride.

MONICA. She did not throw herself.

FLACO. What'd she do, then?

MONICA. Look, let's not talk about it, all right? I didn't come here for that. I came to chill out, have a good time . . . I wish they'd play something. Come on! Make up your mind! I wish they'd play some INXS.

LEE. Why?

MONICA. 'Cause that singer, what was his name . . . he was sexy.

FLACO. Hutcher?

MONICA. Hutchence.

FLACO. Right, Right. Hutchence.

MONICA. He was like Jim Morrison, except skinnier.

LEE. Are you a Jim Morrison freak?

MONICA. No. But sexy's sexy, right?

LEE. If you're into that sort of thing. Where'd Kayla go?

MONICA. Don't worry. She just went to go get some Icees. She'll be back.

FLACO. From the Cuban guy? He's the best. How does he do it?

MONICA. He's got a special ingredient

LEE. I didn't know Kayla liked Icees.

FLACO. I always get the guava when he's here.

MONICA. She likes a lot of things. You should talk to her.

LEE. I do.

MONICA. I mean for real.

LEE. What is it with everybody today? I do talk to people. I do talk for real. What? You want me to spill my guts now?

FLACO. Don't get dramatic.

LEE. I'm not. But first Cory, now you . . .

MONICA. . . . The band's re-grouping. Finally . . .

LEE. Maybe they'll play some INXS just for you.

FLACO. Want me to call something out?

MONICA. No.

FLACO. What do you want to hear?

MONICA. Shh . . . They're starting up.

Music is heard.

LEE. What's that?

FLACO. It sounds familiar.

LEE. But what is it?

FLACO. Music. Music's music.

MONICA. "Love hurts."

LEE. Huh?

MONICA. That's what they're playing except they're not doing the lyrics.

FLACO. What's "Love Hurts"?

MONICA. Old song. My mom sings it sometimes. One of those achy-breaky songs.

FLACO. I don't know it.

MONICA. Of course you do. (*Sings*) "Love hurts . . ." Remember?

FLACO. Never heard of it.

MONICA. The guy who used to sing it . . . his body disappeared.

LEE. Really?

MONICA. That's what my mom used to tell me when she'd sing it. "Monica, the man who sang this song . . . his body got stolen . . ."

FLACO. How'd that happen?

MONICA. I don't know. She wouldn't say.
. . . It's all so creepy: Erika, this song . . . the little boy in the news . . .

LEE. Which boy?

MONICA. Who got killed. In some little town somewhere. It was on the news. Didn't you hear about it? It's everywhere.

LEE. Little kid?

MONICA. Five years old or something. Everything's crazy. Everything's so crazy. That's it. I'm leaving.

FLACO. Where are you going?

MONICA. I gotta go do something. I can't sit around and listen to music while everything's falling apart.

FLACO. What's falling apart?

MONICA. Everything. Everything. Everything. Can't you see?

FLACO. It's just a song, Monica. Look, we'll get them to play INXS or something.

MONICA. No.

FLACO. Monica . . .

She leaves. Pause.

LEE. She's intense.

FLACO. I shouldn't have brought up the Erika thing.

LEE. You didn't on purpose . . .

FLACO. I know, but . . . I just forgot. Wiped it from my mind.

LEE. I'd forgotten too.

FLACO. It was a long time ago.

LEE. Right around the time of the Madrid thing . . .

FLACO. How many people died in that—?

LEE. I don't remember.

> (*Pause. Vaguely recognizable instrumental version of "Suicide Blonde" is heard.*)
>
> I think this is an INXS song. She should've waited . . .
>
> (*Pause.*)
>
> . . . You like this song?

FLACO. I'm whatever . . .

> *Pause.*

LEE. Wanna play some soccer? There's a match starting up over there.

FLACO. Yeah, yeah, let's do that.

7. LIKE VIOLETS

Images of the soccer match, Daniel, and the cliffs and the sea in the background.
In time (after).

LESLIE. I don't always look at the boys. But they were having so much fun
And they were . . . yummy. So, why not look?
Some were in their rock 'n' roll T-shirts.
Others were in little raggedy shorts and no tops.
Really buff in a non-muscleman kind of way.
Others were in soccer clothes. You could tell they played on a team somewhere.
They spoke a different language. I could make out bits of words. Latin-sounding.
One of them told me about Luna Park—another one in some other country—
Where the best musicians play. "Like Madison Square Garden," he said.
Another one told me about a park just like this one, only bigger,

Where families come and spend their weekends.
They all talked about the sun, and time.
Letting time pass, and how in this park named after a moon—
luna, luna, luna—
they felt protected by the sun.
After the match, the boys in the rock 'n' roll shirts headed for
drinks by the stand.
Kayla and Lee met up.
She's sweet on him. I don't know why.
But I waved them on, anyway, 'cause I'm her friend.
The unfamiliar boys wanted to explore the park. I went along
with them.
Most of them came from nervous towns. They knew all about
fear,
How it gets into you, and how it's a very real thing and not
just, you know,
Something somebody talks about scientifically on the TV.
They said they lived with dynamite in their lives,
Daily explosions,
And so they lived with the knowledge
that something awful could happen at any moment . . .
But also how something good can happen too,
And how beautiful that was—
I couldn't make out all their words, but I listened anyway.
Soon we were at the cliffs. Right below.
The sun was beaming something unreal.
There were bands of boys and girls diving, and others by the
pool, making noise.
It was a glorious day. I wanted to scream. In a good way.
But I didn't. I just let one of the boys kiss me.
He was all sweaty from the soccer, and his clothes were
sticky.
He spoke his language. He told me things. He had history in
his eyes.
I touched his chest. He was so strong. But fragile too. He
didn't hide from me.

I told him we could sit by the deep end of the pool, splash
around if we wanted.
He told me the pool-water smelt like violets,
and we could pretend like we were in an ancient place.
I looked up. Flaco and Cory were about to dive. They were a
picture.
Their legs in position, their arms outstretched.
"How beautiful," I said.
My boy whispered something in my ear.
I leaned close.
When I looked back up, no one was in sight.
Images fade.

8. WRITE MY TEARS

Before. Near the cliffs. Leslie and Daniel are sitting. Lee enters.

LEE. Hey, Leslie. You seen Cory around?

LESLIE. No . . . sorry.

DANIEL. Hi. I'm Dani.

LEE. What?

DANIEL. Dani. Daniel.

LEE. Oh. Daniel. Right. You beat my ass at soccer.

DANIEL. Hey. No war.

LEE. No, but I wouldn't mind a rematch sometime. So, you haven't
seen him?

LESLIE. I thought he was with you. Did you call him?

LEE. He's not picking up. Maybe he doesn't have his mobile on.

LESLIE. Cory without his mobile?

LEE. I know. Hard to believe.

DANIEL. We could play now. Come on.

LEE. What?

DANIEL. Get a match going. You and me. A little *futbol*.

LEE. I've had enough soccer for one day.

LESLIE. You want me to call Kayla and ask if she's seen him?

LEE. No, it's all right. I'm sure I'll find him.

LESLIE. If I see him . . .

LEE. Yeah, give me a ring, I'll keep my mobile on. (*Walks away.*)

DANIEL. Bye, then.

LEE. Yeah.

Lee exits.

LESLIE. I wonder where he is.

DANIEL. He's a friend of yours?

LESLIE. He's closer to Flaco and Lee, but . . .
What's that?

DANIEL. What?

LESLIE. Over there. Like out of the sky from this angle.

DANIEL. Maybe it's just a vision of some kind.

LESLIE. In the middle of the day?

DANIEL. We see what we want.

LESLIE. What'd you mean?

DANIEL. We see what we want to see. . . . You wish?

LESLIE. You mean like candles on a cake?

DANIEL. Or on an eyelash.

LESLIE. Sure. We all do. But I don't go around every day wishing for things.

DANIEL. Why not?

LESLIE. No point.

DANIEL. It's good to wish.

LESLIE. Well, sometimes I wish I knew what I wanted. Does that count?

DANIEL. I've had friends die. Just like that.
People I saw practically every day, people I hung out with, spent time . . . routine, right? Nothing you'd think about. And then one day—gone. Wiped out. No reason.

Except hatred. There's lots of that. And that's what I've lived with most of my life.

People all around hating 'cause that's what they know,

That's how they've been raised.

"Hate that one, he's brown, he talks different."

"Hate the other, he's white, he talks different. Or he believes in a different God."

It's hate all the same. Just a fact. No tears. 'Cause well . . . what good are they?

I understand that. Not wanting to cry. Not having to.

'Cause you're spent and can't anymore. So, you bury things. Deep down.

You push everything into a little corner in your brain and just forget

'cause it feels good to forget everything;

To play *futbol*. Soccer, like you say.

Be in the moment.

Live for the now, and just get on with things.

. . . But wishing?

It's always there, kicking about in your system, in the metaphysics of it all . . .

'Cause wishing is elemental. Like breathing almost.

You wish for someone to love you.

You wish for someone to be found.

You wish for silly things, stupid things . . .

Gadgets, games, music

LESLIE. There's so much wishing around music

DANIEL. And then there's

what you wish for

that's totally different . . .

less tangible things,

impossible things

that you think just by wishing

can be possible.

Like I wish I didn't feel pain. Ever. Impossible, right?

I wish there was a feeling of happiness that could last more
than a minute.
I wish everything wasn't such a big deal,
and that we could just talk to each other
without tensing up
and thinking about things we don't want to think about.
Bad memories. Yeah. They flood me. I shrug them off.
That's what I've learnt to do, but it's not what I want.
What I want is
that they would go away
and never come back.
I wish my thoughts wouldn't stray all over the place.
I wish people believed in something and really believed in it
And not just said they did
because it looks good in a newspaper headline.
I wish this park was inside me so I could take it with me
wherever I go,
So I could take you with me . . .
I wish I could go home,
and knew what that meant.
I wish that pool over there smelt of violets instead of chlorine
So we could dip into it and feel the breath of the ancients:
They could give us their wisdom; we could give them our
youth.
I wish I could look at you without thinking about my whole
life . . .

LESLIE. . . . Look.

DANIEL. Hmm?

LESLIE. The divers. Their arms outstretched. Perfect position.

DANIEL. They're wishing.

LESLIE. How beautiful.

> *The two divers, Cory and Flaco, are seen up near the rocks.*
> *A loud explosion.*
> *Freeze, followed by instant darkness.*

The park.
Lee, Kayla, Flaco, Monica, and Leslie are seen in full view.
A mash-up of pop, rock, and classical songs is heard.
An aggressive dance plays out,
a dance of chaos and loss,
of bodies longing and failing, of being cut off and held back.
Occasional solo break-outs occur as someone is too enraged or loss-ridden
and must lash out through movement and gesture.
There should be every effort made that this not seem choreographed and
dancerly, but rather have the impression of improvisation within a form.
The dance builds and builds as bodies exert themselves, and become
fatigued.
As bodies fall and disappear from view, the figure of Cory is seen in perfect
position, ready for everything.

ACT 2

9. CORY DIVES WITHOUT HIS MOBILE

In time (between).

CORY. I fell.
    I kept falling.
    I was a blue light in a wave of dust
    headed
    straight down;
    but in my mind
    I was flying up
    towards the sun,
    'cause that's how it felt
    like I could touch it.
    I am an Icarus for a new age.
    See?
    I pretended I was Morrissey. At the height of everything: all
    fame, all glory.

"I got my hand on you, honey, and we're dancing"
Straight into the sea.
It was all Now Now Now.
Cool heat.
Pure pop songs.
Salt tears.
And falling.
This is my war against sadness.
This is my war against mediocrity.
This is my war against hate.
Will you believe me?
Will you remember me?

The loud explosion repeats, slightly muted.
Kayla starts to sing an original song. She is joined by Leslie
and perhaps some of the others, as Cory's image begins to fade.

Was

(*Verse 1*)

KAYLA (*begins*). This was
   How was
   We were

LESLIE. We were
   We are
   Standing

KAYLA (*and others*). On the beach
   We were
   Staring

   On the cliffs
   We were
   Slim.

   (*Verses alternate between singers now.*)

   (*Verse 2*)
   This was
   How was
   We are

We are
We were
Standing

On the beach
We were
Waving

On the cliffs
We were one

(*Chorus*)
When we
How all
Ending

How this
How all
ends

How this
How all
begins
and then
begins
again.

(*Chorus reprise*)
When we
How all
Ending

How all
We end

How this
How all
Begins

Another day
Ends.
All fades into . . .

Snapshots from the before/after. (This sequence can be pre-recorded.)

LEE. Everything was too beautiful: the sky, the trees, the beach . . .

KAYLA. I felt a breeze skimming in.

It felt good. You need a breeze on a hot day.

MONICA. I was pure adrenaline . . .

Ripped Fuel. That was me.

LESLIE. "How beautiful," I said.

KAYLA. . . . And then there was nothing.

LEE. There was nothing.

MONICA. Everything stopped. Just like that.

LESLIE. No one was in sight.

MONICA. The blur crystallized.

KAYLA. And the last thing I remember

LEE. By the time I looked up . . .

MONICA. Was what Ricky Martin would look like sleeping.

KAYLA. . . . Lee's face.

LEE. Nothing
except for a great big noise this side of—

11. A DAY LIKE A YEAR

*Images of chaos at the park, falling and walking, endless walking in the
background. Gray snapshots of a time past.*

In time (after).

FLACO. We were about to dive when there was this noise.

Real loud. Like when the Shock Drop is at max.

Except louder, more abrupt.

I stopped. I looked toward the noise.

When I turned back

---

4 This scene is optional.

He was gone. Just like that. Cory was gone.

The air got thick.

There was dust everywhere.

There was this smell. Like burning hair.

There was a huge cloud of smoke, and an extraordinary silence.

You couldn't hear anything for a long time.

I think there's something really beautiful about things when they get hushed like that.

Like you can feel the earth, the expanse of it . . . and where you fit in . . .

And then sirens . . . slowly. And screams.

Some people were walking with great purpose

Like they wanted to pretend everything was fine.

Other people were covered in blood.

I thought I was going to die 'cause there was so much smoke,

But I'm okay. I'm lucky.

That's the word you heard the most that day

"Lucky. I feel lucky."

It's not a word I like. It feels small, puny. Life should be more than luck.

Now it's just shock, and wondering why . . .

Who would do such a thing . . .?

. . . Seventy dead, two hundred wounded.

I don't want vengeance.

I'm just curious. 'Cause it can't be just hatred, or evil, or craziness

That makes somebody do something like that . . .

There has to be a legitimate, explainable reason why someone would think

setting off a bomb is the only solution to solve a problem.

I left the park and started walking.

Each siren that cut the air was followed by absolute silence.

I must've walked miles and miles.

It felt as if I was somewhere else, an unfamiliar place.

Even my language changed. I couldn't really talk to people.

Not cool, you know. There was no flow.

It was all nods, looks, shrugs, and hands waving . . .

But somehow the signs got through . . .
Rescue workers labored under the yellow glow of arc lights.
I slowly made my way home, far away from the park.
I thought about Cory and how I swore to myself I wouldn't
tell anybody
He pitched himself off the cliff.
What good would it do to tell anyone now
that he had said goodbye to the world and all that?
Let them think what they like.
I put on a CD. Morrissey.
The song was "Angel, Angel, Down We Go Together."

12. RACING

In time (after).

MONICA. Like nothing
    like running
    like running away
    and not running
    and pretending I'm okay
    and not feeling anything

    just running
    moving
    holding my breath
    releasing
    not thinking
    about anything
    but running
    pulsing
    speeding with light

KAYLA (*appears*). And not telling anyone anything
    because there's nothing

MONICA. But more running
    and keeping up
    and catching up

LESLIE (*appears*). And calling
and seeing if everyone's okay
are you okay are you okay are you all right
call me
yes, let's get together
let's plan
let's do

MONICA. Uh-huh
okay
sure

KAYLA. Later
later
later
and then nothing

MONICA. But waiting

KAYLA. And waiting

MONICA. And this is too long to wait

KAYLA. So, running

LESLIE. Moving
and not waiting
anymore
for anything

MONICA. But this

KAYLA. This

MONICA. This
is what I'm here for.

13. PLACES WE GO TO FORGET

In time (after). Interior. Lee is resting. Flaco is standing.

FLACO. We should go to the club.

LEE. Why?

FLACO. We haven't been.

LEE. I need to sleep.

FLACO. That's all you've been doing.

LEE. Not all . . .

FLACO. Well, I want to go. It's what we do, right?

LEE. What we used to do. It was Cory's thing.

FLACO. So, we go. We celebrate. For him.

LEE. Celebrate what? That everything's screwed up now, even more than before? That we don't know where Cory is, whether he's gone missing or is just plain dead? You may be into the carnival, man, but not me.

FLACO. What's that mean?

LEE. Day of the Dead and all that. Fucking Mardi-Gras.

FLACO. Those are two different things. And anyway, what does that have to do with going to the club?

LEE. I'm not celebrating. Screw Morrissey and his maudlin crap. He's a damn rock star. He can afford to be bleak and get off on it. Well, listen up: I'm not joining the doom parade. Not anymore.

FLACO. Cory would like us to.

LEE. Did he send you a message from the deep blue?

FLACO. . . . . We can't live like this. In hiding.

LEE. I'm not hiding. I'm just not going out. That's all. I'm not exposing myself to potential misery and disaster. Seventy dead, two hundred wounded. Park blown to bits. And the mayor says, "Act like everything's normal." Well, it may be for him, safe in his goddamn mansion, but it sure as hell is not. And the sooner we own up to the fact, the better. And if that means I'm scared? Well, then, guess what? I am. I am damn scared and not afraid to say it.

FLACO. And you think I'm not?

LEE. I don't pretend to know what you're thinking.

FLACO. I'm as affected by losing Cory and everything else that happened that day as much as you are, so don't act like you're the lone survivor here. I was there, too. I was right next to him. Not down below, but right fucking there. And when everything started to burn and blow, I had to figure out a way to get out, and let me tell you, it wasn't easy. 'Cause it was chaos, right? Screams and bodies on fire. And rides falling down in great big pieces. And everybody running every which way. And I made it out, yeah. Just like you. But I'm not staying there in mind . . . I can't. . . I'm going.

LEE. Go ahead.

FLACO. It's *Viva Hate* night. They're only going to play from that CD. All night. An endless loop.

LEE. Endless party.

FLACO. It's just moving. It's just dancing.

LEE. And the singalongs and the contests and the who's got the best hair tonight . . .

FLACO. You used to like it.

LEE. I never liked it. It was a scene. It was fun for a while. I did it. Whatever.

FLACO. . . . Are you going to see Kayla?

LEE. Maybe.

FLACO. You should call her.

LEE. And say what?

FLACO. Just say hey.

LEE. Why? 'Cause we're good together? 'Cause maybe we're destined and all that crap? . . . What if we are? . . . I haven't talked to her since . . . and we're not even . . . we're just connected in some way. It's a good connection. At least I think it is . . . was . . . She's got her friends, you know . . . Screw it. It doesn't feel right.

FLACO. And sleeping does?

LEE. Yeah. Sleeping feels great. Feels just right. I need it.
I haven't slept in . . .
Waking up in the middle of the night . . . every little sound . . .

every siren . . .

people's faces in my dreams . . . dazed and bloody . . .

all that . . . madness, shock . . . dust . . .

What am I supposed to do with all that? Put it away? Forget it all happened?

Seems like that's all everybody wants to do:

get on, come on, move on,

go to the mall, go to the movies, go to a club,

watch the baseball game, the soccer match,

battle your favorite big-eyed, big-breasted, naked anime assassin in cyberspace,

be a fan, cheer on, get on board, get high, get laid, spend everything, forget everything,

and don't talk about anything . . . not really . . . 'cause once you have an opinion

then everybody else has to have one and who knows, there could even be an argument.

And we can't have that. We can't afford a damn argument about anything substantial,

'Cause then how would we go on? How will we call the anti-terrorist hotline, then?

So we talk about salad or cake . . .

We go to great lengths to talk about the many ways you can prepare a salad, and how good it is for digestion, and "did you try it with walnuts or fruit?

And wasn't that dressing better than the other one?"

Entire evenings devoted to the global importance of salad.

Or we wax eternal about chocolate cake,

petty indulgences, guilty pleasures, goddamn dessert.

"Was it dark chocolate or white chocolate, mousse or ice cream? And what was the texture? And how moist was it, and which one is the best one in the city to have?

And where did you have it and why and with whom?

And oh, gotta go there, gotta eat it, gotta fill myself up."

This is what we talk about. Stupid things. Safe things.

'Cause salad and cake are common ground. You can pass the

time talking about them. There's nothing controversial about salad.

And the best thing is you don't have to get angry. Not even a bit.

Well, I want to get angry. I want to get fucking angry about how the World Bank and the IMF have screwed us all over with privatization and globalization and damned multinational corporate deal-making that leave out the poor and make entire populations random targets for go-mad killjoys seeking their brand of righteous vengeance.

I want to get angry about two hundred wounded and seventy dead in Luna Park.

And everywhere else innocents are slaughtered on the left and right side

of the political, ideological, or fanatical profit-making equation.

I want to get angry about Cory disappearing for no reason

and everything else that happened that day

And has been happening and keeps happening;

And how no one is really doing anything about it except saying "Hey, it's a shame,

It's a tragedy, but we got to move on now and not waste time mourning."

Waste time mourning?

Since when did mourning have a damn time limit imposed on it?

Or is it just that it's not comfortable, not pleasant to talk about what happened

and what keeps happening the world over?

But we've no time for that.

No. No time for anger. No time for mourning.

Just salad. Yeah. Cake. Yeah. Morrissey night at the club. Yeah. Viva Hate. Viva everything.

And tell me, once we put all that escapist good after bad, who's to remember? Really remember anything?

I'm sleeping. I don't care how long.

FLACO. . . . You want me to call Kayla for you?

LEE. No.

FLACO. I'll text her, then.

LEE. Don't do anything. If I feel like calling her, I will.

FLACO. You won't.

LEE. Look, you want me to call her, Flaco? Fine. I'll call her.

Lee picks up his mobile. Pause.

FLACO. . . . Well?

LEE. I will.

FLACO. Go on.

LEE. . . . You're going to stand there and stare at me like that?

FLACO. I'm going out.

LEE. Then go out.

FLACO. . . . How's the hair?

LEE. Fine. Just fine.

FLACO. Are you sure? I spent hours on this thing. I want it to look just right.

LEE. You sound just like Cory.

FLACO. Well, we did think alike in a way. Why? Does it freak you out?

LEE. It's kinda nice.

FLACO. So, is it all right?

LEE. Hmm?

FLACO. The hair!

LEE. Killer.

FLACO. Rock 'n' roll, then.

LEE. Rock 'n' roll.

(Flaco leaves.
Lee waits, mobile phone in hand.
Time passes.
Finally, he dials. Waits.)

Hi. Kayla?. . . Kayla?. . . This is Lee. . . Lee. . . Yes. Right. Uh-huh . . . I'm fine. Yeah.

You?. . . Yeah. I know. Not easy . . . Really? Leslie and Daniel?

. . . Great. That's great . . . No. Hadn't heard . . . Kayla? . . .
Kayla? . . . I lost you for a second . . . No, that's fine . . . I just
thought I'd . . . Sure . . . Later.
Phone off.

14. HAVEN'T HAD A DREAM IN A LONG TIME

In time (after). Exterior. Lee and Kayla drinking coffee at a cafe. Silence.

KAYLA. It's good, isn't it?

LEE. It's coffee.

KAYLA. Better than usual, though.

LEE. Yeah. Not as bitter . . . What's that—? Charbucks . . . Old joke.

KAYLA. . . . What have you been doing?

LEE. Nothing. I've been sleeping a lot. You?

KAYLA. You're like on the phone.

LEE. What?

KAYLA. Like on the phone. When you called.

LEE. What does that mean?

KAYLA. Means what it means.

LEE. Should I go? Maybe I should go . . .

KAYLA. No. It's all right. It's good to see you. I just thought . . . I
mean, when you didn't call or e-mail, I . . . I don't know what
I thought.

LEE. I think Cory's dead.

KAYLA. A lot of people died that day.

LEE. Of people I knew, I mean.

KAYLA. Oh. Sorry. . . . I'm really sorry.

LEE. I haven't had a dream in a long time.
Everything's blank. Vague. Unknown.
Fucking joke.

KAYLA. He hasn't been—?

LEE. Found? No.

And the thing is I saw him, right? He was about to dive. And
I thought "Great.

He's not lost. He's just being Cory: flaking out, then popping
up at the last minute."

He goddamn loved Moz. He loved all that bleak mopey British
shit.

When we'd go to the club, it was like he was in heaven. A real
fan, you know.

I don't think I've ever been a fan. Of anything. I mean, I like
stuff, but . . .

I'm not devoted enough. Not even about religion.

My parents tried and tried when I was a kid—catechism classes
and all that—

but it didn't make a difference. I stopped going to Mass after
a while.

I couldn't see the point.

KAYLA. You're Catholic?

LEE. Former lapsed non-believing believer. Why? What are you?

KAYLA. I'm nothing. My parents didn't belong to anything. So, I
didn't either.

LEE. No structure. That's great.

KAYLA. I wouldn't have minded a little bit, even if it was just
something to rebel against.

LEE. It's good to rebel, isn't it?

KAYLA. Feels good. Don't know that it does much good, but . . .

LEE. Of course it does. All those revolutions way back . . . they were
nothing but rebellions that got out of hand. It's apathy that kills.
'Cause that's what they want. That's what the powers-that-be
want: good, dutiful apathetic citizens who feel they can't make a
cent of difference, so they can carry on doing what they're doing
and live in their ever-growing power bubble. You don't think so?

KAYLA. I don't think I can make a judgement about people that I
don't know.

LEE. But you can form an opinion.

KAYLA. So I can have a picture in mind to go with that opinion and have something I can live with? And meanwhile, there are all these other pictures that don't fit, that don't make sense . . . what am I supposed to do with them, Lee? Nothing's neat, nothing's simple. Even simple's complex . . .

LEE. Sorry.

KAYLA. What are you sorry about?

LEE. I don't want to make you upset.

KAYLA. We're just talking. Having coffee . . .

LEE. . . . So, Leslie and Daniel, eh?

KAYLA. Yeah. Can you believe it?

LEE. That's huge.

KAYLA. Marriage. I know. Weird to think about, really.

LEE. Too soon.

KAYLA. And they barely know each other.

LEE. Crazy.

KAYLA. It is what it is.

LEE. But you have to admit, though . . .

KAYLA. I wouldn't do it. No. But if it's what Leslie wants . . . what she thinks she needs . . . Who knows? Maybe they do love each other. Maybe Luna Park was the best thing that could've happened. . . .

LEE. That's morbid.

KAYLA. A lot of people are getting married.

LEE. A lot of people are getting divorced, too.

KAYLA. Yeah, Monica's breaking up with everybody.

LEE. I bet.

KAYLA. What's that mean?

LEE. Monica . . . it seems like something she would do.

KAYLA. Yeah. Well, I'm happy for Leslie. He's a good guy.

LEE. He played mean soccer, that's all I know.

KAYLA. . . . Have you gone back to the park since—?

LEE. No.

KAYLA. They're starting to rebuild, re-landscape . . . They're going to put in a Metropolis ride and everything. A city within a city. It's going to take some time, but . . . they're under way. They showed the plans in the newspaper. Did you see them?

LEE. No.

KAYLA. It's going to look really beautiful.

Pause. He cries.

KAYLA. Are you all right?

LEE. I don't know why I'm crying.

KAYLA. It's a good thing.

LEE. Yeah?

KAYLA. Good to let things out.

A good long cry.

LEE. I'm sorry. I don't usually . . .

KAYLA. It's all right.

He cries a bit more, then recovers a bit.

LEE. . . . Must be the coffee.

KAYLA. Yeah. It's really bad.

LEE. They should give us our money back.

KAYLA. Want me ask them?

LEE. No. No. It's alright. They're making eight dollars an hour anyway.

KAYLA. It's a tough job, too.

LEE. Yeah. People don't realize . . .

KAYLA. Lots of burnt milk and carpal tunnel . . .

LEE. There was this guy as I was coming over here.

KAYLA. Hmm?

LEE. He was walking along. Suit and tie. Going to work probably. He had this bag in his hand. Foreign-brand briefcase. I usually don't notice things like that, but . . .

Anyway, he was just walking. He seemed like a regular guy.
We get to the corner and we both have to wait.
He reaches into his briefcase and then this look came over his
face, panicked, scared.
He looked at me. I didn't say anything. I tried to be as calm as
possible. Non-judgmental. I didn't want to make him think
any the worse of me
for having a mutually fleeting thought that he might have a
bomb in his briefcase.
He reached in and took out a pack of tissues. He had to blow
his nose. That's all.
And then the light went green and we went our separate ways.

KAYLA. We live in a nervous town. Like any other place . . . We're all
the same.

Just luckier than most.

LEE. "Lucky?" I hate that word.

KAYLA. Sometimes there are no words . . .

LEE. Yeah. It's better that way.

Kayla takes his hand. Slight pause. He kisses her.

15. A SMALL REQUEST

In time (after).

MONICA. I just want to not think.
That's all.
To not think about anything.
Nothing.
Nothing at all.
Mmm-hmm.
Nothing.

16. AN AVERAGE LIFE

In time (after). Interior. Leslie is trying on a wedding dress. Kayla watches.

KAYLA. I don't even know why you want a dress.

LESLIE. It's the way it's always been done.

KAYLA. So?

LESLIE. I like tradition. Haven't you always dreamt of wearing a wedding dress?

KAYLA. No.

LESLIE. Not even when you were a little girl?

KAYLA. No.

LESLIE. That's strange.

KAYLA. What's so strange about it?

LESLIE. 'Cause it's what everybody dreams. It's a common dream. Very, very common.

KAYLA. I'm uncommon.

LESLIE. I worry about you.

KAYLA. Don't.

LESLIE. You don't have any focus in your life.

KAYLA. Where's this coming from?

LESLIE. It's true.

KAYLA. I've plenty of focus.

LESLIE. You'll end up like Monica.

KAYLA. Monica's fine.

LESLIE. She's a wreck.

KAYLA. She is not a wreck. She's more together than any of us is. She just has her way of her doing things, that's all. What's happening to you, Leslie? What's going on?

LESLIE. I have priorities now.

KAYLA. Meaning?

LESLIE. Plans, goals . . . I can't live like an adolescent all my life, wasting time, going to the park . . .

KAYLA. You met Daniel in the park.

LESLIE. That's different.

KAYLA. Why is that different?

LESLIE. I don't want to talk about this right now.

KAYLA. You brought it up.

LESLIE. I'm just saying . . .

KAYLA. You don't like Lee, is that it?

LESLIE. I didn't say that.

KAYLA. We're friends. There's nothing at stake.

LESLIE. Precisely.

KAYLA. Look, I'm not planning my whole life around somebody just because I feel I have to.

LESLIE. Is that what you think I—?

KAYLA. You're getting married. Dress and everything.

LESLIE. I love him.

KAYLA. Great. Have a great life.

LESLIE. Go to hell.

KAYLA. . . . I'm here, aren't I?

LESLIE. No, you're not. You're dreaming about I don't know what . . .
We don't know what will happen at any given moment.
And we still act like there's all the time in the world.
It may seem petty and small to you to even consider an average life
but that's exactly what I want: an average, normal, small little life.
I want to get married, and have a legal, spiritual, and emotional bond with someone.
And I'm not some post-feminist chick who needs a man to validate her existence.
That is not what this is about.
I just want to build a life, and not just . . . go about thinking about what's the latest this, and what's the latest that, and let's go shopping and go to the club and pretend the lie we're living is a good honest lie.
And if you think it's funny or stupid or retro, then . . .
I'm sorry. I don't want to be extraordinary.
I want to be completely ordinary. In every way.

KAYLA. What about Daniel?

LESLIE. What about him?

KAYLA. You don't even know him really.

LESLIE. I know him enough.

KAYLA. It seems so much to take on all at once.

LESLIE. We love each other. What's to take on?

KAYLA. Aren't you even a little bit angry?

LESLIE. About what?

KAYLA. You almost got killed.

LESLIE. We almost *all* got killed.
>We lucked out in a way. I know it sounds strange to say that, but . . . we did, right? I mean, we're all right.
>And Dani's healing just fine. He's practically . . . all together, And I'm . . . except for my ear every once in a while—not hearing things—I'm fine.
>So, what have I to get angry about?
>I'm supposed to get all guilty 'cause I'm okay and a lot of people aren't?
>I'm not going to do that. I'm not going to burden myself with guilt because I'm alive. You see, 'cause I'm not good with anger. Never have been.
>(*Referring to bow in back of dress*) Would you fix the bow? I can't . . .

KAYLA. Sure.

LESLIE. It was in this vintage shop.

KAYLA. It's nice.

LESLIE. It is. Isn't it?

KAYLA. Yeah.

LESLIE. The lady at the shop wanted me to take another one they had. From the 1950s, but I said, "No. This one will do."

KAYLA. There.

LESLIE. Yeah?

KAYLA. Perfect.

LESLIE. It's not too frou-frou, is it?

KAYLA. No. It's nice. Pretty.

LESLIE. Yeah?

KAYLA. Yeah.

17. REAL WILD

In time (after). Exterior. Monica and Daniel are drinking coffee at a cafe. He has a crutch next to him.

MONICA. Canada. That's where I'm going.

DANIEL. When?

MONICA. Tomorrow, the next day. I'm packing up and heading out . . .
It's better there. Cleaner, safer . . . unspoiled.

DANIEL. Not all of it.

MONICA. Better than here. Gotta be. More civilized, definitely.

DANIEL. I guess that means no wedding invite for you.

MONICA. No. Sorry. I mean, it's great about you and Leslie . . . But I
can't stick around and do all that chit-chat, hors d'oeuvres, and
wine and cheese wedges things. I'm not good at that, anyway.
I always end up complaining about the wine or the cheese
being too soft or . . . I like the ritual of weddings but not the
fuss. Why not just pledge yourself to each other and break open
a coconut? That's so much simpler and more honest.
Sorry. I don't mean that the way it came out. But you know
what I mean, right?

DANIEL. No circus.

MONICA. Yeah. Exactly.
Although I think you and Leslie should have the best big
wedding you can,
'cause why not, right? You're in it, might as well . . .

DANIEL. I don't know what I'm going to do.
I haven't thought about anything. Nothing at all.

MONICA. Not even when you were in the hospital?

DANIEL. That was a stupid thing. People there with real injuries, real
messed-up shit,

and I'm there with a broken leg. Not even from the blast, but
from running,
from crazy running to get out of the chaos.
Leslie right next to me and I fall.

. . .

I haven't even had time to . . . really think, you know.
Leslie seems so sure . . .

MONICA. And you're not?

DANIEL. I'm all over it. I just . . . I'd like some quiet.

MONICA. Yeah, this city's really noisy. Makes it hard to think. You
should move out to the country.

DANIEL. And do what?

MONICA. Plant things. I have a friend who moved out 'cause she said
she wanted to find her little place in this mad, mad world and
she's growing all these organic vegetables and being really
hippie but in a non-hippie way and she seems really happy.

DANIEL. Even now?

MONICA. Yeah. I e-mailed her when . . . and she was shocked. Sure.
Stunned. But . . . really level, you know. That's what I want.
That's why Canada . . . cause it's so big there and there are all
these moose and ice ponds and hockey and French and Chinese
people—yeah, they have, like, the biggest population of
Chinese outside of China.

DANIEL. Wild.

MONICA. Real wild . . . and not just "la vida loca" but authentic
wildness, you know? Out in the prairie, in the middle of
nothing. Like Newfoundland, right? Can you imagine living
on the tip of a country, just on the edge of a continent?

DANIEL. Like me.

MONICA. What'd you mean?

DANIEL. I'm from one of those "tips," as you say . . . another edge
. . . but yes, very much the same. Just hanging on.

MONICA. And wishing.

DANIEL. I don't do that as much.

MONICA. I'm just starting to again . . . I used to think wishing was, like, for kids, you know. Something you did once and you'd grow out of, but . . . it feels good to wish. And not in a selfish "give me what I want" way but real, you know . . . go ahead. Wish something.

DANIEL. Now?

MONICA. Yeah.

DANIEL. What should I wish for?

MONICA. That they serve better coffee in this place.

DANIEL. I'm not wishing that.

MONICA. I guess it's an impossible . . .

DANIEL. Definitely an impossible.

MONICA. Well, wish for something else, then . . .

DANIEL. . . . Too many wishes.

MONICA. So? Do one at a time. I'll wait.

DANIEL. What about you?

MONICA. I already know what my wish is.

DANIEL. Canada?

MONICA. Absolutely.

DANIEL. You're something else.

MONICA. One day everybody will know that.
   . . . Go on. Do your wishing.

DANIEL. I wish . . .

MONICA. Not out loud! That ruins it.
   Just quiet. Inside. Like you're painting a self-portrait or you're floating on the sea . . .
   That's right. Real quiet.
   And I'll think of Canada . . . And how it'll be . . .

DANIEL. . . . Upwards . . .

MONICA. Yeah. Everything's going upwards . . .

This can be pre-recorded.

CORY. And after
> There was nothing
> But burnt earth

> And tired bodies
> And the endless blue
> And me
> Floating up from out of the sea
> Above everything.
> I had risen up somehow.
> And I could see the whole city . . .
> I could see everything . . .

> Flaco and Leslie and Monica and Lee
> And Kayla
> On the edge of the sand smiling.
> And a young man, too, in soccer clothes,
> Making his way through the trees.

> I keep floating.
> I don't stop.
> I dream of the future.
> The sun touches my skin.
> I live in the most beautiful place in the world.

19. WHAT HAPPENS AFTER

Later. Kayla and Lee in formal dress before the ruins of Luna Park.

LEE. I don't know if I can . . .

KAYLA. We can go back.

LEE. No. I want to be here. Not out of duty . . . I just . . .

KAYLA. We don't have to stay here too long. Just a look.

LEE. Yeah. . . . They've really started to get to work, huh? No time
to waste . . .

KAYLA. They've started to put up the Metropolis . . .
And they're making a garden over there. See?
I think those are hyacinths.

LEE. I'm not good with flowers. I know roses and carnations but anything else . . .

KAYLA. And they're re-doing the bandshell. We could go if you want.

LEE. And do what?

KAYLA. Pretend we're rock stars.

LEE. Moz, eh?

KAYLA. Cobain, Hutchence . . . Ricky Martin . . .

LEE. Stop.

KAYLA. Just joking.

LEE. Not funny.

KAYLA. Sorry.

LEE. . . . At least they haven't let anyone make a big show of their grief with signs and banners and posters and crap . . . I hate it when grief becomes a tourist attraction.

KAYLA. Just some candles and flowers. It's better that way.

LEE. . . . The smell is gone.

KAYLA. Hmm?

LEE. Burning hair . . .

KAYLA. They're cleaning up everything. It's amazing what people can do.

LEE. I wish they'd get rid of it. Just cordon off what's left of the park and leave it alone . . .

KAYLA. It'd be an eyesore.

LEE. So? We can live with that. We should live with that. We should have a reminder: something concrete to look at every day . . . Nothing but erase everything. Build right over, build right away, keep the cultural forgetting machine in motion. So we can keep making promises to ourselves about how we're going to live our lives.

KAYLA. What's wrong with that?

LEE. Well, first of all, it's not true. And second of all . . .

   . . .

   Dammit. I'm crying again.
   Why is it that every time . . .?

KAYLA. . . . It's all right.

LEE. It's not all right. It's not fucking all right. Stop saying that.

   . . .

   Screw it.
   I'll just keep crying.
   He does so. Pause.

KAYLA. We shouldn't have come here.

LEE. I wanted to . . .

   Pause.

KAYLA. . . . It was a nice wedding. Wasn't it?

LEE. Yeah, they did a good job.

KAYLA. I actually think they're going to make it.

LEE. I've never been to one before.

KAYLA. Huh?

LEE. Wedding. First time.

KAYLA. Really?

LEE. No one I've ever known has ever . . .

KAYLA. That's amazing.

LEE. It's what it is.
   I almost lost it, though, when the band broke into . . .

KAYLA. But it's expected, you know. You gotta have at least one godawful song or two at a wedding.

LEE. And Daniel looked good.

KAYLA. He did. Didn't he? He seemed happy. Confused but happy.

LEE. So did Leslie.

KAYLA. Her mind's made up. . . . You think Cory . . .?

LEE. What?

KAYLA. Nothing.

LEE. What is it?

KAYLA. It's stupid.

LEE. Tell me.

KAYLA. I was gonna say . . . you think he can see us?

LEE. You mean, like, from above?

KAYLA. It's crazy, right? To even think . . .

LEE. No. It's not. It's just . . . I don't know. I've never thought about it.

KAYLA. What happens after . . .

LEE. It's unknown. I mean, a tunnel, a bright light . . . that's what we hear, right?

KAYLA. Heaven and hell.

LEE. That, too. But what really happens . . .
I mean, sure, it'd be a riot if he could see us.

KAYLA. What would you say to him?

LEE. . . . Hey.

KAYLA. Is that all?

LEE. It's all speculative, anyway.

Pause.

KAYLA. I could stay here forever.

LEE. We're here already.

*Cory, Flaco, Monica, and Leslie are glimpsed in the background, dancing in an instant memory blur of brilliant, tender ecstasy.
A vision that lasts no more than a moment,
and then it's just Kayla and Lee, and fade.*

The End.